"When the wheels of justice came off the wagon in Iraq."
Bob Reid, Senior Managing Editor, STARS & STRIPES Newspaper, 2017.

"The Department (of Justice) will continue the policies of the previous administrations (i.e., Bush, Obama, and Trump Administrations not supporting intervention into any federal whistle-blower lawsuit). But these lawsuits (i.e., my three federal whistle-blower lawsuits against KBR, CSA, and ITT) are so toxic, so explosive, so radioactive, if they ever saw the light of day they'd bring the whole U.S. government down."
U.S. Attorney-General Jeff Sessions, July 2017.

WHO STOLE IRAQ?

THE REAL REASON THE U.S. INVADED IRAQ
DURING GULF WAR II
Part I of the "KNEW OR SHOULD HAVE KNOWN!" Series

LEONARD H. LE BLANC III

AUTHOR OF "AIR BASE," "THAILAND" & "AFGHANISTAN: LASHKAR GAH: HOME OF THE WARRIORS-I & II"

Taliban Press Imprint
SEATE Services Publishing

This book is dedicated to Alan Grayson, Esq. He was the lawyer who filed my three federal whistle-blower lawsuits against totally corrupt U.S. defense contractors: KBR Services in Iraq, ITT Services in Bosnia, and Combat Support Associates (CSA), Inc., in Kuwait. He is one of only two men in America who fully believed in me and what I was doing. May he continue to win elections for higher public office and continue to serve the great people of the United States with unselfish dedication, honesty, and professionalism.

This book is also dedicated to Victor Kubli, Esq., who was the only other man to believe in me. He fought the good fight against the U.S. "Deep State" for as long as he could until he was overwhelmed by the evil 'Dark Side of The Force' (i.e., Department of Justice (DOJ), Department of Defense (DOD), etc.).

A special thanks goes to my oldest childhood friend, Don Beschle, Esq., Professor of Constitutional Law at the University of Illinois-Chicago law school for checking the book for problems like malice, slander, defamation of character and libel (plus spelling and grammar) to make sure I was on safe legal ground due to the explosive nature of the subject and the many important government and other high-ranking officials plus private individuals involved in this sordid, criminal, and historic saga.

Another special thanks goes to my former U.S. Navy Recruiting District Commanding Officer, Commander (CDR) Mitchell 'Mitch' D. Moore, USN, (Retired), for proofreading and editing my manuscript. He remains the most outstanding officer I ever met in my military service. Any mistakes in the book are my own.

A final special thanks goes to Lieutenant Commander (LCDR) Scott Larkin, USN, (Ret.), for also proofreading and editing my manuscript. He is a true computer savant and computer systems genius.

Originally the book title was called DONALD TRUMPS RUNS THE U.S. "DEEP STATE"! - THE PERFECT EXAMPLE OF A STILL ON-GOING U.S. "DEEP STATE" OPERATION: THE REAL REASON THE U.S. INVADED IRAQ DURING GULF WAR II - Part I and the book series was called WAR WHORES! But Amazon said the title was too "controversial" and the book series title used a "profanity" and they refused to do any advertising for this book. So I simply changed the title WHO STOLE IRAQ? on the advice of legal counsel.

The following "KNEW OR SHOULD HAVE KNOWN!" Series books are planned:

PART II working title will be KNEW OR SHOULD HAVE KNOWN!

PART III working title will be HOW THE DEPARTMENT OF JUSTICE, THE DEPARTMENT OF DEFENSE AND OTHER U.S. GOVERNMENT ORGANIZATIONS PLUS ALL THEIR MINIONS AND LACKEYS CONSPIRED TO COVER UP ALL THE UNBELIEVABLE STEALING IN IRAQ DURING GULF WAR II FROM THE BUSH, OBAMA, AND NOW TRUMP ADMINISTRATION.

PART IV working title will be WHAT KIM KARDASHIAN'S LITTLE SISTER'S BEST FRIEND'S MAID'S DOG HAD FOR BREAKFAST THIS MORNING: HOW "DEMOCRACY DIED IN DARKNESS" BECAUSE THE WASHINGTON POST, THE NEW YORK TIMES, WALL STREET JOURNAL AND THE OTHER BIG MEDIA KILLED THE POWER SWITCH. I WENT TO THE WASHINGTON POST, THE NEW YORK TIMES, WALL STREET JOURNAL AND THE OTHER BIG MEDIA ON ALL OF THIS AND THEY DID . . . . NOTHING, EXCEPT TO TELL ME GO WRITE A BOOK.

PART V working title will be THE DARK SIDE OF THE MOON.

This book title "THE INVASION OF IRAQ" comes by courtesy of Alan Grayson, Esq. It refers to the first time a whistle-blower won a case against a war profiteer, Custer Battles LLC, who operated in Iraq, that went to trial and was finally won on an appeal. It was the second largest recovery by a whistle-blower acting on his own in history. Alan was the lawyer of record. On CNN in April 2006, he used the term "War Whores" to describe the looting of the Iraq's Development Fund.

Printed in Thailand

Back Photo courtesy of ☐☐ عين فى هللا on Unsplash

© 2020.   ISBN 978-1-7923-5241-6
ACKNOWLEDGEMENTS

I want to thank the following great people who helped me write this cast-of-thousands historical book. Their many comments, criticism, corrections, support (even if only verbal), encouragement, feedback (positive and negative), and assistance (or lack thereof which also helped to goad/spur me forward to completion) is sincerely appreciated. They all made this a much better book. The following people helped or were involved in some way, in alphabetical order:

DR. MOHANED T. AL-HAMDI: Associate Professor of Economics, Kansas State University.

MR. MARTY BARON: Executive Editor of the WASHINGTON POST, involved with
11 Pulitzer Prize awards and was featured in the Academy Award-winning Best Picture movie SPOTLIGHT.

MR. WILLIAM BARR, ESQ.: U.S. Attorney General, Trump Administration.

MR. CARL BERNSTEIN: Investigative reporter, author with Bob Woodward of ALL THE PRESIDENT'S MEN.

PROFESSOR (PROF.). DONALD L. ('DON') BESCHLE, ESQ.: Professor of Constitutional Law, John Marshall School of Law, University of Illinois-Chicago, Chicago, Illinois. The only man I know (other than Dr. Darryl R. J. Macer) who got nothing less than A+'s from grade school, through high school, B.A., J.D. to his L.L.M.
degree.

DR. PAT J. BOSCO: Retired Dean of Students and Vice-President of Institutional Advancement, Kansas State University; universally known as 'Mr. K-State,' author of
BOSCOLOGY 101.

MR. STUART W. BOWEN, JR, ESQ.: Attorney-at-Law, Austin, Texas, former Special
Inspector General for Iraq's Reconstruction (SIGIR) (2004-2013), former personal lawyer for George W. Bush who swung Florida's Electoral College votes into the Bush
column and thus, giving him the 2000 U.S. presidential election, author of HARD LESSONS: THE IRAQ RECONSTRUCTION EXPERIENCE.

MR. GORDON CALDECOTT: Retired British Army.

PROF. JOHN W. CARLIN: Professor of Leadership Studies, Kansas State University. Former distinguished and extremely popular two-time Governor (Kansas-D) in a traditionally very heavy Republican state, former National Archivist of the U.S. in the Clinton and the Bush Administrations.

MR. ROBERT A. CARO: Distinguished prolific author of THE POWER BROKER: ROBERT MOSES AND THE FALL OF NEW YORK, THE YEARS OF LYNDON JOHNSON SERIES: THE PATH TO POWER (VOLUME 1), MEANS OF ASCENT (VOLUME 2), MASTER OF THE SENATE (VOLUME 3), THE PASSAGE OF POWER (VOLUME 4), and WORKING; Winner of the 1975 and 1983 Pulitzer Prize for Biography.

MR. THOMAS ('TOM') CROWLEY: Retired U.S. Army officer and wounded Vietnam War veteran, noted author of several fiction and non-fiction books including VIPER'S TAIL, MURDER IN THE SLAUGHTERHOUSE, SHRAPNEL WOUNDS and the forthcoming BANGKOK GAMBLE.

MR. LEONARD ('LEN') DOWNIE, JR.: Retired Executive Editor, THE WASHINGTON POST (1991-2008); author of THE RULES OF THE GAME.

PROF. SUSAN EDGERLEY: Consultant, Department of Journalism & Mass Communications, Kansas State University; Retired Food Editor, Metro Editor and Assistant Managing Editor, NEW YORK TIMES.

DR. JENNIFER ELDRIDGE: Ph.D., Licensed Psychologist.

MR. FRANK FELBER: B.A., Political Science, Kansas State University, Graduate student, University of Arizona.

MRS. LINDA FELBER: Future saint in heaven.

MR. WILLIS ('BILL') FELBER: Retired Executive Editor of the MANHATTAN (Kansas) MERCURY newspaper. Frequent Board Member of assorted Pulitzer Prize Selection Committees. Noteworthy creator of 'Felber-isms' (They are just like 'Yogi-isms' but regionally famous) and prolific author of golf and major league baseball books including THE HOLE TRUTH: DETERMINING THE GREATEST PLAYERS IN GOLF USING SABERMETRICS, A GAME OF BRAWL: THE ORIOLES, THE BEANEATERS, AND THE BATTLE FOR THE 1897 PENNANT, THE BOOK ON THE BOOK: A LANDMARK INQUIRY INTO WHICH STRATEGIES IN THE MODERN GAME ACTUALLY WORK, UNDER PALLOR, UNDER SHADOW: THE 1920 AMERICAN LEAGUE PENNANT RACE THAT RATTLED AND REBUILT BASEBALL and INVENTING BASEBALL: THE 100

GREATEST GAMES OF THE 19TH CENTURY (SABR Digital Library) (Volume 11), one of America's best sports commentators on professional golf and major league baseball.

LIEUTENANT GENERAL (LTGEN) JAY GARNER, USA (RET.): Former head of the U.S. Office of Humanitarian and Reconstruction Agency (OHRA) in Iraq, 2003, precursor organization to Coalition Provisional Agency (CPA).

MR. LARRY GOLSTON, ESQ.: Attorney-at-law with Beasley, Allen Law Firm, Montgomery, Alabama.

MR. GREG GORDON: Retired Washington Correspondent and national investigative reporter, McClatchy News Syndicate.

MR. ALAN M. GRAYSON, ESQ.: Three-time Congressional Representative (Florida -D) and the man who filed my three federal whistle-blower lawsuits against KBR, CSA, and ITT. One of the exceedingly rare honest men in American politics or America. Noted author of HIGH CRIMES: THE IMPEACHMENT OF DONALD TRUMP.

DR. HANNAH GURMAN: Associate Professor, History of the United States, New York University.

MR. SEYMOUR HERSH: Investigative reporter, 1970 Pulitzer Prize winner for International Reporting.

MS. JAMIE IACOCCA: Personal Assistant to the Chief Executive of NEWS CORP., Robert Thompson.

DR. NAJOOD ADNAN ISSA: International Medical Coordinator, Arab Section, Bumrungrad International Hospital, Bangkok, Thailand.

MISS VICTORIA ('TORI') KAMINSKY: Admissions Counsellor, Stone Academy, West Haven, Connecticut.

MR. ZACKERY S. ('ZACK') KOPPLIN: Investigative reporter, Government Accountability Project.

MR. VICTOR A. KUBLI, ESQ.: Attorney-at-Law who took over from Alan Grayson, Esq., to handle my three federal whistle-blower lawsuits when Alan ran for Congress.

MR. DAVID A. LANDRY: Retired U.S. Department of Defense police officer.

LIEUTENANT COMMANDER (LCDR) SCOTT LARKIN, USN (RET.): Former U.S. Navy Intelligence Officer, computer systems genius and computer programming savant.

MR. STEVE LOTZ: Retired John Deere company executive.

DR. DARRYL R. J. MACER: President of the American University of Sovereign

Nations (AUSN), California; Chairman, Accredited Universities of Sovereign Nations (AUSN); Founder and Director of the Eubios Ethics Institute (EEI); Director of the International Peace and Development Ethics Centre, Kaeng Krachan, Thailand; Research Fellow at the Centre for Ethics of Science and Technology. Chulalongkorn University, Bangkok, Thailand; Affiliated Professor in Philosophy, Kumamoto University, Japan; Visiting Professor of Bioethics, University of San Jose-Recoletos, Cebu City, the Philippines; Research Fellow, Center for Ethics of Science & Technology, Chulalongkorn University, Bangkok, Thailand; Adjunct Professor, Institute for Investigation in Bioethics (IIB), Monterrey, Mexico; Senior Research Scholar, Fulbright Academy of Law, Peace & Public Health☐; Visiting Senior Research Fellow at UN University, Institute for the Advanced Study of Sustainability (IAS), Tokyo, Japan; Editor of Eubios Journal of Asian and International Bioethics, and the world's leading expert on Bioethics and Global Public Health. Prolific author of BIOETHICS FOR THE PEOPLE BY THE PEOPLE; SHAPING GENES; ETHICS, LAW & SCIENCE OF USING GENETIC TECHNOLOGY IN MEDICINE & AGRICULTURE; BIOETHICS IS LOVE OF LIFE: AN ALTERNATIVE TEXTBOOK; BIOETHICS AND THE IMPACT OF GENOMICS IN THE 21ST CENTURY: PHARMACOGENOMICS, DNA POLYMORPHISM AND MEDICAL GENETICS SERVICES; ATTITUDES TO GENETIC ENGINEERING: JAPANESE AND INTERNATIONAL COMPARISONS; ENVIRONMENTAL ETHICS IN MANAGING RESOURCES IN THE ASIA PACIFIC WITH RAVICHANDRAN MOORTHY; UNIVERSALISM & ETHICAL VALUES FOR THE ENVIRONMENT WITH JASDEV SINGH RAI, CELIA THORHEIM, ET AL.; LEGACIES OF LOVE, PEACE & HOPE: HOW EDUCATION CAN OVERCOME HATRED AND DIVIDE.

MR. WAYNE T. MATTHEWS: U.S. Army (Ret.).

MR. T. CHRISTIAN MILLER: Investigative Reporter for ProPublica, 2016 Pulitzer Prize winner for Explanatory Journalism.

COMMANDER (CDR) MITCHELL ('MITCH') D. MOORE, USN (RET.): Best officer I ever met in my years of U.S. military service, both U.S. Air Force and U.S. Navy.

SENATOR (SEN.) JERRY MORAN (Kansas-R) and to all his outstanding staff members in Kansas and Washington, D.C., for their constant support and advice.

MR. PAUL MURRAY, ESQ.: Attorney-at-Law, Hafemann, Magee, Thomas, LLC.

MR. RICHARD B. MYERS: President of Kansas State University, retired U.S. Air

Force General (GEN), former Chairman of the Joint Chiefs of Staff (CJCS) in the Bush Administration during GWII, noted author of EYES ON THE HORIZON: SERVING ON THE FRONT LINES OF NATIONAL SECURITY.

DR. & MRS. LEON E. PANETTA: Former White House Chief of Staff in the Clinton Administration, former Director of the Central Intelligence Agency (CIA) and Secretary of Defense (SECDEF) in the Obama Administration, former Congressman (D-California), Directors of The Panetta Institute.

MR. GRANT PECK: Senior Correspondent, Associated Press (AP), Bangkok, Thailand.

MR. ROBERT H. ('BOB') REID: Senior Managing Editor of the official U.S. military newspaper STARS & STRIPES. Retired Senior Editor, Associated Press (AP).

MR. BRYAN RICHARDSON: Executive Editor, THE MANHATTAN (Kansas) MERCURY newspaper.

SENATOR (SEN.) PAT ROBERTS: Long-serving, distinguished Senator (Kansas-R).

MRS. TAGHREED SABEH: Master's degree student, Bioethics & Global Public Health, American University of Sovereign Nations (AUSN).

MS. KELLY SABERI: Producer & Reporter, KSNT-TV, Topeka, Kansas.

MR. HARITH SALIH: Ph.D. student, Kansas State University, veterinary medicine professional, one the world's leading animal-to-human disease transmission experts.

MR. ED SEATON: Owner, Publisher and Editor-in-Chief, THE MANHATTAN (Kansas) MERCURY newspaper.

MR. NED SEATON: Managing Editor, THE MANHATTAN (Kansas) MERCURY newspaper.

MR. JEFF SESSIONS, ESQ.: Former long-serving, distinguished Senator (Alabama -R); former U.S. Attorney-General during the Trump Administration.

MRS. KIMBERLY STAHLMAN: Widow of the murdered Colonel (COL) Michael R. ('Mike') Stahlman, Judge Advocate General (JAG), U.S. Marine Corps (USMC). COL Stahlman investigated the same titanic stealing I did in Iraq and was assassinated.

MRS. KAY STREY: Retiree.

MR. MARK THOMPSON: Retired Senior Military Editor, TIME MAGAZINE, 1985 Pulitzer Prize winner for Public Service. Currently National Security Analyst, Program of Government Oversight (POGO).

MR. JOHN C. TREVOR: One of the greatest marksmen in American history along with
Daniel Boone, Davy Crockett, Billy the Kid, Annie Oakley, Wyatt Earp, Ned Buntline,
'Doc' Holiday, Sergeant (SGT) Alvin C. York (who was a Corporal (CPL) when he won the Congressional Medal of Honor in World War I (WWI)), John Rambo ("NO MAN, NO LAW, NO WAR, NO CORRUPT U.S. DEFENSE CONTRACTOR IN IRAQ, NO CORRUPT U.S. GOVERNMENT CAN STOP HIM!") and Arnold (The 'Terminator'/ex-'Governator') Schwarzenegger.

DR. JON WEFALD: Retired distinguished President of Kansas State University; noted
author of THE TRANSFORMATIVE YEARS AT KANSAS STATE: THE YEARS OF PRESIDENT JON WEFALD FROM 1986 TO 2009.

MR. CRAIG WHITLOCK: Senior Military Reporter, THE WASHINGTON POST.

MR. ROBERT U. ('BOB') WOODWARD: Investigative reporter and award-winning noteworthy prolific author of PLAN OF ATTACK, OBAMA'S WARS, RAGE and FEAR.

PROF. STEPHEN WOLGAST: The Knight Chair in Audience and Community Engagement for News and Professor of the Practice of Journalism, University of Kansas, retired Staff Editor, NEW YORK TIMES, staff member on the NEW YORK TIMES team that received the Pulitzer Prize for Public Service in 2002.

MR. CORWYN WYMAN: Retired. Expert mountaineer, Glacier Chaser, and distinguished outdoorsman.

MR. GEORGE YUHASZ: Retired security expert and consultant, noted children's author of IMAGINE THAT: THE MAGIC OF THE MYSTERIOUS LIGHTS.

And a very special thanks goes to my wonderful family: my beautiful wife, DR. LANA A. LE BLANC: Professor Modern Standard Arabic (MSA) & Social Justice, the American University of Sovereign Nations (AUSN), my handsome son and Lightning McQueen match box car collector fanatic, MASTER LEONARD HENRY ('YUSEF') LE BLANC IV and my beautiful daughter and future YouTube superstar, MISS LUJANE JASMIN ('L.J.') LE BLANC.

THE BLUF[1]

---

[1] The BLUF is a U.S. Army acronym that means BOTTOM-LINE, UP-FRONT. It refers to the lead slide in any U.S. Army Death-by-Power-Point Slide Presentation so the Commander receiving the briefing will have the important summarized information first to not waste the Commander's time. In Hollywood, this would be called the 'denouement,' where all the seemingly unconnected plot lines in a movie are neatly connected or explained at the end of the film for the audience's benefits. In academic journals this is called the abstract.

President Donald Trump runs the U.S. "Deep State." How do I know this? I wrote him and included a brief summary of my book. Several months later he responded with a delightfully useless, flowery, and idiotic two-page letter that lavished praise on his then Attorney-General, Jeff Sessions, and the most wonderful job the Department of Justice (DOJ) was doing to catch assorted evil perpetrators and foul miscreants just like the ones described in my book. Of course, shortly after, Mr. Trump summarily dispensed with the services of Mr. Sessions in the true, grand, imperial Trumpian manner: "YOU'RE FIRED!" Mr. Sessions' crime? He was one of the very rare honest people in the Trump Administration. As we always used to say in the U.S. military: "You are either part of the solution or you are part of the problem." I also wrote to former Presidents Obama, Bush, and Clinton. No response. (Same with all the Attorney-Generals.) In any event, President Trump knows all about the contents of my book as I not only sent him a copy, I also wrote him five or six more times about the matter. He never replied, but he did not deny it either. President Trump runs the U.S. "Deep State." He will hand the responsibility off to the next President who sits in the White House.

The U.S. invasion of Iraq during Gulf War II (GWII) in March 2003 is the biggest foreign policy and military disaster in American history.

Even the most fanatic, bitter, extremist end-of-the-road/dead-ender, hard-core/die-hard Republican Party neo-conservative (neo-con) must admit that GWII was the biggest national debacle at least since the Vietnam War (another war we entered for totally concocted reasons).

Why did the U.S. invade Iraq?

Every reason (or excuse) the Bush Administration used to invade Iraq was either quickly or eventually found to be bogus or invented. All these explanations for the invasion either immediately fell apart or were eventually proven to be outright lies or fantasies. Regardless of the supposed validity of those reasons or excuses, they all included Saddam Hussein:

That he possessed weapons of mass destruction (WMDs) including chemical, biological, and nuclear weapons. (HEY!!! We KNOW he had them!! They were RIGHT here a second ago! Where ARE they?!?!?!?!? DARN!).² Saddam Hussein wanted the western nations to THINK he possessed WMDs so they would NOT attack him. That strategy backfired spectacularly.

That he consorted with, supported or sponsored terrorists and terrorism. (He did not. He never trusted them and would never let any of them inside Iraq).

That he was ready to give nuclear weapons to terrorists. (He did not have any, and even if he did, Saddam would have never given them to terrorists as he was afraid they would use them against HIM! He never trusted terrorists, jihadis or insurgents).

That he wanted to secretly buy yellowcake from Niger to construct more nuclear weapons. (Just more invented lies by the Bush Administration. Just like this incident, the invasion of Iraq was all off of wishful thinking, concocted, easily disproven intelligence and based on bogus, false foreign intelligence reports).

That Osama bin Laden and he were co-conspirators in the attacks against the New York City Twin Towers and the Pentagon on 9/11. (No-Saddam Hussein neither liked or trusted Osama bin Laden-there was never any contact or cooperation between them).

That he was a psychotic dictator and cruel tyrant to his people who brutalized them mercilessly and must be over thrown to 'liberate' the Iraqi people. (It can be difficult to find an honest Iraqi who will freely admit they did not miss Saddam Hussein for many reasons. If someone were found to be corrupt or stealing from the Iraqi government, Saddam would hang the person in a public square as an example to others).

That he was a grave threat to the region's security after invading Iran (1980-88) and Kuwait (1990-91). (In reality, Saddam Hussein was completely contained by the U.S. militarily-imposed Northern and Southern 'No-Fly' Zones and the United Nations (UN)-led sanctions. The sanctions had crushed the population, created widespread hunger and disease, and caused many children dying due to lack of medicine, medical treatment, and malnutrition.

---

² Saddam Hussein got rid of all his WMDs after the end of Gulf War I (GWI) in 1991. He knew they were too dangerous to keep around in his arsenal. The U.S. never found any WMDs after years of intensive searching.

Saddam Hussein was completely hemmed in and no longer posed a threat to anyone either regionally or internationally).

That he had created a separate army with the specific task of invading Israel (like the Iraq would have had any better success than all the other Arab armies that have invaded Israel since 1948).

The U.S. also had many of its own important strategic geopolitical reasons they used to invade Iraq other than just deposing Saddam Hussein:

The U.S. needed to establish Iraq as a bastion of American-sponsored democracy, and have it eventually spread throughout the Middle East (obviously someone forgot to bring democracy in their back packs).

The U.S. would establish Iraq as a true friend to Israel (in your wildest dreams).

The U.S. would make Iraq serve as a strong counter-balance to Iran's long historical attempts at regional hegemony (not a chance: both countries, Iran and Iraq, have Shiite majorities and close, if complex, centuries-long historic, cultural, social, and religious ties).

By establishing true democracy in Iraq, the country would serve as a base to export more democracy throughout the region and replace regional tyrants like Assad in Syria (not a prayer).

The U.S. would win the 'Global War on Terrorism' (GWOT) by overthrowing Saddam Hussein. (Or as my Iraqi-born wife from Basra always says: "Before the Americans invaded Iraq there were no Islamic Jihad terrorists or al-Qaeda, there was no ISIS or Islamic fundamentalists, there were no fanatical Wahabis or insurgents, there were no Shiite and Sunni militiamen death squads. The Americans let them all in or allowed them to be created.").

Iraq would become an oasis of peace, stability, and prosperity (unlike the entire long history of Iraq it has been in the unsettled, chaotic, or war-like state many times before).

Iraq would have become a great business partner for the U.S. The Iraqis would also become a dependable or reliable source of oil to the U.S. Iraq would send us their cheap crude oil in exchange for all manner of consumer, industrial, plus other goods, and services.

It was breathlessly (or blandly) stated that when America invaded Iraq and repaired the decrepit oil industry infrastructure, bringing it up to full production, that the revenues would more than pay for both the complete repair of Iraq's crumbling infrastructure and the U.S. military occupation. It was also stated again and again by the Iraqi exiles to the Clinton and Bush Administration leaders and to high DOD officials, or anyone who would listen, that once the U.S. and Coalition troops crossed the Kuwaiti border into Iraq that they would be met by throngs of people lining the sides of the roads and streets, especially little children, all waiving little American and Iraqi flags and cheering at them on as they sped by on their way to capture Baghdad. Unfortunately that event did not turn out exactly as advertised.

The only problem was they had told the Americans, like everyone always does in the Third World, exactly what they wanted to hear in an effort to get the U.S. to invade Iraq so they could assume power in the vacuum left by Saddam Hussein's removal and start stealing everything. They could have cared less about the Iraqi people and their survival. They wanted one thing and one thing only: total, unrestrained, absolute power. And if they had to spin a bunch of lies, fantasies and pure made-up non-sense to the Clinton and Bush Administrations to get that power, then so be it.

All were lies, inventions, or fantasies at best. Nothing like that even remotely happened.

So why did the U.S. invade Iraq?

If you ask anyone on 'Arab Street'[3] the answer is obvious why the U.S. invaded Iraq: oil. Or more specifically, the U.S. invaded Iraq to steal all of Iraq's oil. But even this reason quickly falls apart on closer examination. If anything, the total OPPOSITE happened. Instead of the U.S. helping themselves to Iraq's oil by furiously pumping it out and spiriting it all away, the company most responsible for boosting oil production, Halliburton, the parent of KBR, under the Restore Iraq's Oil (RIO) Program did the complete opposite. They hindered or retarded Iraq's oil production. Iraqis in the oil

---

[3] A colloquial term for any Arab living in the Middle East/Gulf States or an Arabic speaker.

industry and Iraqi's National Oil Ministry constantly complained about poor service, bad equipment, endless delays and, in general, no real plan to do much of anything except minor repairs. A total failure by all accounts.

Then why did the U.S. invade Iraq?

This question has still remained unanswered for over 17 years. Even though the historic record already has literally thousands of books on the subject and more to come, all these books are the same: They describe the WHO, WHERE, WHEN and WHAT happened in Iraq before and during the GWII, but not the WHY. All these books are not wrong or inaccurate. It is just the real explanation is still missing.

Before we answer that important question we must back-up slightly to see who could have stopped the war from even starting.

Two people could have stopped GWII before it started. Bush Administration National Security Advisor Condoleezza Rice and Secretary of State and retired U.S. Army GEN Colin Powell. Both of them possessed national (even international) prestige in abundance. Their decades-long experience in government, military, academic and/or leadership positions gave them great, even unmatched 'Gravitas' inside the Bush Administration. A firm "No" from either or both of them would have stopped GWII dead in its tracks. They had 'War Veto' power but did not use it.

In retrospect, it is ironic to note that Colin Powell had three chances or opportunities to either correct or change major historic events and failed to do so. The first was as the investigating officer of the My Lai massacre in South Vietnam during the Vietnam War in 1969. For all of Colin Powell's many sterling attributes, he most likely lacked an investigator's instinct or experience-perhaps even called an investigator's 'sixth sense.' He found no evidence of the atrocity after a limited inquiry. Later, Seymour Hersh, an investigative reporter, followed his own finely-honed investigator's instincts about the massacre and won a Pulitzer Prize for reporting on the incident in 1970. The second was what Colin Powell admitted was the worst mistake of his storied career: When he stood up in front of the United Nations General

Assembly in 2003 and stated that Saddam Hussein possessed WMDs. The third time is when I wrote him and Condoleezza Rice about the real reason GWII was started. They could have spoken against it then. But like all good soldiers, they saluted smartly and carried on to the best of their ability in supporting GWII in spite of their grave personal misgivings. They should have listened to their sharply-honed (or accurate) instincts.

Even with the war in progress, only one man could have prevented the insurgency from even starting: Retired U.S. Army LTGEN Jay Garner, who was appointed as the Head of the Office of Reconstruction and Humanitarian Assistance (ORHA). Even then, LTGEN Jay Garner had to literally fight his way through the direct interference, non-cooperation, and mountain of red tape of both Rumsfeld and Cheney on all matters to even get into Iraq. Even though he was supposed to be in charge of Iraq, he and ORHA were treated as an unwanted orphan organization. This was all done deliberately to cause him maximum grief for one outstanding reason.

The one most overwhelmingly important fact of Arabic (and especially Iraqi) culture, far ahead of all the others, is the maintaining of 'Family Honor.' No other aspect of Arab culture is of paramount importance. 'Family Honor' is placed on the male head of the household. It must be maintained or upheld even until death by everyone in the family. It is the one most important aspect of Iraqi and understanding Iraqi culture. The most critical point of the Iraqi people was never even considered by the American military or civilian planners. The vitally important point was irrelevant to them. This failure to take this critically important fact into account would cost many Americans and others their lives and the wounding of thousands more for their fatal lack of cultural understanding.

As an example, what that means is even if the highest-ranking government minister has to work in an completely barren office without a door or glass in the windows, no telephone, no furniture, even if it means they have to sit alone on the barren floor, as long as the minister has their salary being paid on-time, their benefits or perks retained or to be restored at some point, that their official title, personal prestige and 'Family Honor' is preserved and respected, that they can feed and support their families, then they will support the American and Coalition occupiers without question. Not everyone will be happy, but no insurgency can gain the slightest traction in this situation. As Mao Tse-Tung once said: "The guerrilla must move amongst the people as a fish swims in the sea." If the Americans treat the Iraqis with respect, courtesy, and dignity plus maintain their 'Family Honor', then the insurgents will never gain any traction with the Iraqis.

Additionally, if the rest of the country were taken care and looked after: the pensioners, the unemployed, the destitute, the elderly, the incapacitated or crippled, military veterans, retirees of all types, widows, orphans, the military, and security establishment, all the professions, etc., then everyone would have satisfied with the new status quo if they had been taken care of with their salaries and pensions kept intact. Every Iraqi was dependent on the Ba'ath Political Party, and in effect, Saddam Hussein, for some support. To work for the Iraqi government meant you had to be at least a nominal, card-carrying member of the Ba'ath Party. That included every single professional: all doctors, lawyers, nurses, teachers, university professors, engineers, airline pilots, architects, dentists, medical service workers, transportation workers, sanitation workers-literally everyone. It was rare to see a private company in Iraq. And even though there was intense fighting between the Iraqi military and Coalition Forces until Baghdad was captured, almost all of the Iraqi population was sitting on the side lines and waiting to see what the Americans would do once they took control of the country. What the Americans would do would determine if the Iraqi people would support the occupation or oppose it. Initially the people were fully willing to support the occupation of Iraq if the Americans treated them with dignity, respect and guarded or preserved their 'Family Honor.' The U.S. had only one chance to succeed. It completely blew it, but this was all blown deliberately.

If any American knew Iraq and Iraqis better than anyone else, then it was LTGEN Jay Garner. His work with Operation Provide Comfort put him in daily contact with the Kurds in Northern Iraq after Gulf War I (GWI). He was the right man at the right place at the right time for the right mission this time in governing Iraq, a practically impossible job and made even more difficult with the total lack of support he received. He literally received no help.

Quickly, Donald Rumsfeld and Dick Cheney determined they had selected the wrong man for the job running Iraq's occupation. They did everything they could to hamper or stifle LTGEN Jay Garner prior to his departure and while he was in Iraq. In their minds, LTGEN Garner had too many incurable flaws: He was extremely intelligent, very experienced in Iraq, highly respected by the Kurds, independent-minded, no-nonsense, take-charge, honorable, well-organized and was not going to follow any idiotic or non-sensical orders or suggestions from anyone as the appointed Iraqi's Pro-counsel. Rumsfeld and Cheney had to get rid of him as quickly and unceremoniously as possible.

Fortunately, they quickly found a man the complete opposite of LTGEN Jay Garner. Plus, this man met all their exact requirements; a mirror image opposite: This man was politically reliable, he had absolutely no experience in the Middle East, a loyal Republican to a fault, would ignore the obvious (or be blindly oblivious to all the stealing going on in Iraq by KBR and by all the other corrupt U.S. defense contractors who were now pouring into Iraq aided by their Republican congressional 'sponsors' or anyone who had strong ties with the Bush Administration) and would do exactly what he was told to do without any question. The dirty deed was done. The change was immediately announced. LTGEN Garner was quickly, if unceremoniously, bundled off the stage. When former Ambassador L. Paul 'Jerry' Bremer took over power, the first order of business was to throw all Ba'ath Party members out of work and then disband the Iraqi Army and Police plus all the security forces and intelligence agencies. Jerry Bremer instantly made 2.5 million enraged, implacable enemies. He either decided to do that on his own or did what he was ordered to do by Rumsfeld and Cheney. The effect was exactly the same. There would be a very long war with no end. KBR would now steal hundreds of billions of dollars and Iraqi dinars. The insurgency exploded right at that moment exactly as it was planned. America's efforts were doomed. There was no hope.

Post-GWII planning? There are several adjectives used to described it from all the planners: ignored, cursory look at their results, half-hearted, when any plan was completed it was just filed away. Some planners were eerily prescient as to what was going to happen in Iraq post-war end of combat operations. Others who sent in elaborate plans were simply disregarded or shoved to the side lines. Rumsfeld and Cheney deliberately ignored all post-war planning and for one extremely specific reason which was the core of their strategy: deliberate, complete post-war chaos. Who makes money in a short insurgency or war? No one. The U.S. Army furls up its guidons, cases its flags and goes home. The Iraqi Army and Police takes over security. Who makes money in a long insurgency or war? KBR. A long insurgency or war means lots of time to steal hundreds of billions of dollars, defraud the U.S. government and cheat the poor, hapless, benighted taxpayers.

Everyone has been looking through the wrong end of the telescope on this sordid affair (all they are seeing is the eyeball of the startled astronomer). The invasion of Iraq during GWII was the perfect vehicle, the perfect war, the perfect plan executed exactly as planned by the Master-Minds who conceived it and carried it out with rare missteps along the way. Everything unfolded exactly as the Grand Puppet Masters who were secretly working behind-the-scenes as overarching manipulators expected it to happen. It was also a smokescreen, a scam, a ploy, a Kabuki Play, a farce, and all a deliberate scheme. The invasion of Iraq during GWII and the subsequent massive cover-up by DOJ, DOD, et al., is a perfect example of a U.S. "Deep State" operation.

This massive operation was brilliantly planned, precisely executed, and masterfully maintained through almost two decades of subterfuge, lying, dissimilation and stonewalling. The invasion of Iraq and GWII was not to steal oil: as almost every Iraqi, and Arab, will swear on the Koran that was the real reason, but to secretly steal money: hundreds of billions of U.S. dollars and Iraqi dinars and cover their tracks in doing so, including at least one murder of a brave, stalwart USMC JAG COL named Michael R. ('Mike') Stahlman, who was also investigating massive thievery that had been long going on at his base in Camp Ramadi, Anbar Province in 2008. His death was immediately labeled a 'suicide.' The USMC said COL Stahlman killed himself by shooting himself in the left side of the head. But when the USMC Casualty Assistance Officer told this to his widow, Kimberly Stahlman that, she immediately screamed out: "HE'S RIGHT-HANDED!" She soon found out her husband was shot from a distance. (What is wrong with this picture?) The whole affair was quickly covered-up by the USMC and DOD; all the on-scene evidence was quickly destroyed. No one at DOD or the USMC will even speak to Mrs. Stahlman. Everyone continues to completely stonewall her to this day, even their oldest friends that she and her husband had known for more than twenty years since first joining the USMC.

There is one specific reason, but it has nothing to do with stealing oil, bringing democracy to Iraq and the Middle East, finding WMDs, establishing liberty, creating a bastion of regional stability, freeing the Iraqi people from Saddam's tyranny, making Iraq become a friend of Israel, or introducing the blessings of McDonald's Big Mac to the citizens of Iraq.[4]

The invasion of Iraq that kick-started GWII was all thought up and executed by Dick Cheney and Donald Rumsfeld. Working in concert, they planned, executed, and controlled all aspects of the thievery done in Iraq through KBR. The war was merely a cover. KBR did double stealing by overbilling the poor U.S. taxpayers for goods and services and then outright stealing goods, equipment and supplies that supported U.S. military operations. Normally, security investigators inside KBR would have caught the thievery. Except they hired minimal numbers of grossly incompetent, unqualified idiots, even hiring some people with criminal records, who made circus clowns look like seasoned security professionals. At one point, as soon as I connected Cheney, Rumsfeld, and the Deputy Project Manager (DPM) of KBR Operations in Iraq, Remo Butler, all running the massive theft ring, they immediately shut down ALL investigations of KBR country-wide.

---

[4] When my Iraqi-born wife attended an American-based university in Bangkok in 2006 for an M.A. degree in International Relations, she was worried she was not going to be academically prepared as the other graduate students since her undergraduate degree from Basra University was in English (she speaks British English as well as 'Eliza Doolittle' does in MY FAIR LADY: flawlessly). She need not have worried. All the classes were about Iraq and GWII. Everyone was fascinated by my wife's stories about her life inside Iraq and the effect on her from the GWII invasion. She had endless tales to tell. All the students and faculty members told my wife about all the reasons why the U.S. had to invade Iraq. My wife immediately demolished them one-by-one. But the most outrageously silly claim was from one clueless student who told her that the U.S. had the right to invade Iraq to bring the blessings of McDonald's hamburgers to the Iraqi people. My wife went into orbit around Pluto and verbally ripped her into shreds. She did manage to graduate with distinction.

Everything! (What is wrong with this picture?) I was summarily thrown out of KBR Security and soon had trumped-up charges levelled against me. I was illegally terminated as were other honest people who were asking the wrong questions.

I filed a federal whistle-blower lawsuit against KBR in 2007 after I returned to the U.S. After SIX YEARS of investigating, DOJ could NOT FIND ONE INSTANCE of any stealing by KBR in Iraq. After the federal whistle-blower lawsuit was dismissed by the court in exasperation of DOJ's lack of a decision either way on if KBR had stolen anything, I eventually requested all the investigation records on the KBR lawsuit from DOJ. I was expecting several dozen semi-trailer-loads of documents to come rolling in one day. What poured in the old mail chute? Only 220 pages. EXACTLY WHAT WAS GIVEN TO DOJ AT THE START OF THE INVESTIGATION! The actual lawsuit and a few court documents was all I got back. There was NOT A SINGLE SHRED OF EVIDENCE that DOJ had ever done an investigation into KBR's massive stealing. DOJ has NEVER supported a single federal whistle-blower lawsuit in court. They declined to intervene on every single one of them from the Bush, through the Obama and now the Trump Administrations. All the Attorney-Generals were either co-opted or willingly participated in the cover-up. Old English Common Law: "Knew or should have known." They all either knew about it or should have known about it.

Why? The U.S. "Deep State" in perfect operation. There are many players or culprits. Everyone is covering for everyone else. As former Attorney General Jeff Sessions was quoted as saying if these lawsuits ever went forward then the whole U.S. government would collapse.

What about the DOD? There had to be daily reports of major thefts of equipment, supplies and materials that was having a negative effect on the U.S. Army's ability to carry about its mission. I spoke to the former CJCS during GWII, retired GEN Richard B. Myers, USAF in his office as President of Kansas State University briefly one time about it a few years ago. He stated that there was a lot of stealing going on all over Iraq. That is like saying Saudi Arabia has a lot of sand. But Donald Rumsfeld had already anticipated the scam long before he took over as SECDEF. Under the 'guise' of improving and making the Pentagon more efficient or 'transforming' the U.S. military, he carried out a whirlwind of daily verbal abuse, a continual, never-ending barrage of humiliations and personal insults. This was done for only one reason. Like a conjurer who furiously waves their left hand in your face to distract you while they pick your pocket with their right hand. This was all done to keep everyone in the Pentagon completely occupied and focused on the next furious tirade or tongue-lashing. No one was immune, from the CJCS down to the lowest-ranking military member in the Pentagon. It was all an act, a cover, a game. It was only to distract anyone from asking any questions about what was really going on in Iraq or why there was so much stealing going on. Everyone greatly feared Rumsfeld. They dreaded everything about him-for good reason.

Normally, the DOD's Office of the Inspector General (DOD/IG) would have gotten directly involved in this matter. They were completely muzzled by Rumsfeld. During DOJ's investigation into KBR's thievery, after I filed my whistle-blower lawsuit, my lawyer and I met with what I thought were three DOJ's investigators in a meeting in May 2010 inside a DOJ office building. When I sent a Freedom of Information Act (FOIA) to DOD/IG in 2017 for information on any investigation done on KBR, they sent back a transcript of our meeting. The investigators were not from DOJ as I had believed but from DOD/IG. The whole transcript was invented lies. We actually had spent almost six hours in that meeting. We blew right past lunch. I went into great detail how the scam and stealing all worked, all the cover-ups, the connection between Rumsfeld, Cheney, Remo Butler, and the KBR thieves. I also explained in graphic detail how everything was stolen and sold to a massive 100,000-man Iraqi theft ring gang outside the bases was being run by their leader named Mr. Ahmed Abu Kahlem Hassan who ran an army of marauding criminals called the "Hausassem" (thieves in Arabic). They were giving some of the proceeds to the insurgents to buy arms, make more IEDs, weapons to shootdown U.S. Army helicopters (sorry Tammy Duckworth, you can thank KBR for your combat injuries) and hire more insurgents who were then killing more American and Coalition soldiers. Not only were KBR workers and their Iraqi minions thieves, they were also murderers and traitors. I told them all this was set-up by Cheney and Rumsfeld.

In the DOJ meeting the investigators were silent. They took no notes. They asked two unanswerable questions. They acted totally bored to death, as if I were wasting their time. The DOD/IG investigators wrote after our meeting that I did not know why I had filed the federal whistle-blower lawsuit, I had no evidence to offer them, I could not answer any of their questions, I was totally clueless as to why I was even in this meeting and they stated the whole meeting lasted only a few minutes. They recommended dismissal. Another complete cover-up by DOD. All orchestrated by Rumsfeld and Cheney to completely muzzle DOD and DOD/IG plus any subsequent investigation of KBR and every other corrupt U.S. defense contractor in Iraq.

And where is Big Media in all of this? It is America's most self-important, self-absorbed, self-awarding profession who presents itself more honors, awards, prizes, citations, and certificates of merit and congratulations than any other organization in the world (outside of Hollywood and Broadway who vie for a distant second). Surely, how can a blockbuster story of tens (or hundreds?) of thousands of Americans simultaneously betraying their own country (the largest group of Americans to simultaneous do so since the South succeeded from the Union in U.S. Civil War; that betrayal continues to this day); hundreds of billions of U.S. dollars just evaporating in Iraq during GWII; the largest government cover-up in American history including DOD, DOJ and others, stand against the height of Melania's Trump's high heels; that Princess Kate wore the exact same overcoat yesterday that she wore five years ago; what the color, shape, weight and size of the little poop that baby Prince George Albert Louis just had when his mother, Princess Kate, changed his little diapers at Buckingham Palace; or what Kim Kardashian's little sister's best friend's maid's dog has for breakfast this morning, plus Donald Trump's latest tweet? It cannot. It is impossible. There is absolutely no contest.

All the media was totally unanimous in their responses: "GREAT STORY!!!!!!! But, ancient history, not enough manpower, too hard to do." That comment is no doubt true, but peddling extreme trivia is not news, it is just extreme trivia. But Big Media is just trying to give people what they want in order to stay in business. It is just feeding us the drug we cannot get enough of. This drug is endless streams of useless, ultra-fast minutia on a 24/7 hour news cycle. We just cannot get enough of it. Hard news? (Fuhgeddaboudit!) I had long thought Big Media was part of the U.S. "Deep State." But I finally determined they are just simply too lazy to do a REAL news like mine. (And some of them are very rude too.)

The list of American and international media I contacted to no effect would take up a whole book: THE WASHINGTON POST, NEW YORK TIMES, THE NEW YORK POST, THE DAILY NEWS (New York), THE WALL STREET JOURNAL, THE BOSTON GLOBE, VICE, USA TODAY, TIME MAGAZINE, HOUSTON CHRONICLE, THE NEW YORKER MAGAZINE, THE HUFFPO, ABC NEWS, NBC NEWS, CBS NEWS, BLOOMBERG NEWS, SIXTY MINUTES, MSNBC, BREITBART NEWS, CNN, QANON, THE LINCOLN PROJECT, FOX NEWS, MCCLATCHY NEWS SERVICE, the ASSOCIATED PRESS (AP), even THE NATIONAL INQUIRER, was contacted. No one was even interested to reply.

International media included RT-TV (Russia Today), TASS and PRAVDA (all Russia), MANICHI SHMBAUM (Japan), AGENCY FRANCE-PRESSE (AFP) (France), CHINA NEWS SERVICE (China), BRITISH BRODCASTING COMPANY (BCC), THE TIMES OF LONDON, and THE MANCHESTER GUARDIAN (all UK). No replies.

I actually did get a few brief inquiries: AL-JAZEERA, THE WASHINGTON POST and even THE MANHATTAN (Kansas) MERCURY newspaper. But all of them acted like I was some newly-arrived, clueless tourist in some Third World country where they tell you exactly what you want to hear. ("SURE, GREAT STORY! WE'LL GET RIGHT BACK TO YOU ON IT!")

I spoke with Mr. Marty Baron, Executive Editor of THE WASHINGTON POST in April 2017 when he came for an important lecture at Kansas State University. He first stated in public during the Question and Answers (Q&A) session that he was interested in my story. He asked for all the lawsuit and supporting documents. I immediately sent them directly to him. After a month THE WASHINGTON POST's National Military Reporter, Mr. Craig Whitlock, called me. He said they had already done stories on KBR stealing and dismissed me: "Now, go write a book about it." A quick check of THE WASHINGTON POST's morgue (clippings of previous news stories) showed no such KBR story was ever written, but they did do many stories on Stuart W. Bowen, Jr., Special Inspector General for Iraq's Reconstruction (SIGIR) activities, but they had nothing to do with KBR's phenomenal stealing during GWII.

Then a Mr. Phil Rees, Investigative Reporter from AL-JAZEERA, unexpectedly called me out of the blue from Doha, Qatar in December 2017. He said his boss got my letter about my proposed subject and directed Mr. Rees help me write my book about this whole scam. We talked at length about everything. He said AL-JAZEERA would fly me to Washington, D.C. in February 2018 for an interview. February 2018 came and went. I contacted his assistant, Mr. Alex Crutcher, about what happened in March. He said Mr. Rees was busy. The meeting was postponed until late 2018. No one from AL-JAZEERA ever contacted me again.

I even spoke to the Managing Editor, Mr. Ned Seaton, of THE MANHATTAN (Kansas) MERCURY, the local newspaper when I lived there. We spoke at length. He said he was happy to help me, having been on numerous Pulitzer Prize selection committees over the years. He told me he also knew people at THE NEW YORK TIMES, THE WASHINGTON POST and THE WALL STREET JOURNAL. We would try the WALL STREET JOURNAL first, the best fit for the story. He also said he knew Senator Pat Roberts (Kansas-R) quite well. We could also go to see him. I then suddenly realized, just as in the Third World, he was telling me EXACTLY what I wanted to hear (not what I needed to know). He was just trying to get rid of me. He never called me back.

Only one news organization expressed interest. The most venerable, honest, stalwart, and trustworthy newspaper in the USA: the U.S. military's STARS & STRIPES. Already under constant, enormous pressure from the Trump Administration, DOD and the U.S. "Deep State" to cease and desist their unbiased, impartial, and accurate reporting, the Senior Managing Editor, Bob Reid, said they would do a book review once this was published.

Congress? Except for very few stalwarts, like Congressional Representatives Henry Waxman, Maxine Waters and Alan Grayson, all acting as unheard voices in the wilderness, nothing happened. As someone who knows politicians of all stripes very, pointedly explained to me in graphic detail: "No politician in D.C. would dare speak out on the matter. They all knew what was going on in Iraq. All the other politicians would immediately destroy them." I also got a letter in February 2018 from Acting Assistant Attorney General-Civil Division, Chad Readler, who blamed me for everything in that I did not find some deep-pockets law firm to sue KBR on my own without DOJ intervention. Like some law firm would spend many millions of dollars in investigating KBR for a civil court trial without intervention from DOJ. They knew that perfectly well. DOJ rigged it that way including all their internal rules that hampered every whistle-blower who tried to obtain justice. Or as some call DOJ: The "Department of INJUSTICE."

Donald Rumsfeld and Dick Cheney and their thousands of traitorous little minions and lackeys got away with it. It is the largest theft and cover-up in U.S. history, along with many thousands of American betrayers who sold their country out, all being incredibly happy to help these two perps do anything and to protect them completely. The U.S. "Deep State" has succeeded. It continues, all courtesy of President Donald Trump: The Puppet Master. This is all unknown, unwritten history - until now.

President Trump just accused the Pentagon of starting wars and being in bed with the U.S. defense contractors. Remarkably, he is half right. The Pentagon does not start wars, Presidents do that. But this all could not have happened without the connivance of the Pentagon with U.S. defense contractors stealing billions and without the assistance of senior military officers in and out of the Pentagon. Both are totally in a deeply incestuous relationship. They are all one evil unit.

This is the largest theft in U.S. history. This is the largest cover up in U.S. history. It is also the largest scandal and cover-up in USMC history. And this is the biggest simultaneous betrayal of the U.S. by the largest group of Americans since the U.S. Civil War and the longest since it is still on-going to date. President Donald Trump knows about it and does nothing.

	Page
ACKNOWLEDGEMENTS	4
THE BLUF	9
TABLE OF CONTENTS	25
ACRONYMS	30
COLORFUL CAST OF CHARACTERS	38
INTRODUCTION	41

Chapters-Day
1. This was not the first time I had been in Iraq	45
2. Camp Victory-North & Camp Hope	54

AUGUST 2005
3. 01 Camp Hope-Camp Manager's Office	67
4. 14 Camp Hope-Camp Manager's Office	68

JANUARY 2006
5. 15 Camp Hope (E-mail)	69
6. 15 Camp Hope (E-mail)	69
7. 15 Camp Hope-Security Office	70
8. 15 Camp Hope (E-mail)	71
9. 17 Camp Hope (E-mail)	72
10. 17 Camp Victory-North (E-mail)	72
11. 17 Camp Hope (E-mail)	73
12. 17 Camp Victory-North (E-mail)	73

FEBRUARY 2006
13. 02 Camp Hope-Helicopter Landing Pad	73
14. 04 Camp Prosperity-Operations Office	73
15. 04-06 Camp Union III-KBR	76
16. 07 Camp Prosperity-Human Resources (HR) Office	77
17. 07 Camp Prosperity-Camp Managers' Office	79
18. 07 Camp Prosperity-IPBD Co. Managers' Office	79
19. 08 U.S. Embassy Main Building-DCMA's Office	84
20. 08 Camp Prosperity-Main Yard	84
21. 08 Camp Prosperity-IPBD Co. Managers Office	85
22. 10 USMI Compound-KBR Security Office	91
23. 10 Camp Prosperity-Camp Manager's Office	92

24. 11 Camp Prosperity-Main Yard	94
25. 11 Camp Prosperity-HVAC Department	95
26. 11 Camp Union III-Security Office	96
27. 11 Camp Prosperity-Main Yard	98
28. 12 Camp Prosperity-Main Yard	98
29. 12 Camp Prosperity-Main Yard	99
30. 13 Camp Prosperity (E-mail)	100
31. 13 Camp Prosperity-Electrical Department Office	101
32. 13 Camp Prosperity-My Office	101
33. 14 Camp Prosperity (E-mail)	102
34. 14 Camp Prosperity-Mayor's Cell Office	103
35. 14 Camp Prosperity-Mayor's Cell Office	103
36. 14 Camp Prosperity (E-mail)	104
37. 14 Camp Prosperity-My Office	104
38. 15 Camp Union III-KBR Security Office	105
39. 15 Camp Union III-Fuel Point	105
40. 18 Camp Prosperity-Camp General Storage Room Area	107
41. 19 Camp Prosperity (E-mail)	107
42. 19 Camp Prosperity-Main Yard	109
43. 19 Camp Prosperity-IPBD Co. Managers Office	110
44. 20 Camp Prosperity-Main Yard	111
45. 20 Camp Prosperity (E-mail)	112
46. 20 Camp Prosperity-Main Yard	112
47. 20 Camp Prosperity-Main Yard	113
48. 20 Camp Victory-North (E-mail)	114
49. 20 Camp Victory-Main Yard	114
50. 21 Camp Prosperity (E-mail)	114
51. 21 Baghdad Convention Center (BCC)- LN/TCN Badging Application Program Office	117
52. 21 Camp Prosperity (E-mail)	118
53. 21 Camp Prosperity (E-mail)	118
54. 22 Camp Prosperity-Main Yard	119
55. 22 Camp Prosperity-IPBD Co. Managers' Office	120
56. 22 Camp Prosperity-Main Yard	121
57. 23 Camp Prosperity-IPBD Co. Managers' Office	121
58. 23 Camp Prosperity-My Office	126
59. 23 Camp Prosperity (E-mail)	128
60. 23 Camp Prosperity-Main Yard	128
61. 23 Camp Victory-North (E-mail)	131

62. 23 Camp Prosperity (E-mail)	132
63. 23 Camp Prosperity-Operations Office	133
64. 23 Camp Prosperity-Power Gen Department Office	133
65. 23 Camp Prosperity-Main Yard	134
66. 23 Camp Prosperity (E-mail)	136
67. 23 Camp Victory-North (E-mail)	136
68. 25 Camp Prosperity-Main Yard	138
69. 25 Camp Prosperity-Main Yard	139
70. 25 Camp Prosperity-Main Yard	139
71. 25 Camp Prosperity (E-mail)	140
72. 26 Camp Prosperity-My Room	140
73. 26 Camp Prosperity-Baghdad Interrogation Facility (BIF), Ground Floor Cell	142
74. 26 Camp Prosperity-Main Yard	142
75. 26 Camp Union III-Security Office	144
76. 26 Camp Prosperity (E-mail)	145
77. 26 Camp Victory-North (E-mail)	146
78. 26 Camp Prosperity (E-mail)	146
79. 26 Camp Victory-North (E-mail)	147
80. 27 Camp Prosperity (E-mail)	147
81. 27 Camp Prosperity-My Office	147
82. 27 Camp Union III-Security Office	149
83. 27 Camp Prosperity (E- mail)	150
84. 27 Camp Prosperity-Main Yard	151
85. 27 Camp Prosperity (E-mail)	151
86. 27 Camp Prosperity (E-mail)	154
87. 28 Camp Prosperity (E-mail)	154
88. 28 Camp Prosperity-Main Yard	155
89. 28 Camp Prosperity (E-mail)	155
90. 28 Camp Prosperity (E-mail)	158
91. 28 Camp Prosperity (E-mail)	158
92. 28 Camp Victory-North (E-mail)	159
93. 28 Camp Prosperity (E-mail)	159
94. 28 Camp Prosperity (My Room)	159
95. 28 Camp Victory-North (E-mail)	160
96. 28 Camp Prosperity (E-mail)	160
97. 28 Camp Prosperity (E-mail)	160
98. 28 Camp Prosperity (E-mail)	160
99. 28 Camp Prosperity-IPBD Co. Managers' Office	160

99. 28 Camp Prosperity (E-mail)	161
100. 28 Camp Prosperity-Main Yard	162
101. 28 Camp Prosperity (E-mail)	163

MARCH 2006

102. 01 Camp Prosperity (E-mail)	163
103. 01 Camp Prosperity (E-mail)	163
104. 01 Camp Prosperity-Main Yard	164
105. 01 Camp Union III-Fuel Point	165
106. 01 Camp Prosperity (E-mail)	165
107. 01 Camp Victory-North (E-mail)	165
108. 01 Camp Prosperity (E-mail)	166
109. 01 Camp Prosperity-My Office	167
110. 02 Camp Prosperity-My Office	167
111. 02 Camp Prosperity-Main Yard	168
112. 03 Camp Prosperity-IPBD Co. Managers' Office	169
113. 03 Camp Union III-Fuel Point	169
114. 03 U.S. Embassy Main Building-DCMA's Office	171
115. 03 Camp Prosperity (E-mail)	174
116. 03 Camp Prosperity (E-mail)	174
117. 04 Camp Victory-North (E-mail)	175
118. 04 Camp Prosperity (E-mail)	175
119. 04 Camp Prosperity (E-mail)	176
120. 04 Camp Prosperity (E-mail)	177
121. 05 Camp Victory-North (E-mail)	178
122. 05 Camp Prosperity (E-mail)	178
123. 05 Camp Prosperity (E-mail)	179
124. 05 Camp Prosperity-My Office	179
125. 05 Camp Victory-North (E-mail)	180
126. 05 Camp Prosperity (E-mail)	180
127. 05 Camp Prosperity (E-mail)	180
128. 05 Camp Prosperity (E-mail)	182
129. 06 Camp Prosperity (E-mail)	183
130. 06 Camp Victory-North (E-mail)	183
131. 06 Camp Prosperity (E-mail)	184
132. 06 Camp Prosperity-IPBD Co. Managers' Office	186
133. 06 Camp Prosperity (E-mail)	186
134. 07 Camp Prosperity (E-mail)	188
135. 07 Camp Prosperity-IPBD Co. Managers' Office	189

136. 07 Camp Prosperity-Camp Mayor's Cell Office	190
137. 07 Camp Prosperity-Electrical Department Office	191
138. 10 Camp Prosperity-My Office	192
139. 11 Camp Prosperity-Night Patrol	192
140. 11 Camp Prosperity-IBPD Co. Managers' Office	193
141. 11 Camp Prosperity (E-mail)	195
142. 11 Camp Prosperity (E-mail)	196
143. 11 Camp Prosperity-Night Patrol	197
144. 19 Camp Prosperity-IPBD Co. Managers' Office	197
145. 20 Camp Prosperity (E-mail)	200
146. 20 Camp Prosperity (E-mail)	201
147. 20 Camp Prosperity (E-mail)	202
148. 20 Camp Prosperity-My Office	203
149. 21 Camp Victory-North-Security Office	204
Author's Biography	208
Addendums	209

ACRONYMS

14th of July Bridge: Bridge over the Tigris River that connects west and east Baghdad.
It is the main entrance into the "Green Zone." The bridge is named after 14 July 1958

which is the day the Hashemite monarchy was overthrown in a military coup d'état.

9/11: Acronym for the attacks on the Twin Towers and the Pentagon on 11 September 2001 by terrorists.

ACO: U.S. Army Contracts Officer.

A.D.: Anno Domini.

AFOSI: U.S. Air Force Office of Special Investigation. They were responsible for all serious incident investigations inside the International Zone (IZ) or "Green Zone," while the U.S. Air Force Security Forces (SF) were responsible for minor incident investigations in the International Zone (IZ) or "Green Zone." The U.S. Army CID is responsible for serious incident investigations in the rest of Iraq or outside the IZ or "Green Zone."

AMR: U.S. Army Movement Request. An official written request to the U.S. Army to move KBR personnel from Point A to Point B by helicopter, convoy, etc.

AO: Area of Operations.

AP: Associated Press. The international news agency based in New York City, New York.

APO: U.S. Army or U.S. Air Force military post office.

ASAP: As soon as possible.

AUSN: American University of Sovereign Nations, California.

AWOL: Absent without leave from U.S. military service.

B.A.: Bachelor of Arts degree.

BBC: British Broadcasting Company.

BCC: Baghdad Convention Center, "Green Zone," Baghdad, Iraq.

BGEN: U.S. Army, U.S. Air Force or U.S. Marine Corps Brigadier General.

BIAP: Baghdad International Airport. Pronounced "Bye-op."

BIF: Baghdad Interrogation Facility, Camp Prosperity, Baghdad, Iraq.

BLUF: Bottom Line, Up Front means the conclusion or summary is stated on the first slide in U.S. military Power-Point Slide Presentation so the commander's time is not wasted.

B.S.: Bullshit; i.e., lie(s) or falsehood(s).

BTC: KBR's Baghdad Transit Center, Camp Victory-North. All KBR employees coming into or departing Iraq via aircraft at BIAP has be processed through BTC to transit elsewhere. BTC was a complex of offices and bunking facilities operating in converted mobile homes.

BX/PX: U.S. Army or U.S. Air Force base/post exchange. U.S. military's department store.

CAC Card(s): Common Access Card(s). These are U.S. government-issued ID cards with eight colored stripes. This is to identify at a glance the status of the owner/wearer/

bearer on the U.S. military installation. Categories include U.S. military, non-U.S., or foreign military, U.S. contractors, foreign contractors, U.S. and non-U.S. civilian workers, Local Nationals (LNs, i.e., Iraqis), Third-country Nationals (TCNs, i.e., Filipinos, Sri Lankans, etc.) and others. For example, CAC Card with a Yellow-stripe means unrestricted access or entry in all areas and unlimited escort privileges.

CAPT: U.S. Army, U.S. Navy, U.S. Air Force or U.S. Marine Corps Captain.

CC: Courtesy copy on an e-mail to inform other recipient(s) of some information that would be helpful if they had or saw it.

CD(s): Compact Disc(s).

CDR: USN Commander.

CID: U.S. Army Criminal Investigation Division. They are responsible for investigating
  major crimes like murder, rape, armed robbery, treason, sexual harassment, etc., on U.S. Army bases in Iraq except in the "Green Zone" or International Zone (IZ). See USAF OSI.

CJCS: U.S. military's Chairman of the Joint Chiefs of Staff.

CO.: Company.

COBC: KBR's Code of Business Conduct.

COL: U.S. Army, U.S. Air Force or U.S. Marine Corps Colonel.

CONEX BOX: Short for 'container express,' i.e., a shipping container.

CORP.: Corporation.

CPA: Coalition Provisional Authority. CPA governed Iraq from the start of Gulf War II (GWII) until its disbandment on 28 June 2004.

CSA: Combat Support Associates, Ltd. A completely corrupt U.S. defense contractor
  that had the U.S. military support contract at Camp Doha, Kuwait I worked for in 2001
  -02.

CVN: Camp Victory-North.

CVS: Camp Victory-South.

D: U.S. Democratic political party.

D.C.: Washington, District of Columbia, Capital of the U.S.

DCIS: U.S. Defense Criminal Investigative Service.

DCMA: U.S. Defense Contracts Management Agency.

DFAC: Dining facility, sometimes called the chow hall.

DI: Drill Instructor.

DOD: Department of Defense.

DOD/IG: Department of Defense Inspector General.

DOJ: Department of Justice.

DOS: Department of State.

DPM: KBR Country Deputy Project or Program Manager Iraq or Kuwait.
DR: Doctor.
DVD(s): Digital Video Disc(s).
EFP(s): Explosively-formed projectile(s).
ESQ.: Esquire.
ETF: KBR Eligibility for Transfer Form. Written authorization from HR allowing an employee to be transferred to another base.
EXPAT(S): Short for Expatriate(s); i.e., anyone working or living overseas, usually refers to any Westerner: American, Australian, Briton, Canadian, German, South African, etc.
FBI: U.S. Federal Bureau of Investigation.
FOB: U.S. Army Forward Operating Base.
FOIA: Freedom of Information Act, i.e., a written request for U.S. government records from any organization. They organization has a certain time limit to provide those records unless they request an extension of time if the request is complex or involves many records.
FP STATUS: Short for Force Protection Status. Security term that refers to a percentage of physical security projects that have been completed. For example, a FP status or rating of 90 percent means that 90 percent of the scheduled physical security projects have been completed, i.e., blast walls emplaced, concrete barriers set-up, buildings have been protected by external sandbags, etc.
FWB: Federal whistle-blower.
GCC: Gulf Catering Company. Provided food and manpower services in the Camp Prosperity DFAC and the other U.S. military camps inside the "Green Zone."
GEN: U.S. Army, U.S. Air Force or U.S. Marine Corps General.
GP/GP-ed: Refers to U.S. 'Government Property' (GP) or marked as U.S. government property (GP'ed). Normally a small metallic strip with a single letter and five or six numbers or digits is affixed or attached to identify or label some object so it can be inventoried or accounted for as U.S. government property.
GS: U.S. government service civilian.
GWI: Gulf War I (1990-1991).
GWII: Gulf War II (2003-2012).
GWOT: Global War on Terrorism (2001-date).
H&W's: Health & Welfare inspections. See HSE(s).
HAJI SHOP(s): Any concession company owned by an Iraqi that provided souvenirs, trinkets, gadgets, clothing, electronics, and other exotic items for the U.S. military

troops under contract to the PX/BX. The shops were all located close to the main base

PX/BX on Camp Victory-North.

"HAUSASSEM" (pronounced 'Ha-WAH-Sem'): The 100,000 man theft ring who were

  buying stolen goods from KBR workers and their Iraqi employees and giving a portion

  of the proceeds to the insurgents to keep the war going so KBR could steal more goods.

HEAD MOFO: Head Motherfucker, i.e., the most senior person in charge.

HELO: Short for U.S. Army helicopter, usually a Blackhawk or a Chinook; sometimes referred to as a chopper by older soldiers and civilians.

HQs: Headquarters.

HR: Human Resources.

HSE(s): Health, Safety and Environmental inspection(s). Periodic KBR inspections of all KBR facilities including LSA, buildings, working spaces and other facilities to make sure there are no health, safety or environmental violations or hazards.

HVAC: High-volume air conditioning.

ID: Identification.

IED: Improvised Explosive Device, usually a roadside bomb detonated remotely either

  by wire or electronic signal. A low-cost, very effective way used by the insurgents to fight the U.S. military in asymmetrical warfare when you are militarily weak and your

  opponent is militarily strong.

IPBD: Iraqi Human Resources (HR) company contracted to supply Local National (LN)

  manpower to different KBR Departments at Camp Prosperity and elsewhere.

IR: KBR Security Incident Report. Written report on routine matters, i.e., lost badge, stolen boots, a vehicle left unlocked with valuables inside of it, etc. Also see SIR/SR.

ISIS: Islamic State in Iraq and Syria.

ITT: International Telephone & Telegraph Services, Inc. Another corrupt U.S. defense contractor I worked for in Bosnia in 2002-03. HQs in Colorado Springs, Colorado.

IZ: International Zone. Another name for the "Green Zone" in downtown Baghdad. Also refers to the USAF SF/IZ Police.

JAG: Judge Advocate General; i.e., a military lawyer in any of the U.S. military services.

J.D.: Doctor of Jurisprudence.

KBR: Kellogg, Brown & Root Services, Inc., an unbelievably corrupt U.S. government
 defense contractor that operated in Iraq and Kuwait under the LOGCAP III contract. HQs in Houston, Texas.
KVA: Kilo-volt-ampere (or written kVa).
LDD Report: KBR written report of any lost, damaged, or destroyed U.S. government property. The report is initiated by the Property Department and the Security Department is then tasked with investigating to see what happened to it. If KBR lost/destroyed it, then KBR pays for the unit to be replaced at their expense. If it was lost/damaged through the U.S. military's use of it, then KBR gets permission to order a replacement unit.
L.L.M: Master of Laws & Letters.
LN(s): Local National(s), i.e., usually refers to any Iraqi(s) working on a U.S. military base.
LOGCAP III: Logistic Civil Augmentation Program, Part III.
LSA(s): Living Space Area(s), i.e., trailer parks or housing areas.
LT: Lieutenant, all U.S. military services.
LTC: Lieutenant Colonel, U.S. Army, U.S. Air Force or U.S. Marine Corps.
LTGEN: U.S. Army, U.S. Air Force or U.S. Marine Corps Lieutenant General.
LWOP: Leave without pay.
MAJ: U.S. Army, U.S. Air Force or U.S. Marine Corps Major.
MI: Military Intelligence in all military services.
MM: Millimeter.
MNF-I: Multi-national Forces-Iraq, i.e., all the Coalition Forces in Iraq. MNF-I HQs was in the Al-Faw Palace located at CVS, Baghdad, Iraq.
MOBE: Short for mobilization onto the LOGCAP III contract. Essentially it means you
 have been hired by KBR and sent to Iraq or overseas somewhere. Rhymes with "lobe."
 Also see De-mobe.
MOFO: Short for "Motherfucker," i.e., a slang word for the person in charge usually at
 a lower supervisory level. See Head MoFo.
MP: U.S. Army Military Police. They investigate minor crimes and offenses on all U.S.
 Army bases in Iraq except in the "Green Zone" which were handled by the USAF SF or IZ Police.
MRE: Meals-Ready-to-Eat. Portable meals used by troops in the field that could be self

-heated or activated when pouring water into a bag of chemical mix allowing heat to be generated thus cooking the meal. (When you are in the field and very hungry, they are great when you have nothing else to eat.)

MSGT: U.S. Army or U.S. Air Force Master Sergeant.

MSR: Main Supply Route.

MWR: Morale, Welfare and Recreation. KBR Department that provides recreational activities like TV, ping-pong tables, pool tables, board games, video games, darts, etc.,
to U.S. military members and KBR employees.

NGO(s): Non-government organization(s).

NTR/NSTR: KBR Security shorthand for 'Nothing to report' or 'Nothing serious to report.' It means nothing happened on the base in the previous 24 hours or since the last daily report.

OPS: Operations.

ORHA: Office of Reconstruction and Humanitarian Assistance. LTGEN Jay Garner, USA (Ret.) was in charge until he was unceremoniously kicked out of Iraq by Vice-President Dick Cheney and SECDEF Donald Rumsfeld and replaced by former Ambassador L. Paul 'Jerry' Bremer. The OHRA was then re-named the Coalition Provisional Authority (CPA).

O/T: Over-time. (Very restrictive or very limited, required higher headquarters authority
in every case.)

PM: Project Manager or Program Manager. Overall Manager for KBR Iraq or Kuwait Country Operations.

POGO: Project on Government Oversight, Washington, D.C.

POW(s): Prisoner(s) of War.

PPE: Personal protective equipment, i.e., gas mask, yellow-colored chemical/biological
/nuclear contamination bio-hazard suit, rubber boots and gloves, flak vest and ballistic
helmet.

PROF.: Professor.

Q&A: Question and Answer period.

R: U.S. Republican political party.

R&R: Rest and relaxation, i.e., scheduled vacation from the project taken outside Iraq.

RET: Retired.

RHINO(s): Heavily armored bus(es) that transfer U.S. Army, civilian and KBR personnel between CVS and the "Green Zone" daily. Usually they departed at 03:00 when the insurgents were all supposed to be asleep.

RIO: Halliburton Company contract entitled 'Restore Iraq's Oil' that operated in Kuwait and Iraq.
RPG(s): Rocket propelled grenade(s).
RTI: Research Triangle Institute. A North Carolina-based research firm.
RTII: KBR Security Department Request to Initiate an Investigation. A formal request from KBR Security to outside contracted 'corporate' investigators located in Dubai, U.A.E., all sitting fat, dumb and happy in a very plush high-rise office building, to come into Iraq and take over an investigation initiated by KBR Security involving some major crime; major theft, major embezzlement, rape, murder, etc.
RT-TV: Russia Today Television, Moscow, Russia.
S-2: U.S. Army Military Intelligence.
SCW(s): Service Contract Worker(s), i.e., another term for a TCN employee.
SEAL: U.S. Navy Special Warfare member. The acronym is for Sea-Air-Land.
SECDEF: U.S. Secretary of Defense.
SEN: U.S. Senator.
SF: U.S. Army Special Forces.
SF: U.S. Air Force Security Forces.
SGT: U.S. Army, U.S. Air Force or U.S. Marine Corps Sergeant.
SIGIR: Special Inspector General for Iraq's Reconstruction, Stuart Bowen, Esq.; appointed to his position by Congress.
SIR/SR: Serious Incident Report, i.e., alcohol possession, weapons or drug possession, other contraband confiscation, rape, murder, fighting, major injury, major stealing, etc.
SITREP: Situation Report, i.e. KBR Security Report about any incident.
SOR(s): Service Order Request(s).
SSGT: U.S. Army or U.S. Air Force Staff Sergeant.
SST: Shit Sucking Truck, i.e., large sewage waste truck with suction houses to extract human waste from stand-alone Port-A-Potties or other latrines.
SUV(s): Sports Utility Vehicle(s).
TCN(s): Third-country National(s), i.e., any non-Western and non-Iraqi base worker in
   Iraq. A Sri Lankan, Filipino or an Indian worker for KBR is called a TCN, but not an American, Briton, Australian, German, New Zealander or an Iraqi.
THE CLIENT: What KBR calls the U.S. Army.
U.A.E.: United Arab Emirates.
UFN: Unknown first name.
U.K.: United Kingdom.
ULN: Unknown last name.
U.S.: United States.

U.S.A./USA: United States Army or United States of America.
U.S.A.F./USAF: United States Air Force.
U.S. Air Force OSI/AFOSI: U.S. Air Force Office of Special Investigations.
U.S. Air Force SF: U.S. Air Force Security Forces (SF). Previously called Security Police (SP) and before that Air Police (AP). It serves the same basic functions or roles as the U.S. Army Military Police (MP).
U.S.M.C./USMC: U.S. Marine Corps.
USMI: U.S. Mission-Iraq, i.e., KBR's contract to support the U.S. Embassy and its compound area and operations in the "Green Zone" that is not part of the LOGCAP III
contract.
U.S.N./USN: U.S. Navy.
WMD(s): Weapon(s) of mass destruction, i.e., biological, chemical, and nuclear weapons.
Z-100: Inside KBR Security joke. A fictional KBR base somewhere in Iraq far, far away
from everywhere which is the last place you want to get transferred to.

Note: U.S. military time is used throughout the book series. So 1:00AM in civilian time is 01:00 in military time. 1:00PM in civilian time is 13:00 in military time; 7:00PM in civilian time is 19:00 in military time; 12:00AM midnight in civilian time is 24:00 in military time; and Noon or 12:00PM in civilian time is 12:00 in military time.

Note: The were two systems to identify U.S. Army bases in Iraq. The U.S. Army used designated names for military bases (i.e., Camp Cropper or Camp Honor). But KBR used letter and number combinations to identify the bases, which they called sites, that they supported (i.e., D-2 was Camp Prosperity in the "Green Zone," D-1a later combined with D-14 was Camp War Eagle/Hope in Sadr City; F-1 was Camp Victory-North (or CVN) outside of Baghdad International Airport (BIAP); F-2 was Camp Victory-South (or CSV) also outside BIAP; F-5 was BIAP, D-7 was Camp Rustimayah. KBR generally classified the U.S. Army bases in a rough north to south direction, with 'A'-designated sites (or bases) in the farthest north part of Iraq, then 'B'-designated sites below them, then 'C'-sites going down to 'I'-sites at the most southern part of Iraq, in general. Some of the U.S. Army base names changed over time causing great confusion for everyone. For example, Forward Operating Base (FOB) War Eagle was changed to FOB Hope in 2005 and the name Camp Victory-North (CVN) was changed to Camp Liberty in 2004, but that term was rarely heard or used. (The base was also called Camp al-Tahreer (or 'Liberation') in Arabic). Some of the camp names were interchangeable. At one time there were two completely different Camp Hopes at the same time plus a helicopter landing zone called Washington Field, Camp Hope in the "Green Zone."

COLORFUL CAST OF CHARACTERS (Alphabetical order-in Iraq 2005-06.)

ROBERT ('ROB') AKERS (Minor Character): KBR Security Department Manager, USMI, USMI Compound.
KENNETH ('KEN') ANDERSON (Major Character): KBR Security Coordinator, Camp Prosperity.
RONALD ('RON') BATTLE (Minor Character): KBR Electrical Department Foreman,
Camp Prosperity.
ROBERT J. BROWN (Minor Character): Acting KBR Plumbing Department Manager,
Camp Prosperity.
LAMEL BURGESS (Minor Character): KBR Fuels Specialist, Camp Union III.
ROBERT ('BOBBY') BURNS (Major Character): KBR Camp Manager, Camp Prosperity.

REMO BUTLER (Major Character): Retired U.S. Army Special Forces (SF) Brigadier
  General (BGEN). KBR Deputy Project Manager (DPM) for Iraq and Program Manager (PM) for Kuwait, CVS.
R.C. CALLIGAN (Major Character): KBR Security Technician, Camp Prosperity.
JOHN ('JACK') CALLISON (Minor Character): KBR HVAC Technician, Camp Prosperity.
SANDY DARDEN (Minor Character): KBR Security Manager, Central Iraq Sites, CVN, replaced Frank Russell when he de-mobed.
WILLIAM ('BILLY') DICKENS (Minor Character): KBR F-Sites Security Manager, CVN.
ROGER DOUGHTERY (Minor Character): KBR Carpentry Department Manager, Camp Prosperity.
LEE EVANS (Minor Character): KBR Fuel Point Department Manager, Camp Union III.
JAY FREEMAN (Minor Character): KBR HVAC Department Technician, Camp Prosperity.
JEFF FUSCO (Minor Character): KBR Security Senior Technician, Camp Prosperity.
PHILLIP GREENWOOD (Minor Character): KBR Electrical Department worker, Camp Prosperity.
JENE HARPER (Minor Character): KBR Senior Human Resources Manager-Iraq, CVN.
GARFIELD ('JOE') HARRIS (Minor Character): AFOSI Special Agent, "Green Zone," Baghdad.
NICHOLAS ('NICK THE PLUMBER') HECKMAN (Minor Character): KBR Plumbing Department Manager, Camp Prosperity.
RUSSELL HILL (Major Character): KBR HVAC Department Manager, Camp Prosperity.
FERGUS ('RED') JOHNSON (Minor Character): Former KBR Assistant Power Gen Department Manager, Camp Prosperity.
SSGT UFN JORDAN, U.S. ARMY (Minor Character): Camp Mayor, Camp Prosperity.
TIM KNISLEY (Major Character): KBR Security Technician, Camp Prosperity.
JOHN ('JACK') LIANG (Minor Character): KBR Labor Department Manager, Camp Prosperity.
DANIEL ('DAN') MCGUIRE (Minor Character): Head of KBR Security-Iraq, CVS.
DOUGLAS MOORE (Minor Character): KBR Operation Department worker, Camp Prosperity.
PATRICIA MURPHY (Major Character): KBR Human Resources (HR)

Representative, Camp Prosperity.
MICHAEL ('MIKE') PETERS (Major Character): KBR HVAC Technician, Camp Prosperity.
JESSIE RICH (Major Character): KBR Camp D, F & I-Sites Area Security Manager, CVN.
FRANK RUSSELL (Minor Character): KBR Security Manager-Central Iraq Sites, CVN.
JOSEPH ('JOE') SALADINO (Major Character): Quality Assurance Representative (QAR) and Defense Contracting Officer (DCO), Defense Contracts Management Agency (DCMA), U.S. Embassy-Baghdad.
J.T. SEMMES (A pseudonym) (Major Character): KBR Senior Security Technician, CVN.
ARTHUR ('ART') SHOOK (Minor Character): KBR Security Manager, USMI, USMI Compound.
SAMUEL ('SAM') SIMPSON (Minor Character): KBR Power Gen Department Manager, Camp Prosperity.
SARAH SMITH (Minor Character): KBR MWR Coordinator, Camp Prosperity.
CAPTAIN (CAPT) CHRISTOPHER ('CHRIS') SPATOLA, U.S. ARMY (Minor Character): LN/TCN Badging Program Manager, Baghdad Convention Center (BCC), "Green Zone," Baghdad.
LYNN SUMMERVILLE (Major Character): Former KBR Power Gen Department Manager, Camp Prosperity, later promoted to Area Power Gen Manager, CVS.
THOMAS ('TOM') TANNAHILL: LN Examination Program (LEP) Screening Supervisor, Baghdad Convention Center (BCC), "Green Zone," Baghdad.
CLINTON TOWERS (Minor Character): KBR HVAC Department Technician, Camp Prosperity.
TYROME TUKES (Minor Character): KBR Security Technician, Camp Hope, later BIAP.
ROBERT UZZLE (Minor Character): KBR Chief of Services, Camp Prosperity.
MATTIE VAN EXEL (Minor Character): KBR Electrical Department worker, Camp Prosperity.
ROBERT ('BOB') VILLA (Minor Character): KBR Former Plumbing Department Manager, Camp Prosperity.
DONALD WALKER (Minor Character): KBR Electrical Department Manager, Camp Prosperity.
TROY WILLIAMS (Minor Character): KBR Power Gen Department Technician, Camp Prosperity.

DAVID WOODHAM (Minor Character): KBR Deputy Camp Manager, Camp Prosperity.

INTRODUCTION

This is a cautionary tale. This long, complex, almost unbelievable, nearly 'Biblical' saga would be worthy of a Frederick Forsythe, John Le Carre or Len Deighton thriller. All except it is completely non-fiction. All of it is true. Robert Caro would jump at the chance to write this historical saga in a series. It is unbelievably rich, deep, and exhausting. 'Plot' elements include total greed; massive thievery; the betrayal of the U.S. by tens (or hundreds) of thousands of Americans; towering arrogance; great deception through a total cover-up by the U.S. defense contractor providing support services in Iraq during GWII: Kellogg, Brown & Root (KBR) Services, Inc.; and almost every level of several U.S. government departments, including the DOJ, DOD, including the Defense Criminal Investigative Service (DCIS) and DOD/IG, the Department of the Army and others inside the U.S. government. Tens of thousands or more people are involved.

This U.S. "Deep State" Operation has continued from the Bush, Obama to the Trump Administration. Also included in this saga is at least one murder in 2008 of a brave, honest COL Michael R. ('Mike') Stahlman, JAG, USMC, who was investigating the massive U.S. defense contractor thievery and USMC's major fraud, waste, abuse and stealing going on at Camp Ramadi, Anbar Province, Iraq where he was assigned. All the other honest people who tried to investigate the stealing merely had false charges trumped-up or made-up against them and were summarily fired. Like a deadly virus in a person, the body's white cells will race to contain and try to kill it. The same is true in any corrupt organization. All the corrupt managers and their minions will race to remove the honest person 'infecting' the organization and expel them quickly lest they 'kill' the organization by exposing it to public or official scrutiny and cause it to collapse. But sunlight has always been the best disinfectant. However, in this case every single U.S. government safeguard absolutely failed, or actually they were all in bed with the bad guys.

This saga will not be about the story of the inner-most workings of the Bush White House. Nor will it be about the grand strategy or tactical movements of the U.S. military in Iraq during GWII. It will not be a treatise on Iraq, Iraqis, the Islamic Jihad, Islamic political thought, the Middle East, or a recounting of the innumerable mistakes made on all sides. It will also not concern itself with what the Doonesbury cartoon character 'Boopsie' once said after the 9/11 attacks: "I no longer care what Madonna had for breakfast." This tale will be at a much more personal, fundamental level at the one end and a perfect example of a U.S. "Deep State" operation at the other end of the spectrum, literally on the 'cutting edge.'

Actually, President Donald Trump did the best summary of GWII in Iraq, when he said: "We spent USD$1.3 trillion dollars in Iraq and all we have to show for it is potholes at home." A large portion of that money was stolen by KBR in some way, shape or form with every investigation was shut down into that monumental thievery, both internally by KBR and externally by the DOD, DOJ, DOD/IG, U.S. Army CID, DCIS, and all others. They are very, very few heroes in this monumental saga. The very few honest people who tried to correct all this evil were transferred to a remote camp, if they were lucky, or fired outright on trumped-up charges. The rest of the remaining people involved fell into two categories. First they were the thieves, or like almost everyone in KBR Security, many who helped the thieves load their trucks with all stolen loot. The others deliberately did not want to know what was going on in Iraq, or they knew exactly what was going on and kept silent about all the massive stealing.

These people were, in effect, trapped in an insolvable, almost wrenching, situation. And KBR knew that very well. If they spoke out to anyone about the massive stealing and fraud they would be immediately fired on trumped-up charges. They would lose their lucrative income stream. By staying silent, and ignoring all the monumental stealing, graft, and corruption they would keep their jobs and no doubt their badly needed income to support themselves and their families. There were no easy choices in the matter. Actually, it was an impossible situation. What could an honest employee do who spoke out against all the stealing and was fired on trumped-up charges? KBR held all the cards; everything was rigged in their favor. To file a lawsuit for unlawful or illegal termination would be very costly, very hard to do and take a long time. And who had the money to do that? Plus KBR had whole battalions of lawyers that would fanatically fight every lawsuit thrown at them. Their corporate lawyers had such notorious reputations that they made nasty, rabid pit-pulls look like little friendly, harmless French poodles. The deck was completely stacked against any former employee who sought justice.

I always felt that if I had to keep my mouth firmly shut while there were high crimes and misdemeanors going on all around me then I was in the wrong company. Plus KBR was PAYING me to DO my job. They were NOT paying me NOT TO DO my job. I did not have a family or anyone to support, so I only had myself to be concerned about. I had nothing to lose by trying to stop the stealing and bring the perpetrators to justice. Unfortunately almost all the KBR employees in Iraq had sold their souls to the Devil by staying silent and doing nothing. However, when the money finally runs out in this Devil's Bargain, then all you have left is neither the cash nor your soul, but your eternal regret for having sold yourself out.

But there actually were a few stalwarts, a few brave souls that continued the fight against this totally corrupt, extremely well-connected U.S. defense contractor. A few very rare honest people were just like me, furiously beating the lid of a garbage can with a large hammer in the vain hopes that someone in charge-anyone-would show up and help clean up the titanic criminal mess. Theoretically that would be the U.S. government investigators from any agency. The remaining few other paladins of excellence working in KBR Security with me, men like J.T. Semmes and Jessie Rich, who quietly worked behind the scenes, under the proverbial radar scope, keeping a very low profile, trying their best to attract no or minimal attention to what they were doing, but methodically worked to undermine the evil KBR structure internally through their own investigations or efforts. They, and a few other brave people, quietly kept records and recorded what evil deeds were being done in the forlorn hopes someone would read about what was happening and ride to the rescue one day.

In the end, the bad guys completely triumphed. They have successfully covered their tracks and banked their enormous ill-gotten gains. They got away with it, thanks to the hordes of traitorous minions and their eager-to-please, willing lackeys in DOD, DOD, DOD/IG, DCIS, U.S. Army CID, and other elements of the U.S. government including the DCIS and in KBR - with Donald Trump covering for them. These next four books are an attempt to establish a historical record for future generations to come so they could see what monstrous evil was done, when, why by whom. It is all I can do now. To set the record straight for those few stalwarts who tried their best to be responsible, honest, and trustworthy American citizens and were done terribly and unfairly wrong by those who cared only for themselves and their insatiable greed and avarice. I can only hope that this book is a permanent testimonial to them and a reminder to all future generations that: "The price of liberty is eternal vigilance."

It is also completely disheartening to know many tens of thousands of U.S. and other Coalition soldiers, American and foreign contract workers and hundreds of thousands of innocent Iraqis were killed, maimed, wounded, and psychologically scarred with everyone's lives shattered. All due to the monstrous greed of two corrupt men and their legions of evil minions and toadying lackeys who were eager to help them succeed by every means possible. It is also tragic to note all these people either died or were wounded for no reason. It was all for nothing. At least this book can serve as a permanent testimonial, or at least a reminder, to their sacrifices.

1. THIS WAS NOT THE FIRST TIME I HAD BEEN IN IRAQ

I was not a newcomer to Iraq or KBR. I had been first introduced back in July 2003 to a Kuwaiti-based support services firm that mainly did work for U.S. military units stationed in Kuwait by a former co-worker, 'Big Al'

Santiago, who offered me a position working in Iraq. This co-worker and I had been on the same contract together back in 2001-02 for a U.S. defense contractor called Combat Support Associates (CSA). Ltd., at Camp Doha, Kuwait. CSA provided support services for the U.S. Army where we worked and for all the U.S. Army and USMC units stationed out in the Kuwait desert plus all the U.S. Air Force (USAF) units at Al-Asad Air Base also in the desert. We always got along very well with each other. I had been summarily fired by CSA on trumped-up charges for loudly reporting and constantly complaining about CSA's monumental stealing and defrauding the U.S. government and its employees through various scams, schemes, and confidence games in June 2002. I went right to Bosnia in July 2002 for another year on another Force Protection contract for ITT Services, Inc., another U.S. defense contractor that was heavily defrauding the U.S. government.

The Kuwaiti company owner was looking for a regional manager for a new enterprise in Iraq bidding on and, if successful, servicing contracts for whatever private firms, non-governmental organizations (NGOs) and U.S. and British military units that were operating in Southern Iraq. Specifically we would try to get whatever sub-contracts we could from KBR stationed at The Palace Complex that was right along the Shatt-al-Arab waterway in Basra. They had the support services contract with the Coalition Provisional Authority (CPA). They also said that since the British Army controlled the southern portion of Iraq, I should seek whatever contracts through them. The Kuwait company owner said I would get all the contracts they received in southern Iraq and manage them for their firm since I would be on the ground. The Kuwaiti owner also told me that he would use Basra as his base of operations to store certain goods and materials in a secure area or storage facility there in Basra for shipment to Baghdad and other parts of Iraq. I thought it sounded good and was interested to accept the job. I said I wanted to think about it first.

My former co-worker, 'Big Al,' was named as their Iraq country manager. I would operate autonomously under his operational structure. As events evolved, I would then spend almost the next year with my own Iraqi company, initially financially supported by the Kuwaitis, then we would be on our own. I would be living and working in south-eastern Iraq in the country's second largest city called Basra, a city of about 1.8 million, founded in 638 A.D. as a trading center. I signed on with the Kuwaiti firm as their company Regional Manager for South Iraq in late August 2003.

I drove up the 'Highway of Death' in the Kuwaiti Desert towards the Iraq until I got to the Abdaly-Safwan border crossing on 01 September 2003. I tucked myself inside a long U.S. Army convoy that was just heading out from the Kuwait border marshalling yard at Abdaly then peeled off when they turned off at the cloverleaf to head north to Baghdad. The directions the Kuwaitis gave me were simple. They handed me USD$25,000 cash in USD$100 bills, an SUV and told me to drive up into Iraq and meet a Mr. Abu Karrar under the cloverleaf bridge at the Safwan superhighway interchange just inside Iraq-Kuwait border. They said he does not speak any English, but a description of me and the vehicle plus the Kuwaiti license plate number has been given to him. They explained that he will contact me at 13:00. Be early and park the vehicle by the side of the road; follow him to Basra; rent an office or a home in town; staff it, then start doing whatever business I could scratch up with the Americans, British or anyone else I can find. Simple.

We rolled out north in our two-vehicle convoy. The 45-minute drive north from the Safwan-Abdali border crossing to Basra showed the wide tableau of the war's destruction and devastation. It was like the whole wide, flat, desert landscape had first been hit by an F-5 tornado, then by an enormously powerful Category Five hurricane, followed by a massive off-the-top-of-the-chart 9.9 Richter Scale earthquake. Almost everything has been smashed, looted, flattened, blasted, or wrecked. There were no buildings left that I could see that had not been hit by bombs or bullets or both. It has been said the great tragedy of war is waste. I believed it. The city of Basra looked in slightly better shape since the British Army had swept in quickly. But the city looked more like the worst inner cities in the U.S. due to the decade-long UN sanctions after GWI. No upkeep or maintenance had been done all that time on anything. I stayed at a small hotel in Basra until we got a rented place to stay and work from a few days later. I got no sleep. Every night there was almost continual gunfire, loud explosions going off and other war-like noises that made sleep impossible for me. The day time was slightly less noisy. But you knew you were right in the middle of the Big War Zone every second of the day.

I was back and forth almost every other day between Basra and Kuwait City with no security guards, weapons, or protection. (I know, I was a crazy idiot.) Since the country was so dangerous, the U.S. Army stuffed in independent operators like me into U.S. Army convoys. All the convoys split off to go up the Main Supply Route (MSR) to Baghdad on the interstate at the Safwan cloverleaf just north of the border. The British Army had control of Basra and the surrounding area. So I was stuffed in with the convoy and we rolled out. Then I always got out of the line to go to Basra on the local roads at the right highway exit. There were always U.S. Army convoys moving North, so it was easy to get squeezed in every time I showed up.

I did what the Kuwaitis asked. By mid-September we had a dozen employees, a rented house in a tony suburb and were ready to do business. Although we were technically subordinate to the main country manager in Baghdad, we wound up having little, if any, contact. It was just as well. We were too spread out or far away for any meaningful cooperation. Our communications links would always be barely spotty at the best of times. We had quickly set up shop just six months after the invasion had finished and two weeks after my first arrival in Basra. We tried out a few different company names, but all met with poor local reception until we decided on 'Saif Thi al-Fekar Company, Limited,' (the name means the 'Righteous Sword of the Islamic Revolution'. I was told the name was a very well-known and highly respected one for a budding Iraqi firm-instantly recognizable). We soon had the firm locally registered, so we were 'legally' in business. We were lucky in getting a large manpower provider and services contract fairly quickly as sub-contractors to KBR at The Palace Complex.

Since everyone had been thrown out of work with GWII still raging, jobs were at a premium and very scarce. We were one of the only companies that was hiring. We had some walk-ins for jobs off of word-of-mouth that we were hiring. Also in mid-September one serious-looking woman in her early 30s came to the door and requested to see me. The guards checked with me and I said: "OK, let her speak to me." As soon as I laid eyes on her in the reception room, a Miss Lena: A Miss Melanie Wilkes-clone from "GONE WITH THE WIND." I was immediately struck by her great intelligence, her maturity, and an almost regal bearing with a fierce determination to succeed. What made me decide to hire her right on the spot was when she started speaking the most perfectly fluent British "Eliza Doolittle" (from MY FAIR LADY) English I have ever heard in my life. Not just fluent, flawless. I was immediately intrigued, even fascinated, by her. I could easily see that she was the most highly intelligent women I had ever met.

She literally demanded a job. She said she had been an English language specialist for the Basra Provincial Education Ministry and English language high school teacher. I already knew that to be a professional in Iraq: doctor, engineer, scientist, lawyer, grade school or high school teacher, public official, university professor, bus or train driver, dentist, nurse, government administrator, airline pilot, whatever, you had to be a government employee. She also demanded double the salary of what I was paying my highest-paid engineer. I greatly admired her spunk, complete self-confidence, and bold courage. Had it been anyone else sitting there, I would have just thrown them out the door on their can for being so presumptuous and haughty. But I was not going to let her get away on me.

I replied that if she was as good as I thought she was, then I would put her on half-time, half-salary for a month and see how she did. Then I would give her the full-salary she was asking for, at full-time work, after that time. She accepted but showed some disappointment that she was not going to work full-time immediately. In less than a week she was on full-time, full salary. After a month of being my Assistant General Manager I just turned the company completely over to her and went off doing business development, hunting for more contracts to fill. I trusted her completely. Every day before I departed the company we would sit on the living room couch, drink Iraqi milk tea, and talk about a hundred different subjects. I knew she hated me (all Iraqis had been heavily indoctrinated to hate foreigners especially Americans and the British). But she was stuck as she had no choice. I knew she desperately needed the income to support her family. She always retained her professional composure in spite of her true feelings.

A few days later, Miss Lena's younger sister came to visit her. Lena introduced her as Dr. Najood. She looked like a very statuesque, vivacious Iraqi Celine Dion-clone, strikingly attractive and very energetic. Lena explained that she was a doctor at a local hospital and also studying for her Ph.D. in Family Medicine. I immediately hired her on the spot as the company's part-time doctor and paid her USD$100.00 a month as a retainer to be on-call. I said she was in charge of taking care of everyone's health in the company. All the company's employees and their families could see her, and I would pay the medical bills after the fact. Her English was also near fluent. She was extremely outgoing to everyone, plus she was highly intelligent. I also liked her immediately.

Colloquially, The Palace was not actually one building, but a whole complex of little 'Mini-Me' palaces where the British and the U.S. Consulate-Basra plus KBR had all camped out. Saddam Hussein had built a dozen or so large, very imposing, jewel box-like mansion-style mini-palaces and other buildings all inside a high walled compound right alongside the Shatt al-Arab waterway, close to the Iranian border. Reportedly he only spent one night there.

We competed against two other local firms to provide manpower services for KBR and won the contract in mid-October 2003. We would be operating as labor brokers or manpower specialists. KBR had directly hired about 120 Iraqis in the previous months they were in operation: laborers, electricians, laundry staff, interpreters, translators, carpenters, plumbers, etc. But they said they wanted to get out of the Human Resources (HR) business and have a local firm handle all the headaches, payroll, hiring and firing plus the usual HR paperwork. We quickly moved into an unused double trailer that KBR had provided us and were ready to commence operations of 01 November 2003. Over the next several months we won other smaller contracts, mainly in providing manpower services and staffing for such firms as the British Broadcasting Company (BBC); the South Iraq Police Academy, jointly operated by the British Army and British Police; the British Army units at The Palace Complex that rotated in and out with regularity; RTI (Research Triangle Institute); Erinys Security (UK), and, by extension through KBR, the CPA also operating at The Palace. We also picked up other minor, usually short, one-off contracts in maintenance, manpower, security and providing supplies and other miscellaneous services with other smaller firms.

My own local or Iraqi company headquarters office employees (almost all of whom spoke varying degrees of English) never numbered more than twenty. I was the only 'foreigner.' But KBR and, by association, the CPA, who KBR had as their main support sub-contractor, made us eventually grow with expansion to about 450 locals on our payroll. About 350 of those employees were based at three regional satellite work camps in Rustimayah, Nasiriyah and al-Samawa doing re-construction work. But with a quickly deteriorating security situation all over the country, the camps were permanently closed down after several months of operation. After CPA closed up shop on 28 June 2004, they were replaced by the U.S. Department of State (DOS) Consulate-Southern Iraq, one of several that were opened around the country. The plan was when the U.S. Embassy opened in Baghdad in permanent quarters, the Basra Consulate would close along with all the other consulates scattered about Iraq.

Almost from the first day my staff strongly encouraged me to grow a short, well-trimmed beard (I always had a moustache), wear short, well-trimmed hair (no stretch there again, always had my hair trimmed short) and let the sun darken my skin in an effort to make me look more like an 'Iraqi' and thus disguise myself. Not difficult to do in the summer heat where the temperatures reached past 125oF/52oC. They also recommended I keep to my usual attire of well-tailored pants, polo shirts worn tucked-in, leather belt, dress or running shoes, but no hat. In short, blend in by looking like an 'Iraqi.' I did. I also occasionally wore a dishdasha (or dishdash), a white or black (depending on the season-summer or winter) nightgown-like outer garment some Iraqi men wore, an agal, a rope-like, double-strand thick black cord (actually a rope used by desert dwellers as a camel hobble) to hold my chiffayiah (a long rectangular piece of cloth) to my head, a cotton skull cap to keep the chiffayiah from sliding off plus a pair of leather 'Jesus' sandals. The rest of the attire was a pair of long, loose cotton boxer shorts as an inner garment and a white cotton t-shirt underneath. Add some 'worry' (or prayer) beads in my hand and a tribal leader ring or two and - Voila! My disguise was complete.

With my short gray hair and trimmed beard, everyone in the company swore I could pass for a local tribal leader, a real 'Man of Respect.' Or as Mario Puzo would have said, a "Pezzonovante." My 'Lawrence of Arabia' costume worked perfectly. I have lost count on how many times Iraqis had walked up to me and spoke Arabic, only to find out to their complete surprise (or total horror) they were speaking to an American, or at least a non-Arabic speaking foreigner. I always tried to let my body guards do the talking for me to try and prevent that from happening. I figured as long as I did not act like the usual loud-mouthed, arrogant, obnoxious, know-it-all/seen-it-all/been-there-done/that-got-the-t-shirt -typically clueless American I would be safe. Obviously that plan worked.

I kept myself as inconspicuous as possible. That astute move would greatly increase my chances of survival. It did. But not without more than a few close calls. It also helped I always had at least one armed body guard, sometimes two. I always packed max 'heat' at all times. I eventually rode around town in an Islamic Jihad suicide bomber Iraqi pimpmobile taxi which even lowered my profile since there were so many of them. I slept with a gold-plated Tariq 9mm pistol (belonging to a former Saddam Hussein personal bodyguard, a gift from Miss Lena) under my pillow every night just as a precaution. There were numerous IEDs planted up and down the side of the street where we were (we always had to call the British Army bomb squad to defuse all of them) and the sound of gunfire and explosions, especially at night, was a constant reminder I was very deep in the Big War Zone. We also found out who our next door neighbors across the street were - the Headquarters of local Iranian Intelligence Unit. Our guards and their guards became quite friendly and, since we had far more guards with guns than they had, our guards would watch their compound for thieves trying to break in when they were not there and vice versa.

However, in early November 2003 I was in a convoy close to the Safwan-Abdaly border crossing just inside the Iraq border heading North when the SUV I was driving got hit very hard by some people with a grudge against Americans: regional insurgents, the Islamic Jihad terrorists, Taliban, al-Qaeda, bitter end-of-the-roader ex-Ba'ath Party members, maybe the local

Boy Scout troop testing out their AK-47s on us for fun. It did not matter. I was jamming the accelerator as hard as I could like everyone else to get out of the 'Gauntlet of Death' crossfire ambush. Suddenly my driver's side door window shattered and blew inwards hard. (A conveniently-timed IED that went off right next to me or near me? I was not eager to find out.) The left side of my whole head was completely covered with pieces of glass shrapnel. It was definitely stinging. The blast of glass also got my full attention. Once I got safe outside the 'Kill Zone' and out of harm's way I started gently pulling out glass shards from the side of my face and scalp, which were all bloody. I was also digging them out of my ear for at least the next 15 minutes. Then I staunched the bleeding with my handkerchief. I considered myself lucky. I never wanted to be a Purple Heart recipient, now I was. The U.S. Army convoy rolled on to Baghdad to the northwest at the Safwan cloverleaf and I split off to Basra to the north. I got medical treatment at the closest hospital I could get to which was actually at this point in Basra. There were no U.S. or British military hospitals I knew about anywhere even close by. I was not the only person in the Emergency Room.

By mid-January 2004 we were self-financing (although just breaking even). Our operations, through the earned income from the various sub-contracts that we had managed to quickly win, kept us afloat and running. There were no 'Iraqi' firms with a Westerner at the helm (to cut through language problems and cultural barriers while providing quality 'Western' business practices), which is what the Kuwaitis had hoped for - someone with knowledge of Western business practices.

Well before the CPA had permanently shuttered on 28 June 2004, the proverbial handwriting was on the wall. Contracts we had signed were cancelled, shortened, not started, or indefinitely delayed. Private firms and NGOs were getting out one-by-one for good since the security situation was deteriorating on a daily basis; threats to staff members grew. The U.S. Consulate, as the successor organization to CPA, only hired on five out of the 40 employees that were working with the CPA. And all without a proper by-your-leave to me as they were still my employees. At the same time KBR switched from a 'Construction Phase' at The Palace to an 'Operations and

Maintenance Phase.' That meant instead of 15 carpenters they might only need five, instead of 12 electricians they might only need four and so on.

Also in June all three up-country work sites had to be abandoned due to continual attacks by small arms fire, heavy and increasing mortar and rocket barrages, constant threats from the local insurgents and terrorists and severe re-supply problems. All the workers were paid off and let go. In other words, we were rapidly shrinking. We were not losing money yet, but the income streams were drying up fairly quickly. Plus all my Iraqi staff members were being threatened daily to: "Do not work for the British under penalty of death." (They could not distinguish between Americans and British, so I lumped in with the British since they controlled all of Southern Iraq.) Everyone was under a lot of pressure that was growing worse each day.

On 31 August 2004, while I was out on a well-deserved, semi-annual vacation to visit relatives in Canada, the Kuwaitis told the KBR Site Manager, John Dudfield (a very professional gentleman), by e-mail that I had been replaced by an Iraqi manager and was now no longer an employee. I only found out about my 'termination' because he and I had a good working relationship. John forwarded me a copy of the e-mail that was sent by the Kuwaitis to him. But the Kuwaitis never sent me that e-mail saying I was officially canned. Perhaps they figured on saving my enormous 'Western' salary (they paid me USD$1,400/month plus living expenses) with a new Iraqi general manager they hired (who they promptly paid USD$1,975/month). Ironically, the manager they hired was the same manager I had fired the previous December when I found out he was using both the company name during the day and our employees after working hours as own 'his' firm to do business behind my back with his former foreign business contacts prior to GWII. Since he and one of my deputy managers working with me out at The Palace had taken over the company, they were soon barred from The Palace for 'selling' jobs paid for by desperate people who were hungry for work. They took in enormous bribes from people who they had promised 'jobs' to. No jobs ever appeared. They simply pocketed the cash and made poor excuses about the delay. The KBR Camp Manager, John Dudfield, heard enough complaints, did an internal investigation on his own, found it was all true, and banned them both from reentry to The Palace complex. But the U.S.

Consulate-Basra was soon closed down when the U.S. Embassy in Baghdad commenced operations. The Iraqi company was finally dissolved.

After my trip to Canada, I went to stay with an old pen-pal, Karina, at her home in Germany for several months. The word was no one could get hired by KBR unless they knew someone inside KBR and were recommended. While I was working at Camp McGovern, Brcko, Bosnia-Herzegovina on a U.S. DOD Force Protection contract back in 2002-03 for ITT Services, I became friendly with the KBR Camp Manager since I knew I would not return on this contract after my one year contract finished. After a few conversations to get to know each other he said he would give me a recommendation to be hired by KBR if I ever wanted one. In October 2004, I applied for a KBR security position. I immediately accepted. However, it would not actually be until early March 2005 that I actually went to the KBR training course in Houston, TX.

2. CAMP VICTORY-NORTH AND CAMP HOPE

I departed Houston after two weeks of intensive KBR training, orientation, briefings, a physical exam, shots, and the usual mountain of paperwork on 23 March 2005. I carried my canvas alert bag filled with my U.S. Army ballistic helmet and other Personal Protective Equipment (PPE). Flying directly to Dubai in the United Arab Emirates (U.A.E.) via Paris, we had only a few hours' sleep in a hotel before all being reloaded to Dubai International Airport for our Russian charter airlines flight to Baghdad. The joke in Dubai was if the 'combat' (corkscrew-style) landing was going to be 'hot' (possibility of the plane taking heavy cross-fire or shoulder-launched missiles going in) then the Russian stewardesses were going to be 'hotter.' They were right. All three stewardesses were Anna Kournikova and Maria Sharapova-clones.

We landed at BIAP mid-morning of 25 March 2005. It was bright, clear, breezy and in the low 50soF/10soC. BIAP was formerly known as Saddam Hussein International Airport. The terrain was pancake-flat with some trees, shrubs and greenery scattered about the landscape, albeit dust-covered and desert-hardy. The only physical features of elevation were two man-made sloping, teardrop-based, multitiered mounds in the distance, bristling with U.S. Army antennas. After an hour bus ride through what seemed a continuous series of large U.S. military camps we disembarked at KBR's Baghdad Transit Center (BTC), part of U.S. Army's sprawling Camp Victory-North (or CVN). BTC was the temporary housing spot for transients in both directions; portable trailers with a dozen double bunk beds and a cot for an extra overflow person. I intended to get horizontal quickly after traveling for two days. The whole area was later explained as Saddam's former game preserve/hunting grounds plus a personal zoo. Exotic stray wild animals were said to be seen from time to time, including small deer, desert foxes and large hares. The expansive landscape would not have been out of place on a well-watered section of the Serengeti Plain in East Africa.

The day of my arrival I was met at BTC by a KBR Security Technician named Ron Chavez who had been alerted to intercept me. Ron was gregarious, outgoing, and talkative. He quickly steered me into some 'vacant' hooch that one Security supervisor had left unoccupied due to his extensive stay in the U.S. for some medical problems just to keep me out of the crowded, always noisy BTC trailers. I could see that would be much better there than being stuffed in with new roommates coming and old roommates going around the clock. The next day I heard that Ron had gotten a radio call from someone out at a place called Z-lake on base (shaped like the letter 'Z') the previous evening, reporting there was a real 'emergency'. He immediately responded and found a wild party with a lot of heavy drinking and very belligerent drunks. The radio call was bogus, someone had played a sick practical joke. Details were sketchy on the next turn-of-events, but it appears Ron asked for back up first and then either told everyone to stay put or he had confronted a large group of the worst drunks. There is no question that they promptly and severely beat him senseless with their fists and feet. He was quickly 'medivaced' to the U.S. for several months of rehabilitation and treatment. The perpetrators were eventually found and terminated several weeks later after everyone involved wrote the same exactly worded statement blaming Ron for the whole altercation.

On the following day in the local KBR Security office I met a man named J. T. Semmes or just J. T. (a pseudonym). He was the only one actually working in the CVN's Security office. At first glance, J.T. was a very tall, suave, well-built, extremely likeable, deliberately slow-taking, and formal-in-manner gentleman. He held his cards close-to-his-chest, was methodical in his methods and acted the gracious Southern patriarchal host. He was far too educated to be a good-ol'-boy cracker, ridge-runner or hayseed. He could have been a fancy-vested, string-tied, unflappable Mississippi Riverboat gambler or cool-eyed, steady-handed, unflappable, hard-as-nails, hard-boiled, 'pistolero'/gunslinger-for-hire. ("Nobody was faster!") I immediately liked him for his air of competence, intelligence, and authority. I soon found out he was a former Florida State Highway Patrolman, a former Broward County, Florida sheriff and a former young U.S. Army Special Forces (SF) officer who had done a combat tour of duty early on in the Vietnam War.

I also found out he was a crack shot, one of the best marksmen in U.S. history, J.T. had a closet full of U.S. military and civilian rifle and pistol awards, medals, badges, insignia, and trophies he had won over the decades in various shooting match competitions and exhibitions including the highly prestigious President's Hundred Gold Medal, the most coveted marksmanship award of all U.S. annual national shooting match competitions. He also had a sharp-eyed commentary on all things under the sun and a quick manner to summarize all problems and formulate solutions, if any could be found (or accepted). As Mario Puzo (author of THE GODFATHER) would have put it, he was a real 'Man of Respect.' I found we would have a few rare differences in opinion, but never any disagreements. I came to greatly value his wise counsel, experience in the field and years of accumulated wisdom.

Everyone else in Security was either on the road, or so it was reported that was what they said they were doing (it would be the same for the two plus weeks I was assigned to the Security Department), or off doing 'something' particularly important. I did not even get to meet most of my Security colleagues at CVN. On the rare occasions, that someone did make a very brief, often fleeting, appearance in the office, it would always be on a dead run and always acting like their hair was on fire, too busy even to exchange even basic pleasantries. Everyone vied to see who could be the busiest-acting or busiest-looking security person. I soon found out that the operative word here was 'acting.' I determined that everyone was seeing their girlfriends, shopping for the latest pirated DVDs at the assorted Iraqi-run 'Haji' shops, trolling the PXs, screwing-off, resting from a hard morning's work or other important, 'security-related' matters like watching movies in their hooches or napping. The only person actually doing any security work was J.T.

But I quickly was made to realize from my conversations with J.T. and my own personal observations that not only were my fellow KBR Security cohorts not doing an ounce of security work, they were virtually not even QUALIFIED to do any security work. Their backgrounds were varied, but they were almost all united in one important area: almost none of them from what I could see, except for J.T. and myself, had ever been in security, law enforcement or performed any investigations. These people included a truck driver, a vehicle mechanic (who was also an alcoholic), an ex-U.S. Army infantryman who had been awarded a Silver Star medal for bravery from early in GWII plus a few other assorted ex-U.S. Army soldiers, a former Ukrainian Army SF trooper who barely spoken any English and it was guttural at that (only J.T. could glean or translate what he was trying to say to us), a farmer, and a cowboy (or a wrangler-the jury was still out on that person). A few of them were or seemed young enough to have barely graduated from high school.

While our boss, Jesse Rich, was a retired U.S. Army senior enlisted SF troop and his boss, Frank Russell, who was an ex-USN enlisted Special Warfare operator (SEAL), were both definitely 'highly-qualified' and highly intelligent, but I was sure that neither of them had ever done any formal 'investigations' or police work in their lives. That is not to say they were bad persons, just the opposite. It was just they seemed to have NO experience in security matters from my viewpoint. And what did any of them know about Force Protection or physical security like placing blast walls in the right location, sandbagging a structure to protect it from attack, collecting evidence from a crime scene or interviewing witnesses and suspects, then writing up their conclusions in a formal report? What does a retired U.S. Army SF trooper and ex-USN SEAL know about police-style investigations or any of the above? (Answer: Not much in my book.)

Almost all these other people were apparently or deliberately hired specifically because of their COMPLETE LACK of security or law enforcement qualifications or experience. This was greatly troubling. (I wondered how J.T. or I were even considered for employment by KBR Security, much less having been hired on? Very strange!) And there were darn few of us to boot. Many of the exceedingly small FOBs scattered all around Baghdad and throughout Iraq plus some of the intermediate-sized bases had NO security personnel assigned to them. Even a big, sprawling base like CVN only had perhaps a dozen or so Security people assigned, some of whom I would never see or meet in the time I was there. They simply never came into the Security office. Those scant numbers was far too inadequate to cover what the requirements called for in country. If I had gone out and corralled a class of little third graders they would have been more qualified to handle chores in KBR Security than this general bunch of incompetents, or as unqualified and inexperienced as nearly everyone was. I had no answers. The person hiring all these people must have been just as incompetent, unqualified, or as inexperienced as almost all the people they were hiring. Perhaps there was a method in this madness, but I could not sort it all out. Nothing made any sense.

I then met with Frank Russell, Regional Security Manager, in his office later the same morning. Our almost one-sided conversation lasted probably less than 15 seconds. Frank told me I was to be re-assigned to D-1a (or D-14 as it was also known to KBR, or Camp Hope as it was called by the U.S. Army) over in Sadr City once I had completed two weeks of orientation training at CVN. I mentioned that Houston told me I was being assigned to BIAP (or F-5 in KBR terminology). Frank said Houston decided nothing about any assignments in-country and I was to be sent to where I was needed. He added there were five small D-sites (or U.S. Army camps) scattered in and around Baghdad proper without any KBR security personnel assigned there at all.

However, Frank wanted a thorough turn-over of at least two months so the man I was relieving would not be leaving right away. He wished me well. The conversation was over. Months later I found out the real reason for my new assignment. Frank Russell had promised his 'Main Man'/former 'running buddy' now up at Camp Hope, a man named Tyrome Tukes (who has been there all of four months), that the next warm body that walked in the door would be assigned to relieve him. That was me. I later found out that normally security assignments were for one year. Tyrome Tukes was later sent to the assignment I was promised in Houston-BIAP.

Actually, I had heard all about the small FOB in Sadr 'Murder' City in the news even before I left the U.S. The place was a Baghdad suburb in the northeast part of the sprawling metropolis of about five million. Originally the suburb was named Saddam City. It has been created a number of years ago for the Marsh Arabs who lived in the extensive marshlands just north of Basra. They lived simply, having almost Biblical-Era lives, unchanged for several millennia, residing in reed huts and travelling by reed boats, eating dates and fish. But they were intractable opponents of Saddam Hussein due to their independent streak. Saddam had them all rounded up and sent to Saddam City, a Baghdad suburb he created specifically to house them. Then Saddam totally destroyed the marshland ecology by draining the marshes, cutting down all the date and palm trees and having the marshland all filled in with sand and dirt.

The FOB long had the notorious reputation for being the 'hottest' of 'hot' spots in all of Iraq since being established back in May 2003. It was a combination of Dien Bien Phu/Corregidor/Little Big Horn/Bataan/Masada/the Alamo/Pleiku/Stalingrad all rolled into one. The place was reportedly under constant bombardment by every piece of ordnance in the insurgent arsenal, plus continual small arms, and sniper fire. The insurgents also amused themselves by occasionally tossing grenades over the cinder block walls that encircled the camp. It was exactly where I wanted to be. Having volunteered for active duty in Vietnam (USAF), Bosnia/Balkans, GWI and GWII (USN), I had been turned down each time, much to my chagrin. And it always galled me to no end to see in every war there were always a few people who went AWOL or deserted from the service to avoid combat duty. I volunteered to go to war each time and was repeatedly rejected. I was finally headed into some 'front-line'/in-the-trenches action after more than 30 years of trying. Some people run away from the sound of gunfire; a few people run towards it. I was one of those few.

Later that same day at noon the PM decreed that due to the vicious, unprovoked attack on Ron Chavez the previous evening there would be 100 percent vehicle checks done at the entrance gates to CVN. There were two gates, but the back gate was closed and locked, only opened for large vehicles exiting or entering. There would be perhaps half a dozen Third Country Nationals (TCN) security guards doing the physical inspections; the KBR Security Technicians would supervisor them. There were three-hour shifts set up starting right at noon, around-the-clock coverage was done. That meant walking for three hours, taking a break for three or six hours and then come right back to work again. Also, another inspection team was sent over to the nearby TCN camp entrance gate a few hundred meters away.

I drew 18 three-hour shifts/week; almost three per day. Sometimes someone could not work, so I filled in on short notice since I had volunteered to pick up extra work (and the extra pay). Another Security Technician named Jeff Fusco was soon transferred over from the "Green Zone" from Camp Prosperity in downtown Baghdad to assist. He also drew an equal number of shifts as myself. J.T. drew 15 shifts. Everyone else drew a maximum of six shifts/week, if that many. That would be in line with their very hectic schedules of shopping at the PX/'Haji' shops, seeing girlfriends, watching DVDs, resting a lot and doing related important 'Security' activities.

At first, everyone loudly objected to having their vehicles inspected and having to wait in long lines. It was was no fun (and nearly everyone wanted an exemption from the searches for a wide variety of reasons). Nearly everyone was verbally hostile. There had been no inspections prior to this incident. However, tempers cooled off considerably and quickly, plus the bitching stopped completely, when we started finding bottles of whiskey or alcohol, syringes, assorted weapons (mainly knives of all types) and other contraband like drugs and pornographic magazines. Usually every other day someone would get caught with carrying something illegal hidden inside their vehicles. More than a few people got the 'chicken-or-fish, window-or-aisle' question asked at BIAP after quickly being terminated. Getting caught with anything illegal was an automatic firing offense and a one-way ticket home.

There was an attractive, young Hispanic woman, Marina Galvan, who always came through my security inspection check point every day at about the same time. While we inspected the vehicle she was riding in, I always used to tease her and say: "We have to stop meeting like this, people will start to talk." She always thought that was funny and always smiled at me (so did I).

After nearly three weeks of working at CVN I was informed I would be leaving next evening. My last work day there was also the last day when they stopped doing the vehicle inspections. The schedule had first eased off to random searches of every third vehicle then later on every sixth vehicle. Since I was going to my new assignment, for some very strange reason, I was almost to the point of paranoia in worrying about I would get dumped at the wrong base or hop on the wrong chopper. I have never felt that way before, but I did this time out for no reason I knew of. Just a weird feeling I was going to be misrouted or sent to the wrong place. Perhaps I did not want to embarrass myself by getting lost in the Big War Zone. All I was told is I was going to Camp Hope and to be at the helo pad at Camp Victory-South (CVS) no later than 20:30 next evening with my all luggage (which included one large black plastic footlocker, my alert bag with PPE, one green duffle bag and one company-issued laptop - all carried at once), while wearing my flak vest, helmet, long sleeve shirt and earplugs. I arrived at the helo pad just as it was almost dark. I was out there well before the time, maybe an hour early, just to be safe.

My first e-mail to J.T. described the trip after my arrival. The U.S. Army Flight Operations Sergeant (SGT) says: "Name and Destination?" I say: "Le Blanc, Camp Hope." He shines his flashlight on the manifest and says: "OK, got you, stand way over there by the flight line, helos will be a few minutes late." There are a dozen of us, one other civilian and 10 other U.S. Army troops in full combat gear. Two U.S. Army Blackhawk helicopters landed late at 21:05. We lined up in a single file. A crew member comes over and asks us as loud as he can what our name is and where we are going. I am the last person in line and yell: "Le Blanc, Hope!" He shouts at the top of his lungs: "Second helo!" I line up with five other soldiers and we walk out on the landing pad just outside right next to the second helo door. Another crew member comes over and screams: "Destination?" I bellow: "Hope!" He shouts: "OK, get on the helo!"

All five of us quickly load up. The helo lifts off and we quickly zigzag our way due East. In about 10 minutes (no more, if that) we land at this fairly large helo pad after passing over the western part of the city of Baghdad. And I am thinking: "Damn! They said this would be a 25-minute flight and this is a sure damn big helo pad for such a small base." The crew member comes over, opens the door and shouts at the top of his lungs: "Camp Hope, everyone out!" I grab all my stuff, instinctively bend low to avoid the spinning rotors, quickly scramble out and jog over to the edge of the helo pad. No civilians at all. It is all just U.S. Army troops and lots of them. All just hanging or milling around waiting for helo rides to somewhere else.

I have super-heated steam coming out of my ears by now. No Tyrome Tukes. I wander over to the small entrance gate. There are these uniformed Global Risk security guards there, Nepalese I see. I say: "This Camp Hope?" They all reply: "Yes, this is Camp Hope." And right there at the entrance gate is a big arching sign over the roadway entrance reading: "Welcome to Camp Hope-Washington Field." So I know I am not lost, I was very worried about that. I say I am looking for KBR Operations. They say they do not know but check this other big entrance gate down the street. I cart all my stuff over there. Damn! This place is really big. I am thinking, much bigger than what was told to me, but then again no one has ever been out here to see it. I check in at this big gate and there are more Global Security Company guards. I ask for KBR Operations. The Head MoFo says go this way and then that way about half a mile down the street. Damn! This place is huge! They are nice enough to let me stash my gear with them and go wandering down the street. I do find the KBR area, eventually find the KBR Gate, and actually find a KBR Technician, but he is a Bosnian. There are more KBR Sector Security guys too, maybe Indian or Nepalese or Filipinos. I say: "I am looking for a guy named Tyrome Tukes, I am replacing him." The guy thinks and says: "Hmmmmm. No, we do not have any Tyrome here, but Hey! We did have

Tyrome over at the Fuel Point, but he quit six months ago." I loudly exclaimed: "WHAT?!?!?!?"

Anyway, now it is late in the evening, and the guy sees I am really beat. So he says: "Look, I'll run you over to Billeting after we get your gear at this other gate and we'll get you all sorted out tomorrow morning." I said OK. Anyway, we are driving along this road and this whole place is massive, nothing like what was described to me. And he is talking about the "Green Zone" this and the "Green Zone" that and I say to him: "Green Zone? I am supposed to be at Camp War Eagle/Hope in Sadr City." He says: "Sadr City? No, you are at Camp Hope in the "Green Zone." OH SHIT! He asks me what kind of badge I have. I show him I have a DoD Badge/CAC Card and my KBR ID badge. The guy says: "Not even ass-wipe here, completely 100 percent No Speed/Total High-Drag stuff."

He explains that not only do I need this Special High-Speed/Low-Drag Special KBR ID badge but I need at least 15-16 other Special U.S. Embassy Badges too. I cannot go to the chow hall, the PX, in fact if the guards only see I have these poor piddly-ass badges they will probably just shoot me for being an Islamic Jihad terrorist or something for having these No-Load badges! Just great! I said: "I am on a KBR base with a KBR ID badge." The guy tells me: "Nada actionamundo-totally useless. You have to have this Special KBR Identification (ID) badge in the "Green Zone to do anything." We finally get to billeting and the billeting guy is gone, it takes 30 minutes to roust him out of whatever he is doing. Who knows?

Anyway, the billeting guy takes mercy on me and assigns me to the 'Big Room' in the barracks, fortunately very close by. I drag my stuff over there with some clean sheets and blankets the guy gave me. First guy I meet coming out of the barracks, now well after midnight, is holding an Iron City longneck in his hand. OH! Just great! Then once I get inside I get hit with these dense clouds of marijuana smoke billowing out of the place like a heavy fog. Just fun! Of course. the room is on the 2nd floor about a quarter of a mile away from the entrance. I have a devil of a time finding the room. I finally get in and there are multiple bunk-beds beds-it is a huge dormitory room on the second floor, but only one guy in the room: not snoring, not breathing, not moving-whatever. Finally, I get set up to hit the sack and my head hits the pillow and then there is this: "BOOM, BOOM, BOOM!" sound. Fairly close. I am thinking: "Damn! They are setting the record for car bombs or mortar rounds tonight."

All night the explosions goes off periodically: "BOOM, BOOM, BOOM!" I get absolutely no sleep. About 04:00 there is a commotion. I think they came to drag this poor dead guy's body away. Then about 05:00 a bunch of new transients noisily enter the room. I hit the can at 06:30. I finally find out what is going "BOOM! BOOM! BOOM!" all night. It is the very heavy bathroom door. It slowly closes with a loud "BOOM!" But since there is no door closer on the door it somehow rebounds two more times with a loud "BOOM!" sound each time before finally closing. I get over to Billeting sometime after that. No breakfast, of course. I have no little Special CAC, ID, or any other card for the "Green Zone." Come to find out there is not only ONE Camp Hope, but THREE Camp Hopes. One here in the "Green Zone", one is D-1a/War Eagle and the third one is D-12. I got routed to the wrong one by mistake or misunderstanding. Just my luck.

While at Billeting I find out that there is an APB (All-Points Bulletin) out on my sorry butt from various organizations, mainly being from the Camp Hope bubbas. Apparently they started calling around last night when I no-showed at the helo pad, assuming there was even a helo flight in there. Who knows? Billeting has confirmed that they physically have me and will hold on to me before being turned over to competent authority. I am advised by Billeting to check-in and seek guidance from Human Resources (HR) on transportation to my final destination. I also ripped-off an MRE from Billeting (actually several, which will come in very handy I find out later-this is going to be breakfast) and head over to the HR office. One nice HR lady takes my case and makes numerous phone calls on my behalf. She finally gives up after an hour of getting totally nowhere, and in exasperation (just to get me out of her hair), calls Security. They come over and snatch me. Then this good-ol'-boy Security bubba named Scott (nice guy) shows up about 10:45. He grabs me then we drive over to Camp Honor III to visit their little trailer/office. I meet Scott's boss, Roger, a real gung-ho hard-charger.

Roger has an extremely good take on the personnel/situation at CVN. We immediately compare notes and agree on everything for operations (or lack thereof), organization (or lack thereof), management (ditto comments), little 'favorites' (too many), level of workload (way uneven at best), etc. Then who waltzes in the door, but Jeff Fusco. I tell Roger that Jeff was a real trooper in that he did as many shifts as I did these past three weeks of vehicle inspections and easily double (or triple) what the 'favorites' did. Instead of praising Jeff for a good job done, Roger then rips into Jeff big time for being a complete dumb-ass for not calling Roger immediately about being abused or misused and complain about why he had to work far more hours than these other 'favorite' no-loads, and why was not the schedule being made fair for all? He said he would have called down immediately there had he known and ripped some new assholes (that was very believable). I tactfully change the subject.

Now Security has decided on Plan A. I am to be shipped in some fashion BACK to CVN today, perhaps soon, for another try at this movement. I immediately veto that plan. I said there is NO WAY I am going back to start this 'journey' all over again. I said there has to be some way for me to get from Point B (where I am now) to Point C (where I need to be). Roger has the Main Operations Guy called (his Main Man/Good Buddy) to come. He arrives. He is Roger's best pal. He says let us try the Camp helipad for transport to Camp Hope for Plan B. Roger has Jeff bring me back over to the Camp Hope helipad where we see the Flight Operations SGT. The Flight Operations SGT says he has heard of Camp Hope and can see it on the map. But he has never heard of any helicopters flying there and doubts the office report. Roger decides that I am to be given lunch (being Noonish), the Grand Tour of all the bases in the "Green Zone" by Jeff while they all figure out a new Plan C.

We see everything there is to see, have lunch, hit the PX (microscopic by the way, very disappointing). We also have to stay away all afternoon as his office is being used by Corporate Security Head MoFo for some big investigation. We all toddle back into the office about 17:00. Now the Main Ops Guy has Plan C ready. If they send a chit up to God Almighty today for a chop then it takes 48-72 hours to come back down and THEN they can

APPLY for me being ground transported by 'Rhino' convoy to Camp Hope once God, Jesus, Mohammed, Buddha, and the New Pope all chop this request off. Maybe in another one-two+ days after that, even IF they even have a convoy going up to War Eagle/Hope/D-1a/D-14/whatever. It could be longer. Who knew? Not much goes up to Camp War Eagle, maybe every few weeks or so. But the Security Main MoFo vetoes Plan C. He wants me out of here and moving TODAY! Maybe he is taking mercy on me for being jerked around badly; maybe he wants me out of his hair. Who knows? Anyway, so the Main Operations guy calls his 'Main Man' at the helipad to check out a flight to see if there is any way to get me heloed out of here to there and-sure enough-there IS a helicopter shuttle going to Camp Hope or Camp War Eagle late this very afternoon! It is called the 'Marne Shuttle' and it makes like 8-10 stops, a regularly scheduled daily shuttle. PLAN D!

When the helicopter finally landed late that afternoon at Camp Hope after three quick stops, I was met by someone from Operations. They had been alerted I was finally coming in. I loaded my gear into their vehicle, then we drove off. The trip was a long one, lasting perhaps 15-20 seconds to the Operations trailer. Just as the helicopter started to lift off and turn back to their next stop on the circuit of dropping off and taking on passengers, suddenly there was a loud whoosh followed by a loud explosion on the other side of the camp wall. Some bad guy just fired an RPG round in trying to bring the chopper down and just missed it. I thought grimly: "Welcome to Camp Hope! The red carpet has been rolled out!" I sent an e-mail back to my KBR recruiter and reminded him of his promise that we would not be attacked in Iraq, i.e., the war was over. Obviously not yet.

I finally got to meet Tyrome Tukes, the man I was replacing. He was a young man. Black, short, muscular, gregarious-perhaps irrepressible and in outstanding physical condition. He explained he was a former U.S. Army SF SGT vehicle mechanic. He showed me his room; a converted conex box made into a living quarters with a toilet. On the wall was a made-up photo of him as TIME MAGAZINE's 'Man-of-the-Year.' It was a posed shot of him dressed as a U.S. Army SGT with a SF tab on his shoulder on the Magazine's front cover in an acrylic picture frame. Anyone could have made up anything exactly like that photoshopped at any BX/PX specialty shop like TIME MAGAZINE's phony front cover picture.

If Tyrome Tukes was a former U.S. Army SF SGT then he was either the worst soldier in the history of the U.S. Army, got himself courts-martialed fast, or I was the King of Siam. At least the Drill Instructor (DI) in Boot Camp would have taken him behind the barracks and kicked the living shit out of him for his stupid attitude, or the SF instructors would have washed him out of school fast after beating him up for good measure because of his wise-ass, smart mouth. He was one of the most undisciplined people I have ever met, like his brain and personality was still stuck in Kindergarten. I dismissed the matter from my mind. However, he did give me one of the best pieces of advice I have ever gotten for a security person: "Be friendly to everyone, be friends with no one." That sage advice has served me very well since then.

He gave me the grand tour of Camp Hope which lasted twenty minutes, at best. There was not much to see. The place was no larger than a city park in a medium-sized U.S. city. There were a few clustered permanent adobe buildings, the rest were converted conex boxes for offices, LSAs and storage or concerted mobile homes plus a few wooden buildings. The place was surrounded by a high cinder block wall with two gates. My luck held as right before I arrived the two warring factions in Sadr City (Shiite and Sunni) had declared a truce or a cease-fire of sorts, so the daily attacks and bombardment had slowed, but it had never completely stopped. Since the base was so small it was rare anything got stolen. And if it was reported as stolen, it soon re-appeared after the item was found having rolled under a bed, simply misplaced, dropped in a latrine stall, or left behind something on the person's desk.

I could not exactly call this an idyllic, laid-back vacation, but I admit I was lightly tasked. I did a three times/day walk-around 'inspection' of the whole camp to 'show the flag' and let people see me. 'Le Blanc Luck' still held. We would have numerous stray mortar rounds and rocket barrages each week. But when the rounds imploded I was always walking in another part of the camp. 'Le Blanc Luck': Bad luck to be in a place that gets constantly mortared and rocketed, but good luck to be in another place where the rounds did not strike or explode next to me. However, I was doing one of my walk around inspections one fine afternoon, I hear this big swoosh go right past my head and over a cinder brick wall. A huge crash reverberated back as the ground shook underneath me. I trotted around the wall to look at what had suddenly landed. It was a 122mm rocket that had penetrated a conex box filled with construction materials in the Lay-down Yard in the area right next to where I was walking. A dud, inert. It failed to explode. 'Le Blanc Luck had held again.

I quickly found out that Tyrome Tukes was a serial practical joker. Nothing pleased him more than goading someone into losing their temper to the point of punching him in the mouth for his merciless taunting. He was like a rabid pit bull as soon as he found someone's weakness or sore spot and he almost always did. Only the camp manager seemed to be immune to his antics. He was irrepressible. I think he spent all of his day either in the gym working out or thinking up new ways to infuriate everyone on the camp. By all accounts he did a brilliant job at both. When he departed for good he was not missed or lamented. I am sure everyone breathed a sigh of relief. I was happy to see him go myself.

3. 01 AUGUST 2005-CAMP HOPE-CAMP MANAGER'S OFFICE

Camp managers seem to be rotated in and out every few months. No one stayed very long. I did not pay a lot of attention to them. I just did my business and kept my opinion to myself. We always seemed to get along as I kept out of their hair and vice versa. They were all professionals with a lot of experience. I never had a single problem with any of them. The next Camp Manager in was Robert 'Bobby' Burns. Bobby was a big mover and shaker from Louisiana. He knew his business and was a decisive supervisor. He had his rules, you followed them. He was very straightforward with you, no mincing of words. In a word, he was 'fair.' You always knew where you stood with him because he told you straight out in no uncertain terms. You never had to guess with him. Bobby was one of the longer-employed camp managers at KBR. I quickly found out that Bobby was always talking about his 'honor.'

Like he was some sort of antebellum Southern large plantation owner where matters of 'honor' were-life-and-death-matters from pre-Civil War times, only to be finally resolved at the front end of dueling pistols or revolvers at ten paces. Bobby was as autonomous as a ship's captain and expected his orders to be immediately obeyed. And they were.

4. 14 OCTOBER 2005-CAMP HOPE-CAMP MANAGER'S OFFICE

There was one strange incident that made no sense at the time, but perfect sense later in the grand scheme of things. Some ex-coworkers I was friendly with and had worked security in Kuwait and Bosnia maintained a network of contacts via e-mail. Any hint of contract or available work was immediately passed around. A former USAF SF Master Sergeant (MSGT) that I knew from our working together at CSA in Kuwait asked me for some help getting work with KBR in Iraq. I said send me your resume and I will hand it to HR when I get to training. By October he sent an e-mail saying he had not heard anything back either way. I knew he was perfectly well-qualified for the job. I went to Bobby Burns and said how do I check on this guy's resume. He said through KBR Security, not HR. I thought that very strange as all HR departments handle recruiting. I said OK, I will check with the Area Security Manager, Frank Russell. He gave me a tight grimace and said: "I'd advise you not to do that." His remark was even stranger.

I called Frank Russell. I have been chewed-out, balled out, yelled at, dressed-down, belittled, verbally reprimanded, and blasted before by some real professionals in my time. But I have never, ever seen anything like THE-SCREAMING-AT-THE-TOP-OF-YOUR-LUNGS insanely berserk tirade I got over my cell phone. "HOW DARE YOU EVEN TRY TO RECOMMEND SOMEONE FOR KBR SECURITY!!!!!!!!" he started in. "HOW DARE YOU EVEN THINK ABOUT DOING THAT!!!!!!!!" "HOW DARE YOU EVEN TRY TO CONTACT HOUSTON DIRECTLY ABOUT RECRUITING ANYONE INTO SECURITY!!!!!!!!" This out-of-control insanity continued for several minutes. It got so bad I had to hold the phone away from my ear. He probably climbed up on his desk to try to scream louder. I got the message, and an earache.

I went back to Bobby Burns and told him what happened. He gave me another grim look and only said: "I told you not to call him." Yes, you did.

5. 15 JANUARY 2006-CAMP HOPE (E-MAIL)

I tell J.T. that all AMRs continue to be denied-to date, even the LOGCAP III convoys out to Camp Rustimayah have seats unfilled. (What is wrong with this picture?) However, the Camp Manager has stated that KBR Regional Command HQs is working on an AMR to extract 20 of the final survivors from FOB Little Big Horn on 03 February 2006. That 31 of us are still here and people are moving out painfully slow (if at all), I wonder. We will see. I am not holding my breath. The Army Contracts Officer (ACO) and DPM or someone is coming out here tomorrow for a look/see. Maybe some other guys here can hi-jack their helo and escape.

It was announced by the manufacturer that the famous Winchester '73 repeating rifle will be discontinued. Another sad end to a historic legacy. How is your collection stacked? Is this like when an artist dies everyone runs out and buys their albums? Need more of them?

6. 15 JANUARY 2006-CAMP HOPE (E-MAIL)

I say to J.T. I can see right now unless something dramatic happens there will be quite a few people headed into the POW 'cooler' when FOB Stalingrad gets overrun. Then we will either have to hitch rides in HUMVEEs when the Army unit withdraws about mid-February from the FOB for good. (Theoretically.) Or maybe we can just stay here, idling our time with the remaining 20-25 trainers/advisors. They do have billions of paperback books consolidated into their little library from all over the whole camp. I can always demolish the assorted W.E.B. Griffin series books again. Hey! MUCH better than hanging down at Camp Prosperity playing no-win political games and being low-man-on-totem pole, right? I just WISH I had not sent off all my stuff. Maybe I can wind up looking like Robinson Crusoe: rags, long scraggly beard, walking stick, got to get a 'Main Man' named 'Friday' to help me out though, lose some weight, plenty of time to write my memoirs. "TRAPPED IN SADR CITY!" I can see the headlines!! A budding bestseller. Some guys are really freaking out up here. I am starting to think this is turning into a farce personally. Really-some of these people are becoming, well . . . . very strange, as the walls slowly close in on them/us. Very interesting to see how this plays out every day as some people become more and more frantic. Sort of like being trapped in a submarine and sending out underwater messages, tapping out Morse Code on the pipes: HELP! But no one is answering! AAAAHHHH! No submarine rescue submersible vehicles are coming! I will let you know what happens, but this whole situation is really putting a very bad taste in people's mouths. Film at 11. Glug-glug!

7. 15 JANUARY 2006-CAMP HOPE-SECURITY OFFICE

We knew Camp Hope was going to close in early February 2006, so my boss, Jessie Rich, contacted me in early December 2005 and said I could have my pick of any base I wanted since there were so many without a single Security person assigned. I immediately said KBR Camp F-9, the U.S. Army SF compound. It was right next to CVN, small like Camp Hope, quiet, secure and the only people who were allowed in there were the people who worked there or had official business. A perfect place for me to hideout indefinitely and not be bothered by anyone.

A month later my boss Jessie e-mailed me and said I was being transferred to the "Green Zone": Camp Prosperity. I was not happy. I knew the "Green Zone" was a festering cesspool of continual, unrelenting sin, debauchery, and depravity. It was said the "Green Zone" had 10,000 residents during the day and 20,000 residents at night. Outside the little heavily fortified U.S. military camps that peppered the insides of the "Green Zone," the rest of it would have made Sodom and Gomorrah, or Bangkok for that matter, look like a Girl Scout camp or Disneyland. You could literally have anything, and anyone, at any time, day, or night: bars, discos, brothels, drugs, weapons, explosives, gambling, sex. There was no vice barred for the right amount of money-and if you knew where to look. I did not envy the U.S. Army Military

Police (MPs) in their daytime and night time patrols. I am sure they had their hands full every day.

The whole place was pure evil. It was worse than being sent to seventh or lowest level of Hades. I said there was going to be trouble if I went, that I was honest and would not roll over on all the stealing, thievery, and graft there. He explained that a Security Technician named Jeff Fusco just quit. The two remaining Security Technicians needed 'adult supervision.' He said he had no choice. I was the only Senior Security Technician available for the assignment. I resigned myself to my fate. This was not going to end well at all. I was going to cause myself a tremendous amount of trouble.

I was right.

8. 15 JANUARY 2006-CAMP HOPE (E-MAIL)

I tell J.T.-Jessie just sent me an e-mail. An 'Offer I Can't Refuse' accompanied with the head of a camel under the proverbial sheets. I am headed to Camp Prosperity in the "Green Zone" shortly. I 'sleep with the fishes.' Some bubba named Fusco just resigned down there and they are also short-handed. At least 'Luca Brazi' (or Jessie) asked me what my feelings were about the move which I did not indicate ('Laws of Omerta'/"Never let anyone what you are thinking; never let anyone know what you have under your fingernails."). Sh*t! Camp Prosperity is not the LAST place I want to be, but it is sort of close. It is all 100 percent pure political B.S. there, zero percent security. My 'political' skills are non-existent. Just great, I will not cut it down there. It is perfect if you want to get another job with another security firm; it is Ground Center Zero for everything: people, jobs, contacts, contracts, everything, info, the latest hot poop. Except I do not want to get another job with anyone else. I am happy with KBR (well I was until this 'contract' hit the streets). Damn. I will just have to suck it up, and I was looking to going to the SF Camp too. Whatever. I am unhappy. When life hands you lemons, make lemonade. (Ann Landers.) Talk to you soon.

9. 17 JANUARY 2006-CAMP HOPE (E-MAIL)

I say to J.T. we are re-naming our little home, FOB Hope, and start calling it FOB Corregidor. They put in an AMR (Army Movement Request) to get people out of here by helo: denied. The Army is not moving any civilians out of here by helo, military bubbas only. That means we go by convoy, except convoys are moving infrequently and we are not even sure if they will have any seats for any KBR bubbas. NOT looking good up here. Multiple e-mails to the KBR High Supreme Command HQs continue to go unanswered about our little problem. Maybe this place should be called FOB Titanic? I will advise.

10. 17 JANUARY 2006-CAMP VICTORY-NORTH (E-MAIL)

J.T. replies and says DFAC biscuits will knock them out every time, if the Iraqis get hit in the head, or they can knock their own heads together Three Stooges-like in a dive to get them for something to eat.

11. 17 JANUARY 2006-CAMP HOPE (E-MAIL)

I tell J.T. they have 28 good-ol'-boys left and 18 days to get them all out of here. KBR needs to do the math. They have already blown maybe half a dozen opportunities to move people out on convoys before to Camp Rustimayah, but they never pushed the issue-there was ALWAYS TIME. It has always been this very 'manana'-tomorrow-attitude. Then the U.S. Army abruptly cancelled the helo rides in/out 3-4 days ago did not even spook them. But that should have been a big wake-up call to someone somewhere. Now this AMR denial today has them rattled as the days slip by one-by-one. They are hoping for some seats out in tomorrow night's LOGPAC III convoy in/out from Camp Rustimayah. I just sent Jessie a head's-up e-mail saying do not hold your breath waiting for me to relieve Jeff Fusco on 15 February 2006. I said I am essentially at FOB Dien Bien Phu and the KBR High Supreme Transportation/Movement Command HQs has been informed and we have a total non-response-to date. I do not expect him to be able to do anything about it, but at least he will not get sandbagged when it happens. None of us are expecting this Rambo-looking bus to back-haul all of us out of here either. Looking for you to show up in an Islamic Jihad taxi and bail my ass out. See you at the Main Gate soon. Wear your diaper on your head, Jesus sandals and nightie. Got your goodies in a conex box. At least THEY'LL make it out of Camp Little Big Horn.

12. 17 JANUARY 2006-CAMP VICTORY-NORTH (E-MAIL)

J.T. tells me we WILL mount a rescue mission from here, if necessary. A bunch of Haji pickup trucks and a bucket full of DFAC biscuits for ammo.

13. 02 FEBRUARY 2006-CAMP HOPE-HELICOPTER LANDING PAD

My nine months at Camp Hope has been uneventful, except for the regularly scheduled monthly 122mm rocket/mortar barrages (and some occasional sniper fire, random Rocket-propelled Grenade (RPG) rounds or maybe a few stray bullets, mortar rounds and some almost daily unscheduled 122mm rockets).

14. 04 FEBRUARY 2006-CAMP PROSPERITY-OPERATIONS OFFICE

Camp Hope was formally turned over to the Iraqi Army in mid-December 2005 and we prepared to leave. There was only going to be a small U.S. Army training unit that would remain. I was seated and strapped in on the last helicopter out at Midnight on 02 February 2006 and rode it back to CVS. After two days I rode the Rhino to the "Green Zone." Someone was waiting to meet me from Camp Prosperity Operations at the pick-up point. We rode his SUV over there. I got signed in and he explained due to the shortage of available bunks I would have to sleep in the same bed of someone who was away on a long leave. They had put me on the waiting list to move up to my own room. Also there were some LSAs being built to handle all the people assigned to Camp Prosperity opening up soon. The room was in a nearby one-story masonry administration building. Some ply-wood walls had been thrown up as partitions throughout the building to make little sleeping spaces.

Mine was no bigger than a large walk-in closet. I called it home until they got some something bigger and more permanent. I got a few hours' sleep and was back in Operations the next building over at 08:00. They told me to grab some breakfast at the DFAC, come back to process in and then fill-out your check-in list to process in with all the other departments. I did. First on the list: Property. I had to draw my laptop, radio and whatever else I needed. In a funny coincidence, the Property Department equipment issue window was just catty-corner to my bedroom. I handed my check-in list to the man behind the half-way split top-open door that also served as a counter. Immediately the man looked at my check-in sheet, saw I was in Security and then asked me why wasn't anyone in Security doing any investigations into all the a/c units being stolen in droves? I said I would find out and get back to him. I immediately knew this situation was going to get very messy very fast. How little did I know.

Once I had completed my check-in list I started my walk-around tour to get the lay-of-the-land. Although a/c unit theft was the first problem that confronted me on the first morning of my arrival, it was the Power Generation and Distribution (Power Gen) Department that occupied my time for the first few days after I got settled in and oriented to the base. I was immediately approached on my first walk-around inspection tour of the camp by one of the Iraqi camp workers. He said he was the Foreman of all the Iraqi Power Gen workers and his name was Ahmed Naji (forever known as 'Haji Naji' since he had been on the Hajj or religious pilgrimage to Mecca). He had stopped me and had introduced himself since he needed my help. Obviously he had been alerted to my arrival that day. He wanted to discuss all the massive thievery of all the Power Gen equipment, spare parts, tools generator units and literally everything else everywhere. It turned out Haji Naji was one of the rarest of Iraqis: honest and appalled by all the continual stealing. He said he was employed by an Iraqi manpower firm called IPBD Company (Co.), Ltd., in Baghdad, a subcontractor to KBR. They had their office located at Camp

Prosperity. They supplied skilled workers or labor into all the KBR departments under the LOGCAP III contract.

He started complaining about how whole generator sets had been stolen and moved out of the "Green Zone" by KBR and Iraqi Power Gen workers working in cooperation. These thefts has been going on for almost three years, or since GWII started in March 2003 and there were other witnesses who would verify what he was saying. I told him that I wanted to speak to the IBPD Manager in their office first before I did anything else as a courtesy to him.

It had been a long morning and I was only getting started. Getting started? I had just barely lifted my foot off the ground to take the first step and I knew I was in way over my head. Haji Naji then left. I then decided then it would be a good time to pay a courtesy call on the IPBD Co. Manager and see what they had to say when I was then intercepted outside of the Power Gen Office by my two new Security cohorts: R. C. Calligan (R.C.) and Tim Knisley (Tim). Since they were Security Technicians and I was a Senior Security Technician that made me their boss. They were the only remaining Security guys left in the "Green Zone." We exchanged pleasantries. Both of them briefed me on the past history of KBR Security on Camp Prosperity: too many bases to cover, never enough manpower to do it.

They explained my predecessor, Jeff Fusco, resigned after a failed romantic, if purely platonic, affair with a female KBR employee named Sarah Smith. The main problem we had was we had to cover over a half a dozen large bases and an equal number of smaller compounds, all inside the "Green Zone." There were only three of us when there should have been at least many dozens of Security guys. KBR Security was always extremely short-handed, but this was ridiculous. The only exception was the U.S. Embassy compound which was handled by another KBR section under a completely different contract, called the U.S. Mission-Iraq (USMI). Maybe a dozen camps, thousands of U.S. troops and American civilian and contract workers, all manner of Iraqi and foreign contract workers, 20,000 Iraqis living there at night and just the three of us to cover the "Green Zone." Calling this situation 'short-handed' did not even begin to cover it.

R.C. and Tim both seemed very happy to see me. Obviously they were sizing me up to see what type of person I was going to be and what I would do in Security. The first thing they did was to get me my own Security vehicle so I could have mobility. Then we all loaded up and caravanned over to the Security office on Camp Honor, a few minutes-drive away. The Security office was in a non-descript sand-colored half-conex box with no windows, a few desks, filing cabinets, wall maps, chairs and peg boards with the usual safety and health notices tacked up. The place was a total disaster zone. Thick just and sand covered everything. Small mountains of papers were stacked up high on desks, in cardboard boxes on the floor, on top of the filing cabinets and scattered about everywhere. The place obviously had not been used in months if that short a time. I told them both that the first order of business was to straighten up the Security office. I would see to that chore myself. They handed me a spare key to the only door and departed.

15. 04-06 FEBRUARY 2006-CAMP UNION III-KBR SECURITY OFFICE

For the next two full days I worked in the Security office. Organizing messy, disorganized offices was a specialty of mine. I enjoyed the satisfaction of putting the place back into order. It was a tall order. There were U.S. Army regulations that were way out of date, some were issued right after GWII started three years before. Almost everything was obsolete, long past superseded, date expired, no longer applicable, and virtually all of it useless. Some of it did not even apply to KBR Security. I even found some classified material, but none of us had a security clearance or a 'need-to-know' the information. Plus, it was all long obsolescent. Most of it was marked CONFIDENTIAL, a few documents were stamped SECRET. I emptied out a box of useless, superseded documents and placed everything marked classified in it for disposal at the nearest U.S. Army unit that had a burn bag. The few still applicable or current items I put into alphabetical files that were easily searchable and re-organized everything. The vast majority of it was headed for the Dempster Dumpster. It was starting to look better.

On the last day I was working in the office Tim walked in to check up on me. I had my hands full of paperwork. He asked me what I was doing. I said I was getting ready to throw nine copies of the same obsolete U.S. Army regulation from 2004 into the trash pile. He reacted in mock horror: "YOU CAN'T THROW AWAY VALUABLE ARMY REGULATIONS!!!!!!" he nearly shouted. I patiently explained what I had found, what I was doing and how things were going. He said I could get into a lot of trouble for throwing away all these important U.S. Army and KBR papers, regulations, and documents. I replied nearly everything was long out-of-date, did not apply to us at all or was long superseded. No one would blink an eyelash at what I was doing. He departed.

Of course, the very next day I got this 'hot' e-mail in from my boss, Jessie Rich, the F-Sites Area Security Coordinator. He berated me for throwing out valuable U.S. Army regulations and other documents. I patiently explained to him what I had found, what I was doing and what I would finish to do. I never heard from him about the matter again. But I quickly learned how much support I could expect to receive from Tim. None. It was his first, but not last, attempt to get me into trouble - or fired. It was not very often that I went back into the Security office.

16. 06 FEBRUARY 2006-CAMP PROSPERITY-HR OFFICE

Before I could even put myself into gear with the Power Gen Shop investigation, I had to run in to HR about a routine matter about adding more pages to my U.S. passport late that same afternoon. The Camp's HR Representative, Patricia Murphy, immediately buttoned-holed me and 'informally' cautioned me not to talk about any of my preliminary investigations to anyone.

After concluding that little statement she emphatically and specifically told me NOT to talk about Russell Hill, the HVAC Department Manager or any of the other HVAC Department Technicians. I replied I did not understand what she was talking about. She said she had heard from other people on the camp that they heard me say that I was out to "get the HVAC shop people," or

I was "out to get them" plus I had said that I would "take them down" and "arrest them," "put them in jail" or words to that effect. I replied I had no idea what she was talking about and added I do not talk to anyone about my investigations other than people in Security like my boss, Jessie Rich. What wicked crack cocaine was this woman smoking? I had not even started in on the HVAC shop investigations, much less talk to anyone about the HVAC Department or anything else. I had never said a word to anyone. What was she doing by threatening me?

She further cautioned me that if I did not stop or desist from using rumors, innuendo, hearsay, false statements and the like that KBR could be sued for slander or defamation by these individuals, that the company could pay out tens of millions of dollars in compensation, that the company would receive a very public black eye and that this would come back to seriously hurt or gravely damage KBR Security, the implication that it would come back to hurt or gravely damage me personally. Again I said I had no idea what she was talking about. However at no time did Ms. Murphy ask me for my side of the story or act like she was being impartial. She just immediately outright accused me of making these statements as if I actually had made them. Although Ms. Murphy was cautioning me from using rumors, innuendo, hearsay, false statements and the like I felt that Ms. Murphy was obviously using rumors, innuendo, hearsay, false statements, and the like against me for some unknown reason.

It was obviously she was going to impede, hamper or block my investigation of the HVAC Department and, specifically, Russell Hill to the best of her ability. The only unanswered question was why. I was not picking up any allies at Camp Prosperity. This was going to be a long uphill battle.

17. 07 FEBRUARY 2006-CAMP PROSPERITY-CAMP MANAGER'S OFFICE

I met with the Camp Manager, Robert 'Bobby' Burns. We had worked together for a few months in 2005 at Camp Hope when Bobby was assigned as Camp Manager there. I planned to meet him almost every day to keep him up on what I was doing. It was just a courtesy. Technically, we did not work for the Camp Manager. We were considered more like advisors. But I knew the fastest way to get Bobby on my side and keep him there was to keep him abreast of what was happening on his camp on any security matters so he would not get bushwhacked or surprised by anything under my bailiwick. Plus I needed him to support me with all the other KBR workers since I already knew I was going to be stepping on people's toes, a lot of them, and very shortly.

Bobby mentioned one thing that instantly caught my attention. He said that back in January 2006, the Defense Contracts Management Authority (DCMA) representative who worked at the U.S. Embassy was passing under the 14th of July Bridge in the "Green Zone" when he spotted a KBR truck and some Americans and Iraqis who were quickly loading up two Iraqi taxis with package a/c units. Bobby said the DCMA representative had his driver stop, took some photographs and license plate numbers of the two taxis plus descriptions of the vehicles and perps before everyone had scattered. He filed a complaint. KBR Security traced everything to the HVAC Shop and there was an interview conducted with Russell Hill, the HVAC Department Manager shortly after. Bobby said he attended, as did the Camp HR Representative, Patricia Murphy, and some USMI Security representatives, but nothing ever came of it. That perked my interest right up. I said I would go over to see the DCMA at the U.S. Embassy myself in a few days.

18. 07 FEBRUARY 2006-CAMP PROSPERITY-IPBD CO. MANAGERS' OFFICE

Now it was time to see the IPBD Company (Co.) Manager in their office. They were sub-contractors to KBR who supplied skilled and semi-skilled workers to all of Camp Prosperity's departments, including Power Gen, HVAC, Plumbing, Carpentry, Labor, Electrical, Billeting and Operations and I assumed provided manpower services for the rest of the "Green Zone" camps. They were operating out of a converted house trailer set up at a two-story high level on support blocks in the back of the camp placed well away from everything else. I quickly found out there were two co-managers, not one, of the Iraqi manpower company. Both managers spoke near fluent English, and both of them were very anxious to have someone listen to their many problems. Their names were Mr. Ali and Mr. Khalid. They quickly poured out all their company headaches.

First was they had no control over their employees. They said they were managers in name only. Virtually every KBR Department had an Iraqi 'boss' who ran or controlled all the other employees. They told the two IPBD managers who they wanted hired and firing anyone at will if they proved to be honest or uncooperative. If they remained in the face of all the stealing going on in their own department and kept quiet, then they could stay. The managers said the Iraqis worked closely with the KBR employees in coordination to steal whatever they could get their hands on. They also added that they had continually gone to KBR Security to have all this massive thievery investigated and stopped. Nothing was ever done. They were not even listened to by a single person.

There was more. They explained that everything was being stolen, not only at Camp Prosperity and inside the whole "Green Zone", but throughout the entire country. Everything purloined was all sold off to a 100,000-man theft ring, or a virtual massive army of thieves. This huge 'army' operated country-wide, stealing from all the bases, every camp and facility. It was based in Baghdad and run by a mastermind named Mr. Ahmed Abu Kahlem Hassan who ran this huge gang of criminals called the "Hausassem" (Arabic for thieves or literally predatory cockroaches who sprang up suddenly out of nowhere with the war's start). They said they greatly feared for their lives, taking different routes to Camp Prosperity every day. They explained it would be simple to have someone kill them. They went on and said the "Hausassem" paid for the goods in cash, gold, whatever the sellers wanted to be paid with and then re-sold the loot on the Black Market.

But the "Hausassem" retained a percentage of these massive profits then handed it over to the insurgents. This ill-gotten loot helped bankroll the insurgents to buy weapons and ammunition, hire new recruits and pay their salaries plus purchase more and more IEDs from experienced bomb-makers. They added that anything made of aluminum went straight to Iran where their

Revolutionary Guards bombmakers, who specialized in making EFPs, or Explosively-Formed Projectiles, were making EFPs as fast as humanly possible for export right back to Iraq. These bombs had aluminum tips that were shaped into charges and would easily penetrate the hardest armor-plating on any vehicle the U.S. had in its inventory, like a hot knife through soft butter.

I had heard that rumor when I was up at Camp Hope in 2005 about the call for any stolen aluminum that was being shipped directly to Iran, but I did not know exactly why (I thought it was for sale as scrap metal). I also heard the call for any aluminum when I was down in Basra working for the Kuwaitis back in 2003-04. Back then thieves would topple dozens (or hundreds) of long-distance electric power towers and sell the aluminum wire and the whole tower frames to the Iranians. Now I knew why.

We were not done yet. There was even more startling news. They reason they said they knew all about this the huge, nation-wide theft ring operation was that one of their few honest employees was their spy inside the theft ring. They attended the periodic big meetings that were held. They also added that R.C. also attended the meetings. That settled where R.C.'s loyalties lay. Like Tim, R.C. was going to be totally untrustworthy. I would have to be especially careful around them from this moment on. Tim and R.C. were going to sell me out in a heartbeat.

I was totally stunned (or like the British always say: "Gob-smacked"). Not only were KBR employees thieves, but traitors in aiding and abetting the murder of U.S. troops and civilian contract workers all over Iraq while they were fueling and expanding the raging insurgency. This was pure insanity. KBR was lining its pockets with the re-orders of stolen goods under the LOGCAP III contract; its employees were getting rich off of whatever they stole, and the company was paying for the bad guys to keep the war running. A Win-Win for KBR and many of its corrupt employees in Iraq, the "Hausassem" and the insurgents. A Lose-Lose for the poor, snake-bit, hapless U.S. taxpayers, the U.S. government and the U.S. troops being murdered plus anyone honest enough (or dumb enough) to investigate the whole titanic mess. Now I was right square in the middle of all of it.

I explained what we could do to take control back from the employees. At least Mr. Ali and Mr. Khalid would get their company back. They would announce that everyone was terminated. We would start first with the Power Gen Department. However, if anyone walked in and made a written statement confessing or implicating the others, if they had no part in their thievery, then they would keep their jobs. I said I had to tell the Camp Manager, Bobby Burns what IPBD was planning on doing, if they agreed to the plan. He had to agree to it. But there were plenty of out-of-work carpenters, plumbers, electricians, and other skilled craftsmen so the work would not be impacted much. New replacement workers could be very quickly hired and better monitored. It was not as if there was a shortage out of skilled workers in the "Red Zone." Plus, a lot was at stake. The lives of U.S. and other Coalition Forces soldiers and civilian contractors of many nations for one thing.

Both managers immediately agreed to my plan. I said just let me clear it with Bobby Burns first. Bobby saw me immediately. He said that he had no control over IPBD, who they hired or fired. They were just a sub-contractor providing manpower services. He said he could live with the drop in productivity for a few days while IPBD hired new replacements. It was done.

I returned and informed Mr. Ali and Mr. Khalid they could fire everyone except for anyone who wanted to make a written statement about what was going on about all the stealing in the Power Gen Department. Then they could keep their jobs. Only Haji Naji immediately accepted. He went in to write out his statement in the IBPD Managers' Office. After a few days to think about it, about half a dozen other Power Gen workers came back in one-by-one to write out their statements and were re-hired. Both managers were relieved and happy. They had begun to take back control of their company.

The managers and the workers all explained how there were several KBR managers and employees who were central to all the criminal activity. The ringleader was the former Power Gen Department Manager, a man called Lynn Summerville, now just promoted to Area Power Gen Manager just prior to my arrival. Other perpetrators included the Assistant Power Gen

Department Manager named Fergus 'Red' Johnson, Technicians named Troy Williams, Leath Shea, Tony Ame Noail and an Electrical Department worker named Phillip Greenwood. The main Iraqi Power Gen Department ringleader was a man named Reayth Jameel.

Since both Tim and R.C. were incapable of being trusted in the slightest, I knew they would undermine me or at least try to get me fired if given the slightest chance. So I devised a plan to use 'Reverse Psychology' on them. This was to throw them off balance and keep them there. Then I would work on getting them transferred to other bases as soon as I could and out of my hair. So at every instance I praised them to their faces and to our boss Jessie in my e-mails with 'cc's' back to them. I never said a single bad word even though I knew they were doing their utmost to stab me in the back and have me summarily fired.

19. 08 FEBRUARY 2006-U.S. EMBASSY MAIN BUILDING, DCMA'S OFFICE

I met with Joseph 'Joe' Saladino in his office. He was the DCMA Quality Assurance Manager (QAR). He said he was a retired New York City policeman. He immediately started slamming KBR Security for conducting a sham interview of Russell Hill and a non-investigation into the thefts of the package a/c units. He explained the 'interview' only consisted of a few perfunctory questions of Hill and they wrapped everything up when he denied he was under the 14th of July Bridge or that anything had been stolen in his department. Mr. Saladino complained it was all a sham investigation and a bogus interview. Nothing was ever done past that point. Then he started loudly complaining of daily sightings of all manner of things being stolen which he constantly reported to the USMI Security, U.S. Army MPs, the USAF SF/IZ Police, the AFOSI and anyone in charge of law enforcement in the "Green Zone." All of his complaints fell on deaf ears. No one did anything. In fact, he said he complained about the thefts to everyone he could find. He added that a few people said this was all minor stuff and not to worry about it when they clearly were not.

He explained what he saw that day. It was in late January 2006 when he was being driven around the "Green Zone." They used the U-turn under the 14th of July Bridge when he spotted two Iraqi taxis and a KBR pick-up truck parked off to the side. Three men transferring package (or window) a/c units into the taxis' trunks. He immediately had his driver stop. He grabbed his camera and took some photographs of the taxis as they started to drive away and then out of the "Green Zone." He got an accurate description of the KBR employee and wrote down the taxis' license plates. I took down everything he told me. I said I could not promise him anything, but I'd see what I could so. He said I was the very first person to show any interest in what he was saying. I explained I had Russell Hill and the HVAC Shop in my sights. There were too many reports of stolen a/c units of all sizes to ignore.

20. 08 FEBRUARY 2006-CAMP PROSPERITY-MAIN YARD

Along with all the conex boxes being unlocked and most of them wide-open, I also saw the usual line of maybe a dozen KBR work vehicles parked in front of Operations also in the Main Yard right across from the row of conex boxes. Not only were all the vehicles left unlocked, all of them had the keys left sitting in their ignition. Plus almost all of them had very valuable precision measurement instruments, expensive calibration sets, whole sets of toolboxes stuffed with high-priced tools and a wide assortment of other costly goodies that would bring someone a pretty penny out in the Black Market if purloined. All of them were ripe for the picking by anyone passing by who wanted to help themselves with no one the wiser.

I immediately started looting all the vehicles of keys, vehicle registrations, fuel cards and as many valuable tools or equipment as I could carry. Before departing I left a sweet little 'love note' on the steering wheel that said: "See Bobby!" Then I locked the vehicle up. Off I went to see Bobby with the loot, vehicle keys and all the vehicle's paperwork sitting in the glove compartment. I walked directly to the Camp Manager's office. Usually Bobby was away at meetings, so I deposited the 'loot' with Bobby's Deputy Camp Manager, David Woodham.

The outrage from all the stung parties was immediate and loud. I was roundly cursed and berated. All I replied to every single person was: "Lock your stuff up!" and walked away. Soon, if slowly, people got the message. However, I caught one Power Gen Department vehicle parked outside the Power Gen shop left with the keys in the ignition and the usual very expensive goodies sitting inside and outside. However, the very next day the SAME vehicle was left in the very same spot unlocked AGAIN with the same goodies for easy pickings. The stupid idiot driver had not let the message sink in. I loudly kept muttering to myself over and over all the way over to Bobby's office: "IT'S THE SAME DAMN VEHICLE!" Obviously the dummy did not let the tongue-lashing Bobby undoubtedly gave that person the previous day be absorbed.

Bobby grew tired of the growing mound of daily 'stolen' equipment, tools, measuring instruments and the like sitting in his office. He said just take the keys, vehicle registration and fuel card and he would deal with the problem on his end. Finally, after a few weeks of effort, I could not ambush a single vehicle that was left unlocked. Everyone had gotten the message: "Lock your stuff up!" I would attack the unlocked conex boxes the same way.

21. 08 FEBRUARY 2006-CAMP PROSPERTY-IPBD CO. MANAGERS' OFFICE

It did not take long for the Power Gen Department witnesses to come in to save their jobs. Over the next several days they all described how many dozens of generator sets and other light units were stolen, later replaced, then stolen again in a never-ending cycle of thievery. Haji Naji detailed the many occasions and slick, underhanded techniques that Summerville used to steal U.S. Army generators. The first scam was to schedule large U.S. Army generator sets, that were the size of shipping containers, for 'routine maintenance.' Then Summerville deliberately caused minor damage to the generator sets to take them off-line for 'repair' in the Power Gen repair shop. Then Summerville reported to the U.S. Army that the generator sets were unrepairable. He sent in requests through KBR Procurement, then approved by the U.S. Army, for replacement. The 'unrepairable' generator units were then shifted for storage to an adjacent 'scrap' yard near the Power Gen Shop. These units all quickly disappeared from KBR's property records. The fraudulently removed generators were then stripped of all removeable parts that were taken out of the "Green Zone" for re-sale on the Black Market or to pre-arranged customers. The remaining empty generator shells that could not be stripped-down further of any parts were loaded on a flatbed truck at night and hauled out to the "Red Zone" and sold. This cycle was repeated over and over.

All the witnesses confirmed that Summerville used any small problem, like a clogged air or oil filter, to take a generator unit off-line for repair, when the problem could have been easily been solved or fixed on the site with replacing the filters. Summerville would tell the U.S. Army that the generator unit was "no good." He explained it had to be taken back to the Power Gen Department for repairs. Summerville removed the generator units and placed them in the scrap yard. Then Summerville and his cohorts broke down the generator units into smaller pieces or parts and had them carried out of the "Green Zone." Some of the witnesses said they had no idea what happened to some generator units, they just simply disappeared. But Summerville always had KBR order replacement generator units at the U.S. government's expense.

According to another Power Gen Department employee, Ahmed Chasib Luaaby, in a verbal and later written statement, he detailed one instance when Summerville declared ten small generator sets used for lighting at the various "Green Zone" gates, as 'unserviceable' after he had deliberately disabled them. Then he identified small, minor problems with each to the U.S. Army. Luaaby explained these so-called problems did not in any way actually render the ten generator sets unfit for their intended use. Summerville had these lighting units moved to the scrap yard for dismantling and removal. Summerville reported the lighting sets as 'inoperative.' KBR automatically ordered new units.

The witnesses also told how Summerville assigned a KBR staffer with a CAC card to escort Shea, Noail and Jameel out of the "Green Zone" with all the stolen items each time. Summerville did not work to steal just Power Gen equipment. He coordinated the removal of equipment, spare parts, and supplies from other KBR Departments, especially Electrical and Plumbing, so it would all go out the gate at the same time. The witnesses detailed how the IBPD Electrical Shop workers used a yellow table saw to cut down large electrical power cables to a portable size. Then either Shea or Williams carried the U.S. government property out of the "Green Zone" in vehicles during the evening.

Luaaby continued his detailed explanations of how Lynn Summerville placed them out in the Black Market fully repaired for sale for a more lucrative return. In two specific instances, Summerville ordered 10 generator sets removed from the scrap yard after they had been completely repaired then loaded onto a flatbed truck in order. At Summerville's direction, these generator sets were driven out of the "Green Zone" by Shea, Noail and Jameel and delivered to different locations in Baghdad and sold for between USD$30,000-50,000 in cash each. Phillip Greenwood acted as the escort.

At least four generator sets wound up in Sadr City, a notorious insurgent stronghold and my first assignment. Once in place, they required a reliable supply of fuel and spare parts for maintenance to generate power. Summerville supplied both-for a price. Almost every other day, Summerville had Troy Williams arrange for Iraqi IPBD Power Gen employees to supply fuel and any spare parts needed to keep all the generator sets in the "Red Zone" in operation. All courtesy of U.S. government property purchased under the KBR LOGCAP III contract. Summerville shared the profits generated from the sale of power, the stolen parts, generators, and fuel with his cohorts: Shea, Noail and Jameel.

In the second specific instance, Luaaby explained about two large portable U.S. military floodlights (called light-alls) that were being used at Checkpoint #12 for illumination in the "Green Zone." Summerville and his henchmen told the U.S. Army they were removing them for 'servicing', then ordered replacement units through KBR. He sold the stolen light-alls for USD$10,000 each in one of the Baghdad 'souks' (Arabic for market). Haji Naji and other witnesses explained how Summerville and his other Power Gen henchmen also falsified purchase requests to replace supposedly 'damaged and unserviceable' generator unit starter motors, plumbing pumps, skid pumps and macerator pumps from a local supplier. All these 'damaged' starters and pumps were then sold for a hefty profit in the "Red Zone."

Haji Naji told me that he asked Summerville why all these generators and their parts were being taken out of the "Green Zone." Summerville explained they were being sent out for repairs, but that was both absurd and a lie. Haji Naji added that he asked Summerville on several occasions why the stolen generator units were not being repaired in the Power Gen Shop, Summerville told him it was none of his business. Summerville and Shea both told Haji Naji to "forget" about generator and parts. At one point, a certain part was needed to keep a U.S. military generator in operation. Haji Naji explained to me that he recalled the part had been taken out of that particular generator and sold out in an Iraqi market. When Haji Naji said when he asked Summerville about this, Summerville advised Haji Naji "to compromise (i.e., forget about his) remembrance." All the Power Gen workers plus other departments routinely used the terms 'scrap,' 'unserviceable,' and 'broken' to justify submitting purchase requests for re-ordering new property that was stolen and resold. The lack of property records being maintained made such actions simple and easy to do since there was no accounting or oversight from the department supervisors.

Luaaby told me that he reported the theft and fraud sometime around 2004 or 2005 that was endemic to the Power Gen Shop and to Summerville's supervisors in the chain-of-command, named Patrick, Russ, and Conrad. None of them would take any action against Summerville because he was a close personal friend of Remo Butler, KBR's Iraq DPM and KBR PM for Kuwait. I soon found out the real power in Iraq, as far as KBR was concerned, was Remo Butler. The witnesses explained that Summerville was personally recruited and hired by Butler. They knew for a fact that Butler agreed to protect Summerville and his activities by dealing with anyone foolish enough to file a complaint against Summerville in one of three ways: 1) having the person transferred to another camp or into another department (if they were lucky), 2) threatening the person with termination if they persisted or 3) terminating the person outright. That Remo Butler, in the most powerful position in Iraq, who controlled both the Operations and Security chains-of-command from the top, would see everything that was going on at every base since both chains reported directly to him. That Butler personally hired Summerville and was protecting him was obviously not a good sign for me.

Aside from Haji Naji, there were several other Iraqi and KBR Power Gen workers who refused to participate in the thievery or fraud perpetrated by Summerville. Many of these individuals had trumped-up or bogus charges filed against them by Summerville and were terminated or at least suspended. Specifically, Naji told me that Americans named Emil Patrick and Conrad plus another worker from the Philippines were all fired outright.

It was the height of irony that Luaaby said that Summerville blamed all the thievery on the local Power Gen Iraqi staff. In 2005, the local Iraqi Power Gen staff was paid between USD$15.00-18.00/day. When the subject of a raise was brought up, Summerville strongly opposed it because he said the Iraqi staff was engaged in the widespread theft of supplies and equipment. Luaaby and Naji explained that as a result of the fraud and thefts, Summerville and Shea received payments in cash, gold, presents, food, jewelry, and other valuables from the Iraqis who received the power generator units and spare parts for sale in the "Red Zone." They said these funds allowed Summerville to live ostentatiously.

At one point, as Luaaby explained, there was a Power Gen mechanic named Michael Canino complained to Summerville about his USD$100.00/month cell phone bill. Luaaby said Summerville roared with laughter and told Canino his cell phone bill was USD$3,000/month. Luaaby continued on his lengthy narrative. He stated either in 2004 or 2005 that KBR-owned Volvo generator fuel pumps were largely unavailable in the "Red Zone" and only available in the "Green Zone." All these pumps were sent to the scrap yard or hidden in other Power Gen areas.

All were all sold off for USD$1,000 each in the "Red Zone" Black Market. Some of the parts were already missing or stripped out by the KBR employees from the stolen fuel pumps when they were sold or prior to being sent to the scrap yard. But eventually everything was eventually stripped out and the remainder disappeared from public view in the scrap yard, all sold in the "Red Zone" Black Market.

Both Haji Naji and Luaaby explained that sometimes Summerville and Williams found they had generator units or parts in 2004 and 2005 that were too large or heavy to move outside the "Green Zone" by pick-up truck. They contacted another KBR employee named Philip or Felipe who they believed was stationed at the KBR Fuel Point just outside Camp Union III who had access to a large flat-bed semi-trailer truck. He would transport the items out of the "Green Zone" over the 14th of July Bridge into the "Red Zone."

The biggest revelation by all the witnesses was that Summerville had set up and was operating his own personal, massive Black Market 'utility' company out in various areas of Baghdad, all at the U.S. government and ultimately the U.S. taxpayer's expense. They explained in either 2004 or 2005 that seven generator sets were taken out of the gate at one time. All of them ended up in the al-Shala area in North Baghdad, explained to be a low-class area of the city, for use by private Iraqi citizens. Summerville used the generator sets to sell electricity to anyone who could pay the going rate, all for Summerville's personal profit. If anything broke down, Summerville provided fuel, spare parts, oil, and anything else needed to keep the generators running full-time. When Summerville's customers out in the "Red Zone" needed another generator set or a specific spare part for one unit, they placed an 'order' with Summerville. He promptly stole the needed item or items from the LOGCAP III-purchased supplies.

Luaaby stated that on one occasion in 2004 or 2005 Williams induced Jameel to order a DOID-type 750kVA generator set and spare parts through LOGCAP III ostensibly for a need in Sadr City, supposedly at Camp Hope (my last assignment). Jameel bought the generator set for USD$10,000 in cash. He told Shea this was to be given to some unnamed operator out in the "Red Zone" and he was merely the go-between. In reality, Jameel was the purchaser and flipped the generator set to some Iraqi buyer for USD$30,000 out on the open Black Market pocketing the difference. The witnesses concluded the thievery at Camp Prosperity with a story how one of the IPBD Power Gen workers named Ali Moshinali, went to KBR Security, and filed a formal complaint about all the rampant thievery that was going on in the department. KBR Security people did nothing.

Summerville and his merry band of thieves were not just isolated at Camp Prosperity. The whole "Green Zone" was fair game and ripe for stealing generators. By this time the U.S. Army was returning camps and other areas they did not need to the Iraqi government. In December 2005, there was an adjacent base close by Camp Prosperity called Camp Honor. There were separate Power Gen operations there until the camp was returned to the Iraqi military. In addition to the normal stealing of U.S-owned generator sets, Summerville, Shea, Williams, Johnson Noail and Jameel also stole fifty generator sets that belonged to the pre-war Iraqi government. They were easily identified since they were either gray or green in color. All these generator sets had been seized by the U.S. Army and turned over to KBR to be kept at Camp Honor for safe-keeping. At the time of actual turnover of Camp Honor in December 2005 every Iraqi generator set had been stolen and most of the generator sets purchased under LOGCAP III were also gone. Apparently, none of the Iraqi generator sets were never recorded on KBR Power Gen property records thus making it a breeze to truck them all out of the "Green Zone" for sale.

Back in October 2005, when it was apparent Camp Hope would be closed down and handed back to the Iraqis, KBR started transferring people out in small numbers, two or three people at a time, each week to other camps throughout Iraq. By the time I boarded the last helicopter in early February 2006 there were perhaps twenty of us left out of the original 65 staffers. As I walked around Camp Prosperity I eventually met six co-workers I knew from Camp Hope. A few said they had been transferred directly to Camp Prosperity, the others said they were transferred in from other bases that either that were also closing down or transferred by manpower needs to here. All of them told me the exact same story without any prompting: that there was massive thievery going on at the bases they were assigned to, no one in KBR Security was doing any investigating even if they had any Security people assigned there. I knew that many small bases or FOBs had no Security staff. KBR Security as a whole was always the least-manned department in all of

KBR by a wide margin. They said the thieves were having a field day by helping themselves to everything.

22. 10 FEBRUARY 2006-USMI COMPOUND-KBR SECURITY OFFICE

I paid a routine courtesy call to the KBR Security people at the USMI compound close to the U.S. Embassy. Jessie said it would be a good idea to at least get to meet the Security folks working there. It turned out not to be a fun trip. If KBR Security manning in Iraq was as thin as a destitute church mouse's wallet, the manning level at USMI was at 100 percent. I was also informed that Camp Prosperity Security has been under the operational 'control' of USMI, although my boss, Jessie, was my direct supervisor, the day-to-day 'control' was handled by USMI, Art Shook. They had a weekly staff meeting every week that a Camp Prosperity representative always attended. It was scheduled for tomorrow. I decided to attend.

After pleasantries and introductions, I departed. The next day's 10:00 staff meeting was the worst staff meeting I haver have had the displeasure to sit through. Some U.S. Army MP patrol vehicle had stopped a wrecker truck with a broken tail light the day before. The description of the routine traffic stop was seen by one of the KBR Security people who happened to be passing by at the time. They stopped and observed the traffic stop until both vehicles had departed. That traffic stop was described in nauseating minutia and took 30 minutes of excruciatingly boring detail. The two-hour meeting went the same way. I vowed: 1) Never to attend another USMI Security meeting and 2) we would revert to the operational control of my supervisor. I informed Jessie of my decision. He agreed.

23. 10 FEBRUARY 2006-CAMP PROSPERITY-CAMP MANAGER'S OFFICE

Bobby called me into his office and asked me if the Security Department could support the sub-contractor LN/TCN IZ Badging Program effective immediately. They had no one else to spare. He explained that Ms. Sarah Smith, a Morale, Welfare & Recreation (MWR) Coordinator, had been tasked to handle this program, in addition to her MWR Departmental duties, but she was leaving for R&R in 10 days. He added that she could no longer be taking responsibility for the program any longer as per the direction of her Supervisor, Walter Straub. I said we could do so, but I needed to check with my boss, Jessie Rich, to make sure it was OK, as a courtesy. I asked Bobby about the major problems I was going to face. He told me that all the department managers were not supporting Ms. Smith in having their people appear for their scheduled appointments. I asked Bobby for his support on the matter and he pledged to me that is any department manager failed to help my efforts on making appointments he would take immediate corrective action.

The whole badging operation had fallen into complete chaos. I checked with Jessie and he said go straighten out the mess. I quickly found out two things from 'The Usual Suspects': 1) Ms. Sarah Smith was the woman Jeff Fusco had fallen madly in love with (he was married). When she finally spurned his advances (after she had led him on for months), he was crushed and quit on the spot, broken-hearted. That was when Jessie switched me from the SF Camp to Camp Prosperity in mid-January, and 2) she had long been informing the GCC and IPBD supervisors the day before (or the day of) the interview appointments. Everything has ground to a complete halt. The supervisors could not react fast enough to get their people together in time for the scheduled bus ride to the Baghdad Convention Center (BCC) (being busy with other things).

I contacted Ms. Smith. We began an immediate turn-over. She brought me down to the BCC where the IZ badging was accomplished for all the LNs and TCNs who worked for IBPD and GCC. She quickly showed me around the facility and introduced me to the U.S. Army and civilian staff who did the interviews and badge processing. She explained the basic system and how LNs and TCNs were processed for badges. I told Ms. Smith that due to the very detailed and complicated procedures, wide coordination efforts were needed among the many people who were involved. I said the high level of specific information she was passing me at a very high flow rate over several hours that I would need several dry-runs to understand the processing system.

I would need several whole days to absorb all the information she was passing me. She promised that by the time she departed for R&R I would be full briefed-up on all the procedures.

She also informed me that that her biggest problem was having all the department managers have their people at the scheduled appointment time/date. I told her that Bobby Burns had assured me that I had his full support. She told me that she had completely guaranteed to the Camp Manager, Bobby, her supervisor, Walter Straub, and all the U.S. Army and civilian LN/TCN IZ Badge Processing personnel at the BCC she would do a proper turn-over. She would contact me the next day.

She lied about everything.

After that day she immediately disappeared for one full week. I could not contact her by cell phone or in person. Like she had disappeared off the face of the earth. I was too busy doing other investigations to chase her around. Finally I got in touch with her after one solid week. We set up an appointment on 18 February, but with five more major investigations opening up that day I had to cancel. Ms. Smith promised to contact me the next day, but she disappeared for two more full days. She made herself completely unavailable to be contacted in spite of my continued efforts to reach her. I was very frustrated, but I had other fish to fry.

24. 11 FEBRUARY 2006-CAMP PROSPERITY-MAIN YARD

R.C. and I met in the Main Yard beside the long row of conex boxes filled with spare parts and equipment. He wanted to brief me on the unreported and underreported theft of plumbing supplies from the Plumbing Department. The Department Head, Nicholas 'Nick the Plumber' Heckman, had been turning in Lost, Damaged and Destroyed (LDD) Reports for many months that were so incomplete or so vague that any useful information about what exactly was lost or stolen could not be gleaned from the reports themselves. R.C. explained that the faulty LDDs both enabled and hid the widespread thefts in the Plumbing Department.

'Nick the Plumber' was easy to find in the Main Yard since he was walking right past us. I asked him about all of this. He immediately gave me a very flippant attitude about everything. He stated he did not care if the Iraqis stole everything in his Department: "Let them steal everything." He had no explanation of his Department's inadequately completed LDD reports. He also willfully ignored basic security procedures like locking up his conex boxes at night or when not in use during the day. I said anyone could have walked into any of them and walked off with expensive equipment, supplies and materials with no one even noticing. We walked over to one of the open Plumbing Department conex boxes. It was filled with valuable water heaters and brand new water pumps.

I explained to Heckman that, while he did not care, I did. I also explained to him that I was going to be the one responsible to do all the investigations of these stolen items. I also reminded Heckman that we all were on the end of a very long supply chain and that these lost or stolen items were not easily replaced or obtained in a war zone. I calmly explained again that KBR ran a very long supply chain. I reminded him that his full cooperation and support was needed to ensure the security and prevent the unaccounted loss of inventory. Heckman replied: "I don't care if the Iraqis stole everything." R.C. then reminded Heckman of all the incomplete, rejected and poorly written LDDs reports over the past several months that Mr. Heckman had still failed to clear. R.C. also informed Heckman that there were numerous reports of thefts of large amounts of materials, equipment, and supplies in his department with no explanation. I reminded Heckman that I needed his full cooperation and support in assisting us with our security duties. Heckman replied he did not care, then walked off with a wave of his hand. We departed the area.

Later that day I wrote out a statement of our conversation and handed it to the Camp's HR Representative, Patricia Murphy. I heard later that she called him into her office and read him the proverbial Riot Act. Finally, he got the message that he was in serious trouble and might be terminated over his negative attitude. He resigned a few days later and went to work for one of the other big construction contractors in Iraq.

25. 11 FEBRUARY 2006-CAMP PROPSPERITY-HVAC DEPARTMENT

With the Power Gen Shop finally under control by the IPBD Managers, I turned my attention to my original goal: the HVAC Department. Mr. Ali, one of the IPBD Managers, already had told me about one of their employees was eager to tell me all about the thievery inside the HVAC shop. The employee's name was Mr. Basam al-Atar, one of the Iraqi HVAC shop technicians. Mr. Ali told me Mr. al-Atar was already under suspicion USAF SF/IZ Police for HVAC theft. He immediately arranged a meeting between Mr. al-Atar and myself in his office.

Mr. al-Atar explained there were two principal KBR employees involved in the theft of HVACs, spare parts, and equipment: the HVAC Department Manager, Russell Hill and Michael Peters, an HVAC Technician. He added there were two IBPD employees also helping them steal everything: a Mr. Safaa Abd-Wahab Saeed al-Nuamee and a Mr. Raad Eslawa Ajo, a Plumbing Department employee. He detailed how Hill and Peters were doing the same thing Summerville and Williams were doing over in the Power Gen shop in stripping it bare. Several other HVAC employees were interviewed. They told us all the exact same thing. The Iraqi ringleader inside the HVAC Department was a Mr. Ajo. He coordinated all the thefts of everything with Russell Hill and Michael Peters. But they stated he was also involved in stealing equipment and supplies from the Power Gen shop, the Plumbing Department and the U.S. Army's off-load areas, where in-coming container loads of everything are dropped off to be unloaded, sorted out first into their respective areas for later collection or distribution. They added Mr. Ajo also transported stolen items outside the "Green Zone."

However, if Mr. Ajo was coordinating the thefts inside the "Green Zone" of U.S. government property, then they all identified a Mr. Safaa Abd-Wahab Saeed Al-Nuamee as the key contact between the "Hausassem" and

KBR HVAC and other Department personnel. He said that it was Mr. Safaa who coordinated all the thievery and misappropriation activities inside the "Green Zone." Someone in KBR had helped Mr. Safaa illegally obtain a Yellow-stripe CAC card which allowed Mr. Safaa unlimited escort privileges for Iraqis and any others throughout the "Green Zone." I wanted to interview Mr. Safaa. But it had been a long day, so I called it at that.

26. 11 FEBRUARY 2006-CAMP UNION III-KBR SECURITY OFFICE

Tim and I were in the Security Office that morning discussing my investigation of all the stealing going on in the "Green Zone" and things in general, when Michael Peters, HVAC Technician, walked in totally unannounced. He started in to tell us all about the thievery going on in the HVAC Department. (I thought, how can this guy be a successful crook if he blabs everything to the Police? This guy must be an idiot!) This is what we call a spontaneous and voluntary statement in the Security business. He said he was directly involved in illegally arranging a U.S. Army Yellow-Stripe CAC card for a one Mr. Safaa, a LN who also worked for the HVAC Department for IPBD. Peters explained he was the LN Lead Foreman. It was in exchange, as a reward, for Mr. Safaa arranging for the U.S. Army to get three bottles of badly needed, almost very hard to quickly obtain, helium gas for the U.S. Army observation balloon tethered, and always seen in the air, over the "Green Zone." The badge was issued through the Camp Mayor and Badging Office at Camp Union III.

Peters than stated that he and the HVAC Department Manager, Russell Hill, made Mr. Safaa into an exclusive HVAC sub-contractor. And they were also in the process of making him into an official KBR HVAC vendor. Peters then stated that he and Hill were steering substantial HVAC Department work to Mr. Safaa exclusively. He also stated that Mr. Safaa was being given a/c units to be transported off the installation to his work shop to the 215 Apartment Complex, that was just East of Camp Union III. That meant it was out in the "Red Zone." Peters then departed our office.

Tim and I just looked at each other. I already knew that the employment of one person doing two separate jobs, i.e. one for KBR and the other for the U.S. Army, and to be paid for both, was strictly prohibited by KBR Policy. Even worse, the process of any KBR personnel making one non-KBR person both a sub-contractor and/or a vendor without due process or official approval is also completely against KBR company policy. The authorization to steer company work towards one individual or company is also totally against company policy. The release of a/c units or other parts for repair outside the FOB or off-base was also strictly prohibited. The HVAC Department was fully capable to fix any a/c unit whatever the size of the unit was. Sending it off-base to another repair shop was pure fraud, waste, abuse and totally illegal.

27. 11 FEBRUARY 2006-CAMP PROSPERITY-MAIN YARD

I had found out by talking to other KBR employees and the IPBD Managers that the only honest department in the whole camp was Carpentry. The Department Manager, Roger Dougherty, ran a tight ship. All the tools and materials were locked up every day (and night unlike all the other departments) and he had a widely known reputation for honesty and integrity. I never had any problems with them. A very rare exception at Camp Prosperity.

28. 12 FEBRUARY 2006-CAMP PROSPERITY-MAIN YARD

Along with the Power Gen and Plumbing Departments, the Electrical Department left all their conex boxes wide open or unlocked too. Anyone would just waltz in there unannounced at any time of the day or night, help themselves then walk off with all the contents with no one the wiser. There were hundreds of very valuable medium and large circuit breaker switches stored in unlocked conex boxes that lined one side of the Main Yard across from the Operations Department.

One of the IPBD electricians came over to me and said just he saw a semi-trailer driver who had his truck parked in the Main Yard throw a large circuit breaker under his truck. Large vehicles were not allowed to park in the Main Yard due to the possibility of it being a suicide bomber. A truck filled with explosives would take out the whole area if it were detonated. I immediately walked over there. The driver was nowhere to be found, another security violation. I checked under the truck and-sure enough-there was the circuit breaker taken from one of the unlocked conex boxes with the doors wide open. An opportunity theft: the driver could have easily hopped out of his cab, grabbed some circuit breakers and been back inside his cab in a flash.

He just had bad luck. When the driver saw someone looking at what he was doing just at that exact moment, he decided then and there to throw the 'evidence' underneath his truck. I checked inside his cab and the truck underside his truck for more loot. After a thorough search, I came up with a dozen more circuit breakers just like the one I found under his truck. They were hidden everywhere inside the cab. I immediately alerted the Electrical Department. The circuit breakers were the size of a large square loaf of bread. One of the department supervisors arrived said they cost USD$2,000 per pop. The driver showed up just then and saw what was happening. He went white with fear and kept pleading over and over with me saying he was not a thief. I finally grew exasperated at this stupidity and shouted: "YOU ARE A THIEF!" He went sullenly silent in shame having been caught red-handed. The IPBD Managers finally showed up and said they would expel the driver and the truck from the "Green Zone" and terminate his company's contract. Everyone disappeared from the stage.

I met with the Electrical Department Head, Donald Walker, in his office about all his wide-open conex boxes. He explained that he was unable to lock his conex boxes because he could not get any padlocks. I looked at him like he just landed from Mars. I rolled my eyes several times in exasperation. I said there were plenty of strong commercial locks available for sale over at the PX. I would be happy to buy as many as he needed to secure his conex boxes. Walker could replace the locks when he finally got some in later on.

29. 12 FEBRUARY 2006-CAMP PROSPERITY-MAIN YARD

At about 09:30, I was doing a random routine security walk-through the Main Yard to see if any conex boxes were unsecured, based on a theft incident involving Electrical Department materials on the previous day. I immediately discovered that all five Electrical Department conex boxes left unsecured again. The first one I entered had hundreds of medium and large major circuit breaker switches, exactly ten of the same type/model which had been stolen the day before by an LN flatbed driver and eventually retrieved. I immediately contacted the Department Head about the current situation and requested he immediately place locks on all his conex boxes. Walker then proceeded to give me a very long, very convoluted, very complex and ultimately useless 'excuse' why he was unable to do that as there were apparently no available locks in the Materials Department to secure his conex boxes.

I got the very strong impression he had no real desire to secure his conex boxes at all. I immediately directed his attention to the fact that he had several options: 1) see the Camp Manager for some assistance (he stated he had not mentioned this fact to the Camp Manager that they remained unsecured); 2) the Security Department would loan him some locks until his locks from the Materials Department arrived to replace the Security Department locks; 3) he could do a local purchase, with the permission of the Materials Department through a petty cash draw, and buy five perfectly good locks now on sale at the Camp Hope PX; or 4) if he did not put locks on his conex boxes that day the Security Department would put them on and he could come to see me for the keys each time. He did not say or do anything but stare at me. I asked him if he understood, but he continued to stare at me. I checked with the Materials Department Head and they confirmed there were no locks immediately available, but locks could be quickly obtained if someone asked for them.

I went over the next day to the PX and bought half a dozen high security locks and key sets and put them on the conex boxes myself-one set of keys went to the Electrical Department and one set for emergencies went to Operations for their Master Key Box. It only took a month of repeated 'hints' until the Electrical Department replaced my locks with their own high security locks.

Eventually locks were placed on all the Electrical Department conex boxes, but they were the last department to do so (all departments had unsecured conex boxes during the inspection). Actually I had to mention the oversight to Mr. Walker again several days later and then he complied.

30. 13 FEBRUARY 2006-CAMP PROSPERITY (E-MAIL)

I told Jessie I have been investigating the HVAC shop ever since I arrived concerning the major theft of a/c units, spare parts, materials, etc. Wholesale tons of stuff were and had been flying right out the door for a long time. Nothing was ever proven prior to my arrival, but stuff was obviously missing. Making a long, complex story short, confidential information was received naming one LN HVAC worker, named Mr. Safaa, as the contact between the KBR HVAC personnel and the local criminal gangs, etc., moving the stuff to sell off of Camp Prosperity. When I told the HVAC Department Manager, Russell Hill, that we needed to speak to Mr. Safaa briefly (no subject mentioned) several days prior he denied knowing his whereabouts. But we learned later that day from the IBPD Managers that Russell Hill immediately went to Mr. Safaa and warned him to 'disappear.' He disappeared for four days. However, he was been reportedly being seen in the "Green Zone" several times. Mr. Safaa was terminated this morning for failure to appear at work, or explain why he was gone, by IPBD Co. Based on the above I went to the U.S. Army and requested a 'Pick-Up and Detain' Order for Mr. Safaa in connection with the above investigation, since the information on Mr. Safaa also detailed his involvement with assisting the insurgents with information, connections with senior ex-Ba'ath Party members, prostitution, drugs, connections with other theft rings, etc.

31. 13 FEBRUARY 2006-CAMP PROSPERITY-ELECTRICAL DEPARTMENT OFFICE

I was doing a random routine security walk-through inspection of Camp Prosperity department offices when I discovered the Electrical Department office door wide open. I entered and found no personnel were inside. On the center desk was a large ring of dozens of keys in plain view. I waited for five minutes until the Electrical Department Administrative Assistant LN worker finally arrived. I asked him about securing the office and he stated there was only one key to the door and it had to be shared among the expats and no LNs were permitted to have a copy. Later that day I spoke with Walker about his office space door being wide open. He gave me a very long, very convoluted, very complex and ultimately useless 'excuse' why his Department personnel only had one key to this door as to why they could not obtain an extra set of keys. I asked him who he contacted to try and get some extra keys, but he gave an indifferent, not very satisfactory answer. I immediately directed his attention to contact the Camp Manager to have him quickly resolve Walker's extra key problem. He did not strongly indicate he would do that.

32. 13 FEBRUARY 2006-CAMP PROSPERITY-MY OFFICE

Almost from Day One and continuing on, the HR Representative, Patricia Murphy, was a constant thorn in my side. There was not anything she would not do to thwart, hamper, or impede my investigations, especially into the HVAC Shop. She was constantly telling me that what wonderful human beings Russell Hill and Michael Peters were each time we met. Then she would stab me in the back with every manner of nasty comments how I was out to 'get' them unfairly, how I was defaming and slandering them, that what a miserable human being I was, how I had no evidence against them, etc. This investigation, like all the others, was going to be a steep uphill climb. The only problem was hundreds of HVAC a/c units, components, spare parts, equipment, and materials were disappearing at a fast rate and remain unaccounted for. Patricia Murphy warmed me not to talk to anyone about Russell Hill and Michael Peters or any other HVAC Department expats or Iraqi IPBD workers. But at no time did she ever ask me for one single detail about these HVAC Department thefts or my side of the story. (What is wrong with this picture?)

33. 14 FEBRUARY 2006-CAMP PROSPERITY (E-MAIL)

I told Jessie that Mr. Safaa will assist the U.S. Army MPs/CID/U.S. Military Intelligence (S-2), etc. with their inquiries when he is apprehended. I will schedule an appointment with the HR Representative, myself, and Mr. Peters. Perhaps he can expound on the sterling characteristics of Mr. Safaa and delve into more detail exactly how Mr. Safaa was able to do so much work for KBR under a 'No-Bid' contract, his relationships between the KBR HVAC shop, his exchange of industrial gasses for a U.S. Army badge (that he cannot have) and other people of interest, etc. Should be a very interesting conversation. Film at 11. I will let you know.

I added both Tim and R.C. are doing a great job down here. They are really making things happen. Just needed a lot of stuff taken off their shoulders (i.e., USMI) and a direction to go towards. See you shortly, transportation and accommodations are being arranged.

(NOTE: I continued to lie. I sent a 'cc' on the e-mail to both Tim and R.C. By constantly praising them for doing "outstanding work" (they practically do nothing, except a few minor things) this would throw them off balance and keep them guessing what I was thinking and doing.)

34. 14 FEBRUARY 2006-CAMP PROSPERITY-MAYOR'S CELL OFFICE

It was sheer coincidence today that an AFOSI Special Agent, a U.S. Army MP SGT and I all just all happened to be in the Camp Mayor's Cell Office at the exact same time doing different things. While we were waiting we exchanged greetings and what jobs we were doing. We immediately fell into a long conversation about all the massive thefts going on country-wide, not just inside the "Green Zone." The U.S. Army MP SGT told us about what U.S. Army Military Intelligence (S-2) said they had just started to shift their focus away from looking at the insurgency from a strictly military point-of-view or problem and were looking more towards a police problem or criminal point-of-view of the insurgency, i.e., the notorious 100,000-man theft ring called the "Hausassem" being heavily involved as the prime mover or supporter of the insurgency. He added that U.S. Army Intelligence (S-2) finally realized that it was KBR's employees and their Iraqi minions at every base in Iraq who were primarily fueling the insurgency with the stolen goods that were being re-sold in the Black Market with a portion of the proceeds going to the insurgents that allowed them to recruit more troops, pay salaries, pay for IEDs, shoot down helicopters, plant booby traps, and everything else needed to fuel a huge insurgency. Since it was obvious that there was many billions of dollars being stolen all over Iraq, that added up to many hundreds of millions of dollars for the insurgents. Not good.

35. 14 FEBRUARY 2006-CAMP PROSPERITY-CAMP MAYOR'S OFFICE

The U.S. Army MPs told me that Mr. Safaa had just been apprehended at one of the "Green Zone" gates. They said he was handcuffed, hooded, and taken to the Baghdad Interrogation Facility (BIF) in the "Green Zone." Mr. Ajo was also taken into custody at the same time. Michael Peters tried unsuccessfully to have Mr. Safaa released into his custody after arguing that Mr. Safaa's arrest was a 'KBR issue.'

36. 14 FEBRUARY 2006-CAMP PROSPERITY (E-MAIL)

I told Jessie making a very long, very complex story short it appears the AFOSI, USAF SF/IZ Police, U.S. Army CID, U.S. Army Intelligence (S-2), the U.S. Army MPs (and us) are all involved in assorted over-lapping, but inter-locking investigations. A few of us were comparing notes this morning and found out that one local KBR sub-contractor employee (a Mr. Safaa) is essentially tied into all these separate investigations in some way, shape or form. The USAF SF/IZ Police is sitting on the guy right now in the cooler. Everyone is lining up to take a whack at the bubba. He has made a number of voluntary spontaneous statements to me and the U.S. Army MPs concerning his involvement into illegal activities out of the HVAC shop for a start. This is expanding at an expanding rate. Stand-by to stand-by. Bobby is cut in.

37. 14 FEBRUARY 2006-CAMP PROSPERITY-MY OFFICE

Jessie Rich came down on me like a ton of bricks in an e-mail for declaring I was going to 'get' Russell Hill in an e-mail. I never said any such thing. It was J.T. who then explained to me shortly after when I had told him what happened about being verbally blasted by Jessie, that Russell Hill and the Patricia Murphy were 'an item.' She was doing her level best to protect him by making false accusations against me since they were proverbially bumping their bodies together in the horizontal position. I was seen as a direct threat to the both of them. I went back to Jessie and explained the true situation, that he should have looked at both sides of the story first before falsely accusing me of saying something I did not say. I later found out that Jessie and Patricia Murphy were actually good friends. She had used that friendship to try and stop my investigation of Russell Hill's illegal activities. Supposedly Jessie verbally slammed her head into the wall for abusing their friendship. She quickly faded into the background. I never heard any more about the issue from Jessie.

38. 15 FEBRUARY 2006-CAMP UNION III-KBR SECURITY OFFICE

I just collected my thoughts in private. Too many things were happening too fast. I was barely keeping my head above water. I knew it was only going to get much worse before it got any better.

39. 15 FEBRUARY 2006-CAMP UNION III-FUEL POINT

I knew that one of the easiest scams to detect is stealing fuel from the Fuel Point. I first went into the Operations Department and got the latest two monthly lists of assigned vehicles to what department and their license plates that were assigned only to Camp Prosperity plus their mileage for December

2005 and January 2006. They kept the records on mileage driven each month, but not on fuel consumption. I was simply a matter of going over to the Fuel Point, requesting to see the daily logs of what vehicles pulled up and how much fuel they were given in liters. The vehicle's license plate was recorded along with the driver's name, fuel card assigned to that particular vehicle and the time of the day they pumped fuel. Then it was a simple math problem-adding up all the liters drawn for each license plate and adding them up to give me a monthly total for each vehicle. Fuel was only supposed to be dispensed to certain vehicles with the correct fuel card and only those assigned to certain bases in LOGCAP III.

Several problems became immediately apparent. Ten unnamed people had been given fuel cards simply marked #90 through #99. No vehicle numbers were recorded nor were any names listed, just a fuel card with those numbers. Another problem was USMI-assigned vehicles were regularly pumping fuel. I knew they had their own fueling station right inside their compound. USMI vehicles were not authorized to use the Camp Union III Fuel Station. A third problem was anyone and everyone was driving up to refuel there: U.S. Army and other U.S. military vehicles, Iraqi civilian vehicles, Iraqi Army military and government vehicles, other KBR vehicles assigned to camps inside and outside of the "Green Zone." Literally anyone could show up and get all the fuel they wanted with no questions asked.

I spent the rest of the afternoon compiling only Camp Prosperity vehicles fuel draws. Some vehicles came in once a month to refuel. Other vehicles came in daily; a few came in several times a day. Some vehicle fuel draws tallied into the hundreds of liters for the two months, far more than the internal fuel tanks would take. I saw that even if these vehicle were driven for 24 hours per day for 30 days they could not have burned up all that fuel. They must have been filling dozens of jerry cans each time. I totaled up all the fuel and divided it into the mileage reported for the previous two months. Almost half the vehicles drew far more fuel than they needed. Either they were the worst fuel-economy vehicles in the known universe, or someone was getting filthy rich selling fuel off in the Black Market.

The one example was one Camp Prosperity vehicle that was driven eight kilometers in January 2006 consumed 1,640 liters of fuel. The vehicle was assigned to or driven by a 'Douglas Moore' on the Fuel Point records as it came through.

I queried the new Fuel Point supervisor, Lee Evans, about the anonymous fuel cards numbered #90 through #99. He said he did not know who these drivers were, why they were given these cards, or why they by-passed the rules requiring they identify themselves. He said this was all set up and the cards issued prior to his arrival. No one explained anything to him when he took over as supervisor. He did not question why it was done. But Evans did promise me that the next time the drivers came in he would immediately confiscate their cards and deny them any fuel. I also questioned why he allowed USMI vehicles to draw fuel. He said he would direct them back to the USMI Fuel Point. That was as good as I could expect for right now.

I went out to interview the Iraqi Fuel Point workers. They were brazenly honest with me. They said anyone could drive up, fill up and drive away for a carton of cigarettes, a bottle of liquor (Johnny Walker Black or Red was preferred) or even cold hard cash, a USD$20.00 bill was the recommended 'tip' - no questions asked. Anyone could drive up and refuel to their little black heart's content. So much for KBR Supervisors doing their jobs here. I assumed most of the fuel that was stolen was used to power all of KBR's many stolen generator sets out in the "Red Zone." The rest was no doubt sold to whatever Iraqi paid the highest price for it.

After I was done I drove back to Camp Prosperity and sought out Douglas Moore. He was on leave at that time. I would catch him later. When he returned a few days later he was immediately horrified and denied even using the vehicle, much less having drawn that much or any fuel out at all. Obviously someone had been using his name as a cover to steal fuel. Of course, no one checked any CAC or ID cards of the drivers at the Fuel Point.

40. 18 FEBRUARY 2006-CAMP PROSPERITY-CAMP GENERAL STORAGE ROOM AREA

At 17:45 I addressed everyone at the Camp's All-Hands Meeting. Once a month there was a meeting of all KBR staff members who received briefings on health, safety, policy changes, HR, and general subjects. I got up in front and spoke briefly. I reminded everyone to secure all their property, vehicles, and personal property. I also specifically informed everyone that all areas outside the U.S. Army and private security contractor protected FOBs, U.S. controlled areas and sub-contractor camps were strictly off-limits which specifically included the 215 Apartment Complex. Everyone signed the roster at the beginning of the meeting to confirm their participation, including a Troy Williams.

41. 19 FEBRUARY 2006-CAMP PROSPERITY (E-MAIL)

I tell Jessie thanks. The latest is the USAF SF/IZ Police/AFOSI has formally asked to interview Michael Peters concerning the massive HVAC Theft Ring. Bobby and HR are handling that exclusively, we stepped back on their request-not our bailiwick. Apparently the AFOSI has independently gathered more information. They also found and are interviewing/holding the two taxi drivers that drove the four a/c units that got loaded into their taxis from the KBR truck, as photographed by the DCMA down by the 14th of July Bridge last month. Also Mr. Safaa (the HVAC sub-contractor/vendor now in BIF detention) has apparently now given up Michael Peters as one of the ringleaders, so we expect the U.S. Army to weight in for some formal interview requests very quickly.

We expect once Michael Peters cracks he will give up everyone else who is dirty in the shop. We also were informed late today by the Senior Operations Coordinator that a Jay Freeman (HVAC Technician) is also one of the major theft ringleaders based on information/strong circumstantial evidence he had developed (the Senior Operations guy just arrived yesterday from a long R&R). We will be requesting a statement from Jay Freeman shortly. We have another investigation to start very soon (or as soon as we catch our breaths) on the Power Gen shop. Too much stuff missing for way too long.

Rob Akers and two other Security Technicians came in from USMI this afternoon. We had a very friendly sit-down/exchange of info. Final: personal favor. I got the four applications for U.S. Embassy Badges from April at the USMI Security Badge Office on the Embassy for all of us (he said there was already an e-mail in there about me about something - just great, I am really on the radar scope at USMI). I just want to make absolutely sure they will get approved first/in advance before I submit the paperwork. Maybe everyone needs to chop this off for us, but I want to make sure we are OK from the start. Then I will bang in the paperwork in there to April on your OK. It was very interesting to see Macedonian SGTs, Bulgarian 2nd Lieutenants (LTs), Georgian Ensigns, Mongolian Privates ALL with U.S. Embassy Yellow-stripe CAC cards walking around inside or outside the U.S. Embassy, but I have to walk in the back door with the garbage collectors and street sweepers to literally sneak into the place. Anyway, I will not do anything without your personal approval on these U.S. Embassy badges. Thanks-more to follow.

R.C. did an Incident Report (IR). He said that at 20:15 he was called out by Tim to assist him on an unauthorized KBR employee in an unsecured area. When they arrived at the apartment complex known as 215 Apartments, Tim and he recognize some of IPBD LN employees. He asked them was there a KBR employee in the apartments. They all said yes. Tim repeated the same question asking them if they were a 100 percent sure. The two KBR LNs employee said: "Yes, we know him, he comes here every day." Even the kids in the neighborhood also said they recognized the KBR employee. R.C. then asked one of the kids to get the Iraqi Police to come this location. When they arrived we asked them to assist use in locating the KBR employee. The KBR LNs and the kids knew exactly what floor and apartment number where the KBR employer would be located. R.C. said he and the Iraqis police went to the seven floor. The Iraqi Police knocked at the door. An Iraqi female answered. Seconds later Troy Williams came to the door. R.C. then made a positive identification that it was Troy Williams. The neighborhood resident told R.C. that Mr. Troy Williams was asked several times to stay out of that area by the USAF SF/IZ Police. The Police warned Troy that this area was unsecured and unsafe. He then asked Troy where his vehicle was. He said that it was parked on the other side of 215 Apartment Complex. R.C. identified the vehicle, took several pictures because it was also left in unsecured area.

42. 19 FEBRUARY 2006-CAMP PROSPERITY-MAIN YARD

R.C. came to tell me that one of the KBR Power Gen workers, Troy Williams, was running his own personal one-man theft scheme. R.C. explained Williams had an Iraqi 'girlfriend' he has been continuously seeing at a multi-story apartment building in the "Green Zone." The father of Williams' girlfriend threatened Williams by saying he would continue to allow Williams to see his daughter if he delivered U.S. government property to him, all stolen, of course. This included alternators, starter motors and other parts. Williams would load-up his Power Gen Repair truck with all manner of goods and drive it over to his girlfriend's apartment building. Williams readily agreed. While he was upstairs seeing his girlfriend each evening, the girlfriend's father was stripping the truck bare. A quick check with Haji Naji confirmed all of the above had been going on since about 2004. He stated Williams stole a massive amount of U.S. government property to his girlfriend's father who then sold it. Williams and the girl's father split the proceeds.

R.C. and Haji Naji explained that Williams only got into trouble because he started stealing goods that his supervisor, Lynn Summerville, had ear-marked to be stolen by himself. Summerville became very angry and wanted to punish Williams for it. When Summerville learned of a particular time and day Williams was going to be at his girlfriend's apartment building, he enlisted the help of the Iraqi Police.

R.C. explained that he and Tim were going to accompany the Iraqi Police that evening to see the apprehension of Troy Williams at his girlfriend's apartment. Obviously that information came right from Summerville who told it to R.C. directly since he wanted Williams to be terminated.

43. 19 FEBRUARY 2006-CAMP PROSPERITY-IPBD MANAGERS' OFFICE

I had been alerted by the IPBD Managers that Lynn Summerville was coming down for an 'inspection tour' today. I planned on asking him about the massive thievery in the Power Gen Department when he was the Manager. I was sure since he was lighting up half of Baghdad with stolen former Iraqi Army and U.S. government-purchased large generation units while powering them with stolen U.S. government-owned fuel and fixing them with stolen U.S. government-bought spare parts. I was sure he would like to see his lucrative 'utility empire' close-up and personal on this visit. I asked the IBPD Managers to let me know when Summerville would be available for me to ask him a few questions if they did not mind.

A few hours later Summerville appeared. I was taken aback. If he was a criminal 'Mastermind' he did not show any signs of it. He was short, non-descript and completely unremarkable. He could have passed for a small-time, third-rate street hustler in my book. He was very cheerful (as I would be too, making a real fortune off of purloined U.S. government equipment, supplies and materials - all tax-free). We sat outside in the sun on two folding chairs I had set up outside of the Operation Office for our conversation.

He was totally unaware about what I wanted to talk to him about. I started in slowly. I said I had gotten in some reports from some of the Power Gen workers while he was assigned here as the Power Gen Department Manager about some generators sets, light-alls and other equipment that had come up 'missing.' What did he know anything about that? "Nothing" was his simple reply. He kept his smiling, happy demeanor as if I had no idea what I was talking about. I dug in again a little deeper next after firing my first warning shot. I started reading the exact statements I had been given that named him each time as the kingpin of all the thefts in the department including the actual conversations. After the third statement into the pile I was holding, I could see his face slowly start to sag and then he visibly became very angry. Then I innocently added: "I have no idea what all this means. Do you?"

He immediately shouted: "IT'S ALL LIES!!!! THE IRAQIS STOLE EVERYTHING!!!! THEN ARE BLAMING ME FOR THIS STEALING!!!!"

I held up my hand and said almost sweetly: "I want your statement on all of this before you leave tomorrow." He stormed off in a rage. Of course, I had no power to force him to make a statement or do anything. He did not have to do a thing, but I knew I had gotten under his skin and badly rattled him. He knew he had been found out after all these years and was on notice he was being watched (even if no one was actually watching him).

The next day I got his written 'statement' from HR. It was full of venom. He denied everything and we all could go to hell as far as he was concerned. Then he was gone. I thought it might spook him out of KBR. I would see.

44. 20 FEBRUARY 2006-CAMP PROSPERITY-MAIN YARD

R.C. added more details to the narrative of Troy Williams. He said Tim secured Williams' Power Gen truck parked outside. It was jammed full of stolen goods. The truck was loaded with an air compressor a 250-gallon water tank and tool box with his tools all this together is probably valued at well over tens of thousand dollars of government property. KBR immediately fired Williams-not for stealing U.S. government property, but for being in an area that was off-limits to KBR personnel. R.C. also passed a message along to me. He said Remo Butler had just told him: "Don't worry about Le Blanc, I'll take care of him." Warning received. I was now on "Formal Notice" to be "terminated."

45. 20 FEBRUARY 2006-CAMP PROSPERITY (E-MAIL)

I pass to Jessie that a Mr. Troy Williams (Power Gen Technician) was just found in an unauthorized area off the FOB (215 Apartment Complex) and apprehended by the Iraqi Police. R.C. and Tim were notified and then coordinated everything with them. R.C. was present at the apprehension in the seventh floor apartment. Tim secured the KBR vehicle parked some distance away, with KBR Power Gen items all unsecured on/in the vehicle. Mr. Williams was released into KBR Security's custody without being charged and transported back to the FOB. The Camp Manager, HR Rep and Williams' supervisor have all been notified. An IR to follow when HR finishes gathering a written statement from Williams. We have just gathered information that Williams is a strong suspect in many thefts of Power Gen materials over a long period of time. I will let you know as we progress on the matter.

46. 20 FEBRUARY 2006-CAMP PROSPERITY-MAIN YARD

Samuel Simpson, the new Power Gen Department Manager, came over to me after breakfast and reported that a new generator unit had been delivered late yesterday afternoon. He said when he went to inspect it that next morning one of the important parts was missing. I said I would go take a look. The generator would have barely fit on the back of a large semi-trailer flatbed truck. It was so new it must have just had the cellophane ripped off of it, all the shiny parts were still shiny. I walked inside and looked. It did not take an Inspector Jacques Clouseau of the French National Surete to see a part obviously had been removed the size of a child's basketball.

I walked back to the Power Gen shop and asked for the Iraqi Lead Foreman. He was newly hired, about my height, burley, and exuded confidence, even arrogance. Probably ex-military, an Iraqi SF officer with a talent for generators or mechanics or both. He said his name was Mr. Ahmed Joudi. He spoke excellent English. I said: "Come with me." I explained on the way a brand-new generator unit had just shown up last night and a critical part was missing. I added someone from the Power Gen Shop already stole it. He gave me this big smile and said: "How do you know that?"

We walked inside generator unit through the side door. The missing part was obvious, right in plain sight. I said: "Look at where the part was. It is very difficult to remove where it was placed in the unit. But look closer. See any marks, scratches, abrasions, nicks, or tool marks anywhere around the empty space? Only an expert would know exactly how to extract the part without leaving a mark anywhere. Plus, they would also need a specialized set of Power Gen tools to extract the part. An amateur or anyone not knowing what they were doing would have left a lot of marks everywhere in trying to wrestle the part out of its spot."

The Foreman just kept his wide grin and friendly manner. We both walked out of the trailer and parted ways.

Knew or should have known. He either stole it himself or knew who did. I never saw him again. He either walked off the base or went into IPBD and resigned. He knew what was coming next: termination. I never saw him again. He either quit on the spot or just walked out the gate without giving any notice.

47. 20 FEBRUARY 2006-CAMP PROSPERITY-MAIN YARD

About 09:00, the morning of the day Sarah Smith was to depart for her R&R, I called her supervisor, Walter Straub. I asked him to force Ms. Smith to see me and complete the turn-over now within the rapidly dwindling time left for this event. Ms. Smith finally appeared with a breezy attitude. She stated she was really too busy to finish the whole turn-over process, but she would make some time for me due to her busy personal schedule of leaving for R&R at noon to do a quick, abbreviated refresher. She stated she still had many things left to do before her helicopter flight, but she would do what she could for me. She dumped a lot of data on me again quickly and promised to have all the relevant e-mails for scheduled appointments re-routed to me the following day and then from now on.

48. 20 FEBRUARY 2006-CAMP VICTORY-NORTH (E-MAIL)

Jessie informed all of us that there will be additional information to follow on changes that are going to be made within the D-Area Sites Security Department. I am currently in the process of moving the Security Coordinator from Camp Rustimayah (Ken Anderson) over to Camp Prosperity. We should be receiving additional personnel from Houston sometime in the near future and I will be sending them out to the sites. Billy Dickens (the KBR F-Sites Security Manager) will be heading out on R&R from 28 February to mid-March so I will be picking up his camps for those couple of weeks. As such it will be difficult for me to get out to the sites at that point but if there are issues at your site that you believe I need to come down for let me know and I will make it happen. I am here to support each of you and your sites. That is one of the reasons I am requiring more detailed information from each of you on what your daily activities consist of. As I stated before if you have any questions, concerns or issues please contact me by phone or email. Thanks for all the work you are doing at these sites.

49. 20 FEBRUARY 2006-CAMP PROSPERITY-MAIN YARD

I would not find out until much later that Jessie either had been either ordered, or strongly suggested, to transfer Ken Anderson down to the "Green Zone" as the new supervisor. The why would quickly become apparent after the transfer was done. But I strongly suspected where this order had come from. The same place as the 'warning.;

50. 21 FEBRUARY 2006-CAMP PROSPERITY (E-MAIL)

I tell Jessie I am busy as always. The following topics in no order:

HR: One thing that struck me as very strange, when we were interviewing Michael Peters and Russell Hill (HVAC Shop Thefts), was Tim and I were discussing what they had told us in the interview after and were going over the discrepancies in their statements. Patricia Murphy jumped right in and said she did not hear them say anything like that at all. Tim and I looked at each other (he was taking notes and I was making mental notes of any statement discrepancies). He read back to me exactly what both of them had said in several key statements and their discrepancies. I said to Tim that is exactly what he told us word-for-word. She again quickly jumped in and said she did not hear them say that. Tim and I looked at each other again and I thought: "Something is not right here." I may be senile, but I do not have advanced Alzheimer's Disease that bad yet. I just let it go.

But if the HVAC scumballs needed a real friend, they have one in Patricia Murphy in HR. The real person that has been impeding my investigation is her, not the scumballs. I would pitch a guess and say that she is very buddy-buddy with them, or very 'muy simpatico.' She keeps going on how wonderful Russell Hill is, what a fine job they are doing in HVAC, I am just picking on them, defaming them, she's threatening me with the Company will get a massive lawsuit due to my irresponsible actions, unproven slander and silly accusations against them, Security could get a black eye over this, pressuring me, going on how fine they all are, outstanding, upright, pure, blameless, true citizens of high moral fiber and implying/inferring subtly (or actually) I am some kind of low-life, unprofessional, out-of-control, rag-ass renegade. Interesting.

Maybe I am all wrong here, but mega-hundreds of HVAC units, components and spare parts are STILL missing, and no one has seen, heard or knows anything in the HVAC Shop about it. I come in and try to get to the bottom of this cesspool and now I am a total rag-ass renegade from the HR side for trying to do my job. What is wrong with this picture? Patricia Murphy is doing her job here? I have my doubts on the matter.

ELECTRICAL SHOP INVESTIGATION: The Electrical Shop LNs are all reportedly primed to speak to us. We will see soon if they will drop the dime on the expats later this week.

PLUMBING SHOP INVESTIGATION: Ditto the above.

HVAC SHOP INVESTIGATION: I got an interesting call this afternoon from Mr. Safaa's relatives. They are requesting my assistance in having Mr. Safaa (the HVAC Shop LN Foreman still under investigation for these massive thefts) released from the BIF. I said the U.S. Army was preparing to do just that, that he was being out-processed. However, before they did that I was programmed to speak to him about a few minor matters or to have him "assist us in our inquiries" (as the British Police say about suspects). They said they would pressure him into telling me anything I needed to know. I said all I wanted is the whole and complete truth about the inner workings of the HVAC Department and the massive thefts. I said I do not like to put pressure on anyone. But I did feel when we speak that I would have his complete and undivided attention which I felt I did not have before when we last spoke. We will see. I did promise that when I felt he was forthcoming and made a complete breast of everything he was free to go about his business. The USAF SF/IZ Police and I will do a sit-down with the HVAC LNs tomorrow at 13:00. See what happens.

FUEL POINT INVESTIGATION: One Fuel Point lead man just came in off of R&R last night. He is a person of interest to us. We will be speaking very soon in HR. Sit-down already coordinated through HR, his new Manager and Bobby. I have so much info on this scam that it is mind-boggling from the limited work I have done matching/cross-referencing temporary fuel cards/fuel draws to vehicles. Unbelievable.

POWER GEN SHOP INVESTIGATIONS: Lynn Summerville is due to fly in on Sunday for a Power Gen site visit. He is a person of great interest to us. We will be speaking very soon in HR. Sit-down already coordinated through HR and Bobby. I have a ton of Iraqi LN Power Gen detailed verbal statements and info against him.

KEN'S ARRIVAL: Room cleaned and ready, if needed he can use my room as his office (internet connection) since I will be down at the BCC from like 07:00-18:00 every day now anyway, he has that option-his call. If he wants an internet drop into his single-man room we can do so.

51. 21 FEBRUARY 2006-BAGHDAD CONVENTION CENTER (BCC)-LN/TCN BADGING APPLICATIONS PROGRAM OFFICE

At 09:00 I went down to the BCC and contacted the Badging Applications Manager, a U.S. Army CAPT Christopher 'Chris' Spatola and the LN Examination Program (LEP) Screening Supervisor, Thomas 'Tom' Tannahill, and re-established contact from our first meeting. All I could do at this point was wait. I had to place all my investigations on hold to do someone's else job for them. Sarah Smith was supposed to be handling appointments for security background screenings or interviews so the GCC TCNs and IPBD's LNs to get ID badges or CAC cards to be able to work. This involved interviews with a U.S. defense contractor based in the BCC, maybe a ten-minute drive away from Camp Prosperity, that conducted the interviews. Because there were so many TCN workers in the "Green Zone," appointments had to be scheduled each day for them. Then the supervisors had to be notified in plenty of time so they could get their workers together to be assembled for the bus ride down to the BCC for their interviews. Without the security screening being done then the TCN or LN could not start working in the DFAC, repairing electrical problems, doing laundry, cleaning hooches, etc., which meant they were not getting paid, and the GCC and IPBD companies was not making any money until they started their employment.

Sarah Smith thought the whole thing was all a big joke. But it took time and effort to chase her around the camp and get all the information I needed from her. Finally I got it organized and into automatic and coordinated the appointments several days in advance, so the supervisors had plenty of time to get everyone assembled. The system finally worked with a lot of effort. I complained to Sarah Smith's supervisor about her total lack of cooperation. He told me he already had endless headaches with her grade school games. This was the last straw. He fired her on the spot as soon as she came back from her R&R.

52. 21 FEBRUARY 2006-CAMP PROSPERITY (E-MAIL)

I passed to Jessie that he might have to go back to the DPM and informed him we just broke a major theft ring in the Power Gen shop down here as well. The Iraqi Power Gen people were all working in the ring and I have one name of a KBR-expat still working in-country we will need to interview downstream. All the Iraqis are getting fired effective today after statements are taken. I do not have a department scanner, but I can borrow one temporarily. My investigations have been slowed down by HR as I have been informed that I need to wait for the RTII 'Professionals' to come in here and run these four major theft ring investigations we are doing and make doubly sure we do not violate the rights of any KBR employee. I informed HR I will continue to run these investigations to the best of my ability until I am properly relieved. I have been also bogged down by massive LN and TCN badging requirements since the lady handling it went off on R&R yesterday. I am doing the best I can do down here. We are a little busy.

53. 21 FE BRUARY 2006-CAMP PROSPERITY (E-MAIL)

I tell Jessie that the USAF OSI and USAF SF/IZ Police Investigators are still compiling the data (Michael Peters was in there for seven solid hours and Russell Hill was in there for at least two hours). They are probably as backed up as we are right now. I understand informally that Michael Peters gave the Interviewers about 100,000 miles of rope to hang himself and implicated a man named Jay Freeman (also HVAC Shop), a new person of interest and Russell Hill. Russell Hill was questioned and apparently provided satisfactory answers to all their questions. He was released without comment. The USAF SF/IZ Police is continuing their investigation and compiling data. We expect their results/recommendation sometime shortly. We are continuing to receive a steady stream of information about other illegal activities in the HVAC Shop and other trade crafts. I asked Mr. Freeman for a statement and he said he would cooperate with us. He did give us a verbal statement on other HVAC thefts of non-GP'ed a/c units at Camp Freedom yesterday we will pursue involving U.S. Army personnel. I will advise soonest.

54. 22 FEBRUARY 2006-CAMP PROSPERITY-MAIN YARD

R.C. approached me and said he saw a KBR-contracted Human Waste Disposal Truck (always called a Shit-Sucking Truck (SST)) enter Camp

Honor; a former U.S. Army camp adjacent to Camp Prosperity. R.C. said he knew there were no more troops at the camp since it had been closed down in December 2005 and turned back to Iraqi Army control. R.C. went to the Labor Manager, Jack Liang, who was in charge of Human Waste Disposal/SST trucks about the discrepancy. R.C. said Liang told him there were still three U.S. Army soldiers working at Camp Honor and they still needed the three remaining Port-A-Potties still needed daily cleaning. R.C. said he went right to Bobby Burns and Bobby denied there were any soldiers remaining at Camp Honor. Bobby stated categorically all U.S. Army soldiers had been withdrawn. He said Jack Liang failed to adequately explain the discrepancy.

I told R.C. we could all drive over there and see for ourselves. We inspected the Port-A-Potties first. We could not even get within a few meters due to the overpowering stench of human waste. All the Port-A-Potties were overflowing with excrement and urine. None of them had been cleaned or emptied for months. We checked inside the main building. Actually we did find a U.S. Army Major (MAJ) working in an office. He explained they were part of a seven-man training team for the Iraqi Army, but he said they never used the Port-A-Potties for the obvious reasons. He said everyone used the latrines inside the building. Although they were nasty smelling and unclean, they could still be used.

We drove back and saw Jack Liang. We told him what we had found. He muttered that he would cut back on the SST cleaning services at Camp Honor to twice a week. The stupid idiot was splitting the contract profits between the SST company and himself; another complete scam at the U.S. government's expense.

I went and explained everything to Bobby. Within a few days Jack Liang was transferred out to CVN. No punishment was given. We were so jammed up on other investigations we could not check on the SST scam again.

55. 22 FEBRUARY 2006-CAMP PROSPERITY-IPBD CO. MANAGERS' OFFICE

Both Mr. Ali and Mr. Khalid made a joint statement on the shenanigans that had been going on in the Power Gen Department prior to my arrival at Camp Prosperity on 04 February 2006:

"Mr. Laeth Shaie'e Salih has been hiring people who now work under him without our knowledge or approval for at least one year. He does not ask our permission and he gets a final approval from Mr. Lynn Summerville. Mr. Laeth recently hired two workers without our permission. These workers starting working for two or three days when the supervisor of the Power Gen Shop, Mr. Summerville, came to us and said he wanted to hire one new guy and we found out that actually Mr. Laeth was the one who brought him in!

The last time when we transferred from Camp Honor to Camp Prosperity in December 2005, Mr. Laeth stayed at Camp Honor with a pick-up truck and his materials and left the Camp for the "Red Zone" with cable, electrical materials, water tanks and other generator shop materials and equipment!

At one time Mr. Laeth and other workers stayed at Camp Prosperity until everyone left including his friend who should not have stayed behind. The next day, Mr. R.C. Calligan, KBR Security, told me that some materials and parts from several brand new, never used generators were missing. Then Mr. R.C. took to show me the generators then. I told Mr. R.C. about this stuff and my knowledge of the above.

I told all the workers in the shop not to get too near the new generators, adding to the knowledge that anyone who will be close will be in a suspicious position if he gets close to the new generators."

56. 22 FEBRUARY 2006-CAMP PROSPERITY-MAIN YARD

This was not the last we would see of Troy Williams. He was returned to us like a bad penny. On his way out the door, he had already been checked-in for his flight from BIAP to Dubai and sent back home that day. Between the check-in counter and the boarding gate he said he 'lost' his U.S. passport. So he was transferred right back at Camp Prosperity once again, but under restricted movement (confined to his room and only escorted to the DFAC by someone from Operations for each meal) until the U.S. Embassy got him a new emergency-issued U.S. passport. We later heard he had sold his U.S. passport to some Iraqi for the going rate of USD$10,000. With a new U.S. passport he was expelled from Iraq for good.

57. 23 FEBRUARY 2006-CAMP PROSPERITY-IPBD MANAGERS' OFFICE

After the completion of interviewing the Power Gen LN workers at about 16:00, one of the Power Gen LN workers came back into IPBD's offices and requested to make a spontaneous, voluntary statement concerning the theft and misappropriation of Power Gen Department equipment, materials, and supplies at Camp Prosperity. He requested anonymity until his statement could be translated and passed along to a trustworthy person in the Security Department. At the time he stated he did not trust anyone in the Security Department other than me. I promised him his written statement and identity would be held in the strictest confidence and his written statement would be forwarded to my immediate supervisor, Mr. Jessie Rich, CVN, by hand-delivered courier. I took written notes from his verbal statement to me that was translated from Arabic to English through an interpreter. He then immediately afterwards wrote a five page statement detailing what he had just told me.

The Power Gen LN worker stated that the big problem in the Power Gen Department is Mr. Leath (identified as Leath Shea, former Power Gen Department LN Lead Man, now fired) and Mr. Lynn (now identified as Lynn Summerville, former Power Gen Department Head, now Area/Regional Power Gen Manager). He stated that Troy (identified as Troy Williams, former Power Gen Mechanic, now fired) was a 'dumb shit.' He stated that Troy's Iraqi girlfriend took all his money. When he ran out of cash her father went to Troy and said if you want to keep seeing my daughter then bring me something I can sell off out in town, like alternators and other parts, and we will spilt the proceeds. So Troy brought him what he wanted, but all the money wound back up with the girl's father anyway.

The Power Gen LN worker stated that 'Red' (now identified at Fergus Johnson, former KBR Power Gen Assistant Department Head, now de-mobed) saw Troy (now identified as Troy Williams, Power Gen Mechanic) inside one of the conex boxes/shipping containers. He had seen Mr. Williams with two Cummings Model starter motors and an alternator which had not been moved in three months. He stated that 'Red' caught him red-handed inside the conex box with these soon-to-be-stolen parts and started screaming at him: "Do not make trouble for Lynn!," "You can't be this stupid!," "Do not cause problems for Lynn!" and "Just drop it!" (i.e., either the parts he was stealing or the whole matter, not sure).

The Power Gen LN worker stated between six months and one year ago Leath took USD$2.00/day from every worker's salary. For example, if an LN worker had a daily pay rate of USD$11.00 you kicked back USD$2.00/day to Leath and you collected USD$9.00. If an LN worker made USD$13.00/day in salary then you collected USD$11.00/day and gave Leath USD$2.00. If you complained about the kickback system then you were forced to 'quit' your job.

The Power Gen LN worker stated that Lynn Summerville and Leath Shea had a deal going. Leath bought Power Gen parts in the local market place for, say USD$1.00 for example, and then it was sold to KBR at a mark-up. Lynn Summerville told Leath Shea to put USD$20.00 in the invoice and they would split the profits 50 percent-50 percent.

The Power Gen LN worker stated that a Ramos/Ranos(?) Smith (assume an unidentified KBR Power Gen employee no longer in the Department/or with KBR) knew Lynn Summerville was stealing but kept silent and a Russ/Ross (assume an unidentified KBR Power Gen employee no longer in the Department/or with KBR) is a good guy, but he knew everything that was going on.

The Power Gen LN worker stated that there is a 'Fat Man' (an unidentified off-base LN) who is a friend of Lynn Summerville and Leath Shea who provides them things when they need them. The Power Gen LN said there also was another Power Gen LN worker named Ghalib (former unidentified Power Gen LN worker, ULN) who was here six or seven months ago and quit. Also most/all of the Power Gen LN workers stayed back at Camp Honor after the camp closed to help steal things.

The Power Gen LN worker stated that Mr. Ahmed Naji, Mr. Haji Naji (Ahmed Naji is Haji Naji's son) and Mr. Firus Fayick Farach, all these Power Gen LN workers are honest. Mr. Firas is a new guy, has done no stealing and only here in the Power Gen department for twenty days.

The Power Gen LN worker stated that whole generator sets have been stolen. That a new generator set belonging to the U.S. Army was stolen plus fifty other Iraqi generator sets that were either green or gray in color that belonged to Saddam Hussein (i.e., the Iraqi Army) at Camp Honor that the U.S. Army seized during the Liberation of Iraq and were turned over to KBR for safe-keeping were all stolen.

The Power Gen LN worker stated that Lynn got permission to remove the generators when they were stopped or broken for any small problem. He changed/swapped out the whole generator units on even small, 'B.S.' problems over simple items: air filters, fuel pumps, dynamos, water, fuel filters, etc. He did this many times. Lynn Summerville told the U.S. Army all the generator units were 'no good.' He removed all these generator units to the 'scrap yard' or 'scrap area' - both units with GP and non-GP numbers and hid them. Then they were all stripped or broken down into much smaller pieces and transported out of the "Green Zone" or they simply 'disappeared' out of the scrap yard or area.

The Power Gen LN worker stated that ten small generator sets for lighting at the various gates to the "Green Zone" were all declared 'unserviceable' by Lynn and then removed one-by-one after either being deliberately disabled by Lynn Summerville or a small, minor problem was found and then the unit was declared 'unrepairable' and removed to the scrap yard or area. One small generator set is still outside the Camp Prosperity Main Yard as an example.

The Power Gen LN worker stated that KBR-owned Volvo generator fuel pumps, which are not available here outside of the "Green Zone" at any price but are available only in Jordan at USD$1,000/each, were stripped out and sold for far more than that amount out in the "Red Zone." Each Volvo generator unit was sent to the scrap yard or area and stripped. Some parts were already missing from the sets, some were already stripped prior to being sent to the scrap yard or area, but all were eventually completely stripped out and soon the remainder 'disappeared.'

The Power Gen LN worker stated that Leath Shea admitted to taking parts off of generators for re-use on other sets. He was always asked where are these sets? He never gave an answer. He added that Leath Shea also was a 'slave driver.' He also stated that Russ/Ross and Emil (assume an unidentified former KBR Power Gen employee no longer in the Department/or with KBR, ULN) pushed the LN workers to have three sets serviced when one generator set serviced was the norm. He also stated that Lynn Summerville had Emil fired over some 'B.S.' reason.

The Power Gen LN worker asked where did fifty generator sets confiscated by the U.S. Army and turned over to KBR for safe-keeping go off to? He stated Lynn Summerville waltzed them all out of the "Green Zone" to the "Red Zone" with no one the wiser. When Lynn Summerville did that he put the good/honest people out of the picture by forcing them to take from one day to seven day offs without pay or had them working in another area away from Camp Honor all that day.

The Power Gen LN worker stated that Russ/Ross (ULN) wanted to complain to KBR about giving raises to the LN workers that Lynn strongly opposed. Russ/Ross and Lynn sparked and argued over these pay raises. Apparently the LN workers, for example, made USD$15.00/day and Russ/Ross wanted to raise their pay to USD$18.00, but Lynn Summerville was very strongly opposed to that. The Power Gen LN worker also stated four points:

1) Spare parts were constantly being stolen.

2) Whole generator sets were being dismantled and shipped out in sections or parts. The U.S. Army soldiers never checked anything going out the gates.

3) If Lynn Summerville and Troy Williams felt a generator part or piece was too large to move, they contacted a Phillip/Philip/Felipe at the KBR Fuel Point right outside Camp Union III (assume an unidentified former KBR Fuel Point worker no longer with the Department/or with KBR) and he moved it out over the 14th of July Bridge. There were seven generator sets taken out the gate at one time. In the al-Shala Area of North Baghdad these generator sets are still working. Lynn Summerville still gets a cut of the percentage/power used, sort of his personal privately-owned 'Power Company.' If anything breaks down, Lynn Summerville provides everything to fix it: fuel, spare or replacement parts, oil, materials, etc. If customers need a generator set or specific spare parts then they place an order in advance and then the needed generator set, or spare parts are stolen from KBR.

4) Lynn Summerville and Leath Shea have an open exchange of money, gold, presents, food, jewelry, etc., lots of everything.

The Power Gen LN worker stated that Manuel (now identified as Manuel Canino, Power Gen Mechanic) always complains about spending USD$100/month on cell phone calls. Lynn heard this, laughed, and says I am spending USD$3,000/month on cell phone calls.

The Power Gen LN worker stated that Troy Williams got Riyad (now identified as probably Reayeth Jameel al-Dulame, KBR Power Gen LN worker) a DOID (assume a type or brand of generator set) generator set and spare parts for Sadr City. Riyad bought the generator set for USD$10,000, said to be a DOID-type, 750kVa, not operated by air but some other way (not sure of the actual nomenclature). Mr. Riyad told Mr. Leath that the generator set was to be purchased by some unnamed operator in the "Red Zone" and Mr. Riyad was the go-between, but in reality the purchaser of the generator set was actually Mr. Riyad for himself. A DOID generator unit, if purchased at a shop in the "Red Zone" sells for USD$30,000.

The Power Gen LN worker stated that the relationship between Reayeth Shea and Toni/Tony (now identified perhaps as Tony Ame Noail, former KBR Power Gen LN Assistant Department Manager, but unsure if it is the same person) deteriorated as Reayeth Shea became very greedy. Reayeth Shea went to Lynn Summerville and complained so Lynn could fire Tony Ame Noail. Lynn Summerville also started having Tony Ame Noail do very demeaning stuff, leaning on him and causing him to do petty tasks and chores. When relations became too bad then Ali (now identified probably as Ali Moshinali, Power Gen LN worker) went to the KBR Security Department and filed a complaint, but no one did anything about the situation. Apparently Lynn Summerville did fire Tony Ame Noail. Ali (another unidentified Power Gen LN worker also named Ali, unknown who it is) and Riyad said they would 'can' (or fire) Ali (Ali Moshinali) if he (or anyone else) went to the KBR Security Department again. Phillip/Philip/Felipe (unknown former KBR Power Gen worker, ULN) transferred to the Fuel Point now because the relationship between Lynn Summerville and he deteriorated as Summerville and Phillip/Philip/Felipe had a bad falling out.

The Power Gen LN worker stated that Lynn got Emil, Patrick, Conrad, and some Filipino worker (all assumed to be former KBR Power Gen workers) fired. They all knew Lynn Summerville very well, but Summerville found out some 'B.S.' stuff against them, trumped up false charges and got them all fired. Russ/Ross was an honest guy, but apparently he quit in disgust. Jack (unknown current/former KBR Power Gen employee, unknown last name) and Manuel (Canino) are both OK.

58. 23 FEBRUARY 2006-CAMP PROSPERITY-MY OFFICE

At 17:30 an e-mail pours in down the old e-mail chute from CAPT Spatola. He informs me that that we missed 32 appointments that day (which I had no idea we had scheduled, thanks Ms. Smith for screwing me over!). His e-mail also mentioned that over 50 appointments were missed over the past two weeks. (Thanks again Ms. Smith for NOT doing your job!) He stated that effectively immediately KBR was banned from processing any more applications until all the missed appointments were made up. I went back down to the Baghdad Convention Center (BCC) and did a quick check on their Master Appointments Schedule on their Application Status Convention Center computer system which anyone could access. I found out there were almost 100 missed appointments.

I started asking the people who worked there some questions about what happened. They explained that interview appointments were being released at least four days in advance on the Application Status computer at the BCC which would allow plenty of time for the supervisors to arrange for their people to go, but Ms. Smith was only checking the Application Status appointment schedules perhaps every two-three days. She would deliberately wait until the morning of the appointment to inform the department managers to have their people down at the BCC to process their badges. (Stupid 'bimb!) This put an enormous strain on the camp operations due to the total disruption of moving people from remote sites, concentrating them into one location and moving them all by bus down to the BCC in time. The department managers all assumed that it was the BCC's poor planning for the short-fuse scheduling and assumed it was their normal practice. Since Ms. Smith operated independently on detached duty from MWR, and no one was checking up on her activities, she literally had no direct supervisor. It was apparent that she was just breezing in and out of the BCC at will from all reports and remained unsupervised.

After speaking to CAPT Spatola, Mr. Tannahill and the other processing personnel there, they all stated they had bent over backwards to give KBR (and Ms. Smith) many additional appointments due to the fact that KBR had more LNs and TCN personnel (IPBD and GCC sub-contractors) to badge than anyone else. They were noticing that, although Ms. Smith was pushing through enormous numbers of applications on the front end, she failed to properly follow-up on making sure these appointments were being met on the back end. She was also not making up any of this rapidly growing number of missed appointments. CAPT Spatola said he repeatedly cautioned Ms. Smith that she was submitting way too many applications into his office. He added that she was also not doing a very good job at all on ensuring the scheduled appointments were all met. He stated that he repeatedly warned her that if she continued to miss any more appointments he would not accept any further applications. Ms. Smith conveniently did not inform me of that serious situation.

59. 23 FEBRUARY 2006-CAMP PROSPERITY (E-MAIL)

I informed Jessie that KBR remains on the 'No Applications Accepted' List. I explained although I had been working very hard to complete all the missed appointments which are done at a very slow rate; only four LN/TCN applicants and one badged expat escort are processed per day. I further explained that the system is completely unforgiving for anyone who misses an appointment without a prior cancellation. I have done on a deal with CAPT Spatola that when we have all the missed appointments made up, then we can have 10 new applications submitted in the first week, then 20 new applications submitted in the second week and so on up. This is provided we make all our scheduled appointments each week. If not, then we drop back down to the previous week's lower number. We have 104 applications from KBR total remaining to be processed. Normally we are allowed 50 application submissions per week.

60. 23 FEBRUARY 2006-CAMP PROSPERITY (E-MAIL)

Jessie-the following topics in no order. Actually, my reports will end when Ken arrives at Camp Prosperity, as this will be his department after. Needless to say, we are slightly busy.

HVAC THEFT INVESTIGATION: Going on in three areas: 1) I will coordinate with Rob at USMI on the DCMAs statement and see if he can pick Russell Hill (HVAC Dept. Head) out of a line-up as the driver the KBR HVAC truck under the 14th of July Bridge on/about 27 January 2006 transferring HVAC units to Iraqi taxi drivers-I was informed by someone (Patricia Murphy) that we cannot interview or take statements from The Client, but Joe Saladino came to us (after USMI did nothing) with the complaint and demanded some immediate action; it was USMI's investigation to start with; 2) the IBPD Co. KBR sub-contractor Managers have come us to say they were told by their LNs inside HVAC that the other HVAC LNs have specific information on the massive thefts going on, they will be interviewed one-by-one with the notification of HR, Bobby and HVAC Shop in the next few days; 3) Mr. Safaa (HVAC Iraqi Supervisor) will be released from the BIF in a few days, the MI/CID/MPs have said they extracted all the information they can get from him and he is completely dry. They will give us his statement (they said he named specific KBR HVAC shop employee names) and a chance for us to interview him prior to his release very shortly. See what he gives us. I think I have his attention now. I did not before.

FUEL POINT THEFT/MISAPPROPRIATION INVESTIGATION: One Fuel Point guy de-mobed last night, supposedly on the orders of the client (not a direct Security matter with us), but he was the prime suspect on the massive thefts and scams at the Fuel Point. Two others are under investigation. Even from the very limited investigation I have done so far (matching daily fuel records to specific vehicles gassed up, like how much fuel was drawn over the month for January 2006), this was a monumental, 100 percent total scam-my mind is boggled.

POWER GEN INVESTIGATION: IPBD Co. Managers came to me about direct information they had about all their Power Gen LNs being involved in the massive stealing/theft ring over there. They also said they had lost complete control over their employees in the shop, the Power Gen Department Manager said exactly the same thing: He could not control them, they were telling THEM what to do and not the other way around. I coordinated with the KBR Power Gen Department Manager, HR and Bobby and I interviewed all the Power Gen Shop LNs in the IPBD Office. I found enough credible evidence from their statements to recommend to the Power Gen Manager to suspend all their workers pending further investigation. They strongly implicated the KBR Power Gen expats in the massive thefts with detailed information (but rarely themselves) especially Troy Williams, who everyone said was totally dirty, and a Fergus Johnson (now de-mobed). He passed that recommendation to Bobby. Bobby then passed the recommendation to IBPD and they were all suspended until further notice. However, one of the suspended Power Gen LNs came to the IBPD last night and wanted to do a deal-go on record as to very detailed times, dates, places,

GP numbers, etc. on the whole LN crew and KBR Power Gen personnel for running the theft ring in exchange for his old job back. I am coordinating that with Bobby, HR and the Power Gen Shop Manager and I will listen to what he has to say this morning. No promises were made.

HR: It is actually funny as here is Patricia Murphy beating me up severely around the head and shoulders (not daily anyway, almost) over these accusations of me talking about investigations, saying I am going bust to people, slandering/defaming them for this and that (that I am using all unsubstantiated rumors, innuendoes, smoke and hearsay against 'certain people') and then turning right around and using the same type of unsubstantiated rumors, innuendoes, smoke and hearsay against me without even checking into my side of the story, or asking me for my version of events. She is just flailing away at me with a heavy chain. Actually this is really hilarious-the complete irony.

WALK AROUND INSPECTIONS: All of us are finding many instances daily of open/unsecured vehicles with some valuable items inside or in the truck beds, a whole basket load of unsecured items in plain sight in the yard, unlocked/unattended conex boxes with valuable items inside and the actual locks unlocked on hasps, etc. On vehicles-they are being re-locked by me with a note on the steering wheel to "See Bobby!" to re-claim any unattended items which are dropped off to him. On open/unlocked conex boxes, a Security Department padlock goes on them and the owner can get the keys from me when they have a lock in their hands to replace our lock. On lost/found items adrift anywhere on the ground/lying about-item(s) goes to Bobby's office to be re-claimed. People are not yet thinking 'security' of their items/property.

VIOLATION OF OFF-LIMITS AREA INCIDENT: The firing of Troy Williams (the perpetrator) has sent shock-waves through the place. He is the first (and no means the last) to go, and that shook up all the people who needed to be shook up and gave a smile to the faces of the people who were waiting for someone to come in and clean up Dodge City - finally. The word is on the street: clean up your act or be ready to select from a delightfully tasteful chicken-or-fish menu. I can say without fear of contradiction everyone on the FOB now knows we mean business. The accurate depiction of this place being the 'Wild, Wild West' is changing, although slowly.

LN/TCN BADGES: I am processing a total of 680 badges between GCC and IPBD workers down at the Convention Center. I am working on it every day now effective from yesterday. This is an everyday/all day, being a very long, very labor/time intensive effort that will go on for quite a while.

BOBBY: I have 100 percent complete support from Bobby for everything. If Bobby believed the rumors on me/was displeased about anything that I am doing wrong he has not indicated his displeasure to me (and I assume not to you). If he felt I was even getting anywhere close to crossing the line (believe me) Bobby would be speed-dialing you and let you know immediately. He would be booting me right out of here fast and rightfully so. Although Bobby is now out of the loop on our investigations (and so is HR now as per your latest e-mail), I still brief Bobby on internal security matters like open conex boxes (like who it belongs to), unsecured vehicles (ditto), lost-and-found items (he can find the owners-some of these items I can't even imagine who they belong to), but Bobby knows who and he wants to know as well after a little chit-chat with the owners and general overall camp security/safety/other matters or problems we see that he needs to be appraised on. For example, you probably do not need to know what specific HVAC or Labor conex boxes on what specific day we found open, but Bobby does. You need to know we are finding them open in general and working to have them secured at all times as part of our continual, daily, random walking patrols for internal security, i.e. we are doing our jobs. But the main problems we face are security (or general) 'attitudes' (occasionally very bad) here and only Bobby can help us or cause them to be changed.

61. 23 FEBRUARY 2006-CAMP PROSPERITY-MAIN YARD

At 15:00, Mr. Ali and Mr. Khalid contacted me about a Samuel Simpson, Power Gen Department Head. They stated that Simpson has gone to them and requested the IBPD Company find him a young, attractive, intelligent Iraqi LN female to act as his Administrative Assistant/ Secretary in the Power Gen Department. Mr. Ali and Mr. Khalid told Simpson that it was a very strict IBPD Company Policy that no females of any nationality are hired into the "Green Zone" or into their company for work with KBR due to the numerous problems and complaints they had received in the past with young, single/unattached, especially attractive, local females. They also informed Simpson if he needed an Administrative Assistant/Secretary that they had hundreds of highly qualified males with excellent skills ready for immediate employment. All Simpson had to do was go through the proper channels with his formal hiring request and they would fill it quickly. Simpson then departed their offices. They asked me to explain their Company Hiring Policy to Simpson which I did in detail. He acknowledged the briefing.

62. 23 FEBRUARY 2006-CAMP VICTORY-NORTH (E-MAIL)

Jessie tells me you guys are doing a good job down there. (NOTE: My plan to laud Tim and R.C. is working very well.) I am not sure who told you we could not get statements from The Client, but we have in the past and in this case I think we should get a statement from them. I am giving you the approval to attempt to gather statements from The Client on this issue. If they do not want to give you one that is fine but as part of our investigation we would not be doing our job if we did not ask. You are correct in your assessment of what the relationship is between the Security Department and the Camp Manager. I do not need to know the specifics on issues that the Camp Manager does need to know. All I need to know is that there is an issue with that area. Continue your investigations as you are and if someone wants to make a complaint against you or the Security Department then we will deal with it then. At this point no one has filed any type of written complaint, so I am not worried about it. In the future you are still to do your interviews with HR present. But they are only there to witness the interview. How the interview is conducted is not what they are there for. You do it your way and we will deal with any complaints as they come up. I have confidence in your abilities and the abilities of Tim and R.C. If I did not then the three of you would not be down there. Ken's Eligibility to Transfer Form (ETF) has been approved so he can move anytime from this Sunday forward. I will let you know when we have this coordinated. Keep me in the loop and things will be fine. Talk to you soon.

63. 23 FEBRUARY 2006-CAMP PROSPERITY (E-MAIL)

I tell J.T. I agree with you. I just wanted a quick kill to put this investigation out of its misery, instead of a slow painful lingering death. But you are right (I am wrong), there is no way Corporate will allow these slime balls to go to far-off Siberia as ditch diggers, much less as HVAC fix-it guys. This is the one I absolutely want the coffin nails driven into and buried six feet under before I take it to anyone. I have enough strong circumstantial evidence to nail two of them right now (Russell Hill and Michael Peters), but I want it stone cold. I will see what the USAF SF/IZ Police can do for us on Saturday. I believe one of these guys (of not all of them) is going to break under the terrible strain of keeping silent and take them all down. They are physically sick to their stomachs right now, under enormous pressure and great strain. They all look really bad. (Poor babies!) I can wait them out, I have time (I only have at least 7-10 days of investigations and statements to catch up on anyway!). I am really badly far behind. Thanks again for clearing us out from under Patricia's heavy HR thumb. She is more a drag on this investigation than the damn scumball crooks. If we had stayed under her guidance we would never catch any crooks here. Much more to follow.

64. 23 FEBRUARY 2006-CAMP PROSPERITY-OPERATIONS OFFICE

One of the Operations Department people contacted me. They said a copy of letter was just discovered from the U.S. Army's Camp Prosperity Mayor's Cell (signed by the Camp Mayor a certain CAPT UFN Phillips) had been issued to a Jack Liang of the Labor Department authorizing him to remove certain scrap, discarded and other used items from Camp Prosperity, mainly scrap metal, copper parts and other discarded or used material. They told me that this was in direct violation of KBR's Policies and Procedures in that no materials may be removed from the Camp and no personnel are allowed to go directly to the U.S. Army for Policy exceptions and changes unless it is officially authorized. I typed up an IR and sent it to Jessie. I also alerted Bobby to the scam. It was all I could do; my plate was full (actually overflowing to be honest).

65. 23 FEBRUARY 2006-CAMP PROSPERITY-POWER GEN SHOP

I complied my Field Investigator notes after speaking to everyone in the Power Gen Shop:

1. Leath Shea-LN Power Gen Lead Man: Mr. Leath stated that 'Red' (assumed to be Fergus Johnson, former KBR Power Gen Department Head, now de-mobed) knew Troy Williams (former Power Gen Department worker, now fired) had things 'missing' from his truck-some voltmeters, two starters, two alternators and a recorder. The key for the conex box where many other Power Gen items and equipment that were found to be missing was in the possession of Williams.

2. Tony Ame Noail-LN Power Gen Assistant Lead Man: Tony was absent that day.

3. Ahmed Naji-LN Power Gen worker: Ahmed stated that he know of one starter off of a Caterpillar and one voltmeter was stolen. He had no other information to pass to us. (NOTE: IPBD said that Ahmed Naji is the son of Haji Naji and believes him to be innocent.)

4. Reayeth Jameel Al-Dulame-LN Power Gen worker: Reayth initially stated that he had no idea who was doing the stealing and had no information to pass to us. However, he immediately went on to state that he knew of a dynamo, an alternator, a generator starting machine and two other pieces of equipment were stolen by 'Red' (believed to be Fergus Johnson, former Assistant Power Gen Department Head, now de-mobed). 'Red' asked us (LN

Power Gen workers) and Troy Williams (former Power Gen workers, now fired) if we know of anything stolen. However, 'Red' and Troy were the only ones who had the key to the conex box where the stolen items were taken from. Reayth he was standing next to Williams when 'Red' called him on his cell phone and was shouting loudly in a 'Hot conversation' with Williams accusing him of doing bad things and stealing the above missing items. 'Red' told Troy directly to give back the key which he apparently did.

5. Ahmed Chasib Luaaby-LN Power Gen worker: Ahmed stated that Troy Williams (former KBR Power Gen worker, now fired) was a bad worker as he changed the oil in one machine but did a bad job and that shut the machine down or destroyed it. Mr. Ahmed was standing next to 'Red,' (believed to be Fergus Johnson, former KBR Assistant Power Gen Department Head, now de-mobed) when 'Red' started yelling into his cell phone at Troy Williams and said: "He just opened up a newly arrived conex box and two dynamos, a starter motor and other stuff was missing and only Troy had the key to it." Ahmed also stated that two or three Power Gen sets had parts missing and he personally knows of a lot of stuff that is missing from the Power Gen shop, but the problem is the KBR Foreman and LN Power Gen lead man did not ask anyone about the thefts. No one asked the workers about the thefts which he thought was very strange.

6. Ali Moshinali-LN Power Gen worker: Ali stated he had no information to pass to us.

7. Firas Fayick Farach-LN Power Gen worker: Firas stated he had no information to pass to us. He stated he was working here only 20 days.

8. Gasan Jameel Khalaf-LN Power Gen worker: Gasan stated he has been working here for only 50 days. He only heard about 'Red' was the boss, and Troy Williams had the keys to a conex box where some Power Gen equipment was stolen. He had no other information to pass us.

9. Haji Naji-LN Power Gen Administrative Assistant: Haji Naji self-admitted to being a big 'blabbermouth' and cannot keep a secret. Everyone interviewed confirmed Haji Naji's story and stated he cannot stay silent. Hence no one trusted him with any secrets, and he was told nothing. He said he is an 'old timer.' (NOTE: IPBD stated Haji Naji is completely trustworthy, he just talks about everything to everyone. This was also confirmed by everyone who was interviewed. A completely honest, but talkative, person.)

66. 23 FEBRUARY 2006-CAMP PROSPERITY-MAIN YARD

Jay Freeman, an HVAC Technician, approached me and said he wanted to voluntarily give me information about some thefts that had occurred in the "Green Zone." He informed me that he had personal detailed knowledge of the theft or misappropriation of non-GP'ed a/c units and other U.S. Army materials by U.S. Army personnel at Camp Freedom in the "Green Zone." He said he personally witnessed U.S. Army troops handing over these a/c units to some unnamed Iraqis or LNs. I thanked him for the information and said I would put it in an IR to my boss, Jessie Rich.

67. 23 FEBRUARY 2006-CAMP PROSPERITY (E-MAIL)

I thank Jessie for his verbal support. I appreciate it (and need it too). Things are happening here at warp-factor speed. The following topics in no order:

HVAC SHOP LN INTERVIEWS ON THEFT INVESTIGATION: The USAF SF/IZ Police officially requested to be present with us when we interview 20 HVAC Shop LNs concerning this massive theft investigation. Tentatively set for 13:00, Saturday here. I have coordinated with HR and need to coordinate with Bobby and the HVAC Shop Manager. We believe that once that is complete they will start to wrap up their end of this investigation. However, we have additional KBR people they might want to interview after we speak, one name just popped up in the interviews (Jay Freeman).

LET'S MAKE A DEAL/MAKE THEM AN OFFER THEY CAN'T REFUSE: Three/four KBR HVAC guys in the shop from all reports are very badly rattled over the theft investigation. It is the same thing always: we know nothing, we see nothing, we hear nothing. They say this even before I open my mouth to question them about something-real Watergate stuff here. They start answering the questions before we start asking them. We believe now that they (and some others) know exactly what is going on in the HVAC with the massive outflow of a/c units, etc., and either they are silently ignoring the scam or getting paid a small percentage to keep mum. Too much stuff has disappeared for someone not to have seen or heard something. It is like they are all dummies (now zombies). I want your permission (subject to checks with Legal, HR, Corporate HQs, Dan McGuire, the PM, Dick Cheney, etc.) to offer them 'Immunity.' Tell us what you know about the scam in exchange for you to keep your job, get immediately transferred to KBR Site Z-100 in Outer Mongolia and you do not get put on the Government's de-barred from government work 'Black List.' Spill it all and walk away clean, bring down the Kingpin(s) for us. Just a suggestion. Option is to have the USAF SF/IZ Police 'make them an offer they can't refuse' too, only they get no government 'Black List' posting, provided they can crack these guys for us. These guys are in near hysterics over keeping silent on this. They all look like 500 miles of bad road and I have not even questioned two out of the four. And the other two I just asked for brief statements on a related matter in conjunction with the investigation. Your call.

DCMA'S STATEMENT/USMI INVESTIGATION ON HVAC THEFT: I will coordinate with Rob Akers over at USMI and he can do the legwork on re-activating this end of the investigation (with your permission, of course) or maybe you want to hit Art Shook up for it for some 'service' out of 'respect' as equals. I mean it was their investigation in the first place and it went cold after they took statements/interviewed Russell Hill over here at our pad. I am sensitive to avoid getting in their lane over there, but Rob and I have discussed the subject several times in a few schmooze-a-thons, so we are 'muy simpatico'. We have worked on it already. Call it on this one, but we need him to give us a statement and finger Russell Hill out of a photo line-up if they will do it. I will do it myself if Rob Akers can give me the contact info. He is hot to trot on this item and still wants firm answers last time they spoke.

U.S. EMBASSY BADGES: I did not ask him to do so, but R.C. did a schmooze-a-thon with Art and sort of like got him to agree in principal to authorize us to all get U.S. Embassy Badges, like 100 percent approval from Art's end. Anyway, as soon as we catch our breaths we will go for it and submit the paperwork. I was coming out of the Convention Center Complex after four hours of badging procedures today at 18:00 and who did I pass? A bunch of Iraqis who all looked like Islamic Jihad terrorists and all with Yellow-stripe Escort-authorized U.S. Embassy Badges! Amazing!

POWER GEN SHOP THEFT INVESTIGATION: Some of the Power Gen Shop LNs want their jobs back and are willing to make statements (one did today) against three KBR expats in exchange. I got all the approvals to 'discuss' the deal from Bobby, HR, and the new Power Gen Department Head. Pending their completed statements and my evaluation of the accuracy. Of the expats one was a de-mobe, one was Troy Williams (now de-mobed) and the other is the Arca/Regional Power Gen Manager, a guy named Lynn Summerville, a real big wheel somewhere. The other expats either went along in silence or got fired with trumped-up charges. In any event there is a lot of info pouring out of these people now. Horse is out of the barn (I know), but I believe I have enough to easily take down Summerville. Stand-by.

68. 23 FEBRUARY 2006-CAMP VICTORY-NORTH (E-MAIL)

Jessie says thanks for the update. I will check the immunity deal, but I can pretty much bet the answer on it is going to be no. I think that if any of them are involved they have broken so many rules that there is no way the company would consider allowing them to continue working here no matter how much intel they were to give us. I will look into it, but do not hold your breath. The ones that are not guilty of doing anything will eventually come forward to save their jobs or they will start to turn on each other once they realize that this thing is not going to stop. I will try to contact Art Shook tomorrow on the HVAC/DCMA issue and see what I can do. We are doing a couple of H&Ws here tomorrow (one on a camp with 3,000 SCWs) so I will be tied up most of the day. I will get back to you on this. Continue what you guys are doing and keep up the good work.

69. 25 FEBRUARY 2006-CAMP PROSPERITY-MAIN YARD

About 16:00, Mr. Ali and Mr. Khalid contacted me again. They stated Sam Simpson had entered their offices with a young, attractive Iraqi LN female. They stated that he had hired this young woman and pressured them into accepting her as their employee. They hired and enrolled this young woman under Simpson's direct pressure so as not to cause an immediate problem for KBR or themselves. Simpson and the young woman departed the scene after this. Mr. Ali and Mr. Khalid then immediately contacted me and explained the situation. I stated that this young woman could not be hired under any circumstances as per their company policy. I recommended to them she be immediately discharged/not enrolled on their payroll/company. I stated I would seek out Simpson as soon as possible and explain the IBPD Co. Hiring Policy to him more emphatically again. I saw Simpson at approximately 17:00 then forcefully and in great detail explained IBPD Co. Hiring Policy again to him and further explained to him not to go to IBPD Co. with any other potential employees or personnel that he wanted or had already hired under any circumstances. I stated this young woman was not hired by IPBD and would not be hired under any circumstances. He acknowledged the second briefing.

70. 25 FEBRUARY 2006-CAMP PROSPERITY-MAIN YARD

Like Yogi Berra always says: "It's 'Déjà vu' all over again." Same old problems-unlocked conex boxes. It never stops, I was getting no cooperation at all.

71. 25 FEBRUARY 2006-CAMP PROSPERITY-MAIN YARD

Russell Hill, the HVAC Department Manager, also approached me, after Jay Freeman did two days ago, and said he wanted to voluntarily give me information about some thefts that had occurred in the "Green Zone." He informed me that he had personal detailed knowledge of the theft or misappropriation of non-GP'ed a/c units and other U.S. Army materials by U.S. Army personnel at Camp Freedom in the "Green Zone." He said he personally witnessed U.S. Army troops handing over these a/c units to some unnamed Iraqis or LNs. I thanked him for the information and said I'd put it in an IR to my boss, Jessie Rich.

72. 25 FEBRUARY 2006-CAMP PROSPERITY (E-MAIL)

I tell Jessie the following topics in no order:

KEN ANDERSON'S ARRIVAL: I will greatly anticipate Ken's arrival by the end of the month as I am jammed up and back-logged badly with everything. I was averaging a minor investigation every 30 days at Camp Hope. I am averaging a moderate to major investigation every day here and more to come. Just things we never got to because of USMI's control before, now we can get to stuff, and the backlog list is huge.

HVAC Investigation: There has been mega-tonnage of rumors swirling all around theft, misappropriation and disappearance of HVAC supplies, materials, and spare parts since I arrived. Bobby has authorized us to initiate an investigation into this to get to the bottom once and for all. This will be complex, time consuming, long and involved.

USMI BADGES: USMI and Bobby compromised on us not having to individually escort everyone over to USMI for re-badging. We will be replacing all of KBR's Yellow-stripe badges (with US Embassy access) with new KBR Blue-stripe badges with no U.S. Embassy access/escort privileges. We are collecting the Yellow-stripe Badges en masse and turning them in all in batches and they will be re-issued to us in batches. Saves us a lot of work.

NIGHT OPS: R.C. and I were out there (he was supposed to be at the Camp Union III Main Gate and I definitely was at Prosperity Main Gate) from 20:00-22:00 last night. We will try again later tonight and see what happens. (R.C. was supposed to be at the entrance gates to see who was coming through the gate breaking curfew, i.e., no one KBR employee could be outside the camp after dark-an immediate termination offense. I knew the chances of him actually being there was going to like a big fat bird was going to land in the middle of a pack of hungry wolves. He was going to make the rounds of the "Green Zone" night clubs, bars, and dives.)

Each time when I was in to see Patricia Murphy at least three separate times about routine HR business, Murphy repeated the accusations of my using rumors, innuendo, hearsay, false statements, and the like against the HVAC Shop and specifically against Russell Hill. She said she was informally verbally counseling me against doing this. Again said I had no idea what she was talking about. However, at no time did she ask me for my side of the story, or did I feel she was acting impartially or conducting an impartial investigation. I did ask her if any formal complaint had been made against me and she denied that one had.

After an interview with Russell Hill concerning my preliminary investigation on or about 15 February 2006, Tim, Patricia Murphy, and I were in the HR Office. Tim and I were discussing comments on portions of the interview with Hill that Tim had taken written notes of the conversations between us and Hill. I mentioned to Tim that it was an important fact that Hill admitted to giving inoperable KBR a/c units to a Mr. Safaa, his lead LN HVAC Foreman, and these a/c units were authorized by Hill to be transferred off-base to be repaired at the 215 Apartment Complex HVAC Shop that was owned and operated by Mr. Safaa.

I stated that was very important because no a/c units were authorized to be transported off-base plus why would any a/c unit be sent out into town when the HVAC Shop had a full and complete repair facility for every type and size of a/c unit manufactured. I stated that it was completely against KBR Policy to do that. Immediately Murphy stated: "I did not hear Russell Hill say that." Tim and I looked at each other and Tim looked at his written notes and repeated exactly what Hill had said word-for-word. I then stated that that was exactly what I remembered Hill saying word-for-word. Murphy then immediately cut in and said: "I did not hear him say that." Later after the interview Tim informed me that Hill and Murphy were long-time, close personal friends, having been assigned together on Camp Prosperity for quite some time. I felt from the start that Murphy had acted completely unprofessional in her HR duties and at no time ever asked me for my side of the story on her investigation of these allegations. I felt strongly that Murphy had been actively hampering or interfered with my investigations of the theft and misappropriation of U.S. government property from the HVAC Shop due to her attitude and actions.

73. 26 FEBRUARY 2006-CAMP PROSPERITY-MY ROOM

It is well after midnight. I cannot fall asleep even though I am totally exhausted, like every night. This job is literally killing me. It is churning in my mind constantly 24/7. No one wants to help. In fact nearly everyone is pulling hard against me. I knew the day I arrived this was not going to end well for me-at all.

74. 26 FEBRUARY 2006-CAMP PROSPERITY, BAGHDAD INTERRORGATION FACILITY (BIF)-GROUND FLOOR CELL

I went to visit Mr. Safaa at the BIF at 17:00. The U.S. Army MP CAPT at the Front Desk said he did not hold out for too long. He was not tortured or physically abused it was explained, but he was asked a lot of questions (the Iraqi interrogators were screaming at him) until he spilled everything about the whole theft ring scheme and confessed within a day. Once the U.S. Army interrogators and their Iraqi interpreters felt they had drained him dry they left him alone. The MP Captain explained they could only hold him, or anyone, was for 30 days maximum. Then he would be released back out into the "Red Zone." The U.S. Army allowed me access after I properly identified myself. Mr. Safaa looked ragged, exhausted, and totally depressed. Like all criminal 'masterminds' he turned timid when caught. All he wanted to know is who had ordered him to be arrested, incarcerated, and interrogated. I lied and said: "Michael Peters."

Mr. Safaa gave me his voluntary statement about the events inside the HVAC Facility concerning theft and misappropriation of KBR and US Army property and materials. He stated that Jay Freeman and Michael Peters are working together to steal KBR HVAC and U.S. Army a/c units and materials. They are helped, in turn, by a Mr. Ahmed Abu Kahlem Hassan, the King Looter or Chief of the "Hausassem" (Thieves). Most of the stealing that went on before was from Camp Honor before it closed down. According to Mr. Safaa, Mr. Ahmed Abu Kahlem Hassan got a cell phone antenna for Freeman in his Camp Union III LSA room. He also set him up with an internet connection in his room. Mr. Safaa stated that Russell Hill gave Camp Freedom to Freeman exclusively and he is in charge of all the HVAC thefts. He said Freeman also stole a new flex meter that just arrived.

Mr. Safaa went on to state that Hill only steals non-GP'ed a/c units and parts. He does this by pulling or breaking apart these a/c units into four parts in the HVAC Shop on Camp Prosperity all the time and then putting them all into separate conex boxes on Camp Prosperity. No one ever sees these parts or components again. He went on to state that Hill said he went to the Camp Manager and got permission to let him take all the old a/c components and pieces and give them to Mr. Safaa to be sold out in town. Then he authorized Mr. Safaa to go and buy new a/c components and sell them back to KBR.

Mr. Safaa also stated that Peters wrote all the Service Order Requests (SORs) authorizing the work to be done by the U.S. Army. Normally the U.S.

Army writes all the service order requests or provides the information to have it done.

Mr. Safaa started that Freeman switched out all the old a/c units in Building 20 at Camp Freedom four weeks ago. He also stated that these old a/c units were sent off base and new units ordered and put in their place. He also started that the King of the "Hausassem," Mr. Ahmed Hassan, was involved in the transportation of these units.

Mr. Safaa also stated that Hill steals non-GPed items by going into a building he is working in, causing one small part to break, or seeing if any units is slightly damaged he then declares the whole unit to be unserviceable and then orders a completely new unit as a replacement. He then takes the old unit to be sold or moved off base.

I left and never saw him again. But he had ripped the U.S. government off for tens of millions of dollars over three years so he would be living a comfortable retirement somewhere. I had a bad taste in my mouth in turning in Mr. Safaa to the U.S. Army. I dislike doing things like that, but he would get no sympathy from me. I had no other choice but to turn him in and have him interrogated. He was a thief and a criminal.

The U.S. Army MP CAPT promised he would send me a transcript of Mr. Safaa's interviews and full confession once it had been translated and transcribed. It never arrived.

75. 26 FEBRUARY 2006-CAMP PROSPERITY-MAIN YARD

I wrote an IR. At 09:30 hours I was conducting an investigation into the theft of numerous electrical and plumbing supplies from a KBR Plumbing Department locked conex box in the Materials Yard of Camp Prosperity. The theft was reported Robert J. Brown, acting Plumbing Department Head, at 06:30 hours that same morning. Brown stated there were a number of electrical and plumbing supplies placed in the conex box found sometime yesterday afternoon and, upon investigation of his LN workers, no one noticed or stated who had placed some Electrical Department materials in the Plumbing Department conex box. Brown secured the conex box with a padlock at approximately 19:30 hours and departed the area. Brown briefed me about the discrepancies at approximately 22:30 hours and I stated we will investigate the matter tomorrow morning.

When Brown opened the padlocked conex box the next morning the electrical materials were missing. During my interview with Mr. Raad Ajo, Iraqi LN Plumbing Supervisor, IBPD sub-contract worker and other Plumbing Department LNs, several statements were made strongly implicating Mr. Ajo as the ringleader for the theft of Plumbing Department supplies, theft/misappropriation of US Army/Coalition Forces materials by the conex load off the FOB/"Green Zone" and involvement in other thefts and transportation off the FOB/"Green Zone" concerning the HVAC and Power Gen Departments and theft/misappropriation of other US military property and materials off the FOB/"Green Zone."

Based on probable cause and the statements of his co-workers implicating Mr. Ajo and a statement of Mr. Brown stating that only Mr. Ajo and he had the only keys to the conex box. Mr. Ajo was detained by KBR Security and turned over the US Army MPs for further questioning about these alleged thefts/misappropriations.

76. 26 FEBRUARY 2006-CAMP UNON III-KBR SECURITY OFFICE

This morning Mr. Ali had already approached me before about a reoccurring 'personnel problem' about to occur in the Power Gen Department. Mr. Ali explained that the new Power Gen Department Manager, Samuel Simpson, had again gone out on his own and hired a very young, very attractive Iraqi female as his 'personal secretary' (no one in the camp had a 'secretary' -personal, impersonal, or otherwise). No Iraqi woman were allowed to be hired, or at least not allowed to work, in the "Green Zone" by KBR or IPBD Co. under any circumstances. Mr. Ali said he told Simpson to terminate the young lady, but he was adamant she was now his employee. I said I would have a man-to-man talk with Mr. Simpson about the matter at once - again.

Tim and I were sitting in our office that afternoon when Simpson walked in unannounced. I broached the subject. He made a spontaneous, voluntary statement that he had re-hired this young Iraqi woman against what was specifically explained to him twice before by both the IPBD Co. co-General Managers and myself. He stated he was going to convince IPBD Co. to accept this woman as his employee. Simpson also stated that he had given her a typing test on a KBR laptop computer, and she had passed admirably. He then started to wax poetic on how he met this poor, destitute, lovely, out-of-work, out-of-luck young woman somewhere out in the "Green Zone" at some unspecified off-base location and through some personal, but unspecified, contact. He added she had been university professor with good English-speaking and typing skills. He wanted to help her out with a job. Simpson also stated they would be working 'closely' together. He further went on that he liked this young woman a lot.

We explained again that it was against KBR policy and IPBD Co. policy that no Iraqi females were allowed to work for KBR in the "Green Zone." He said he would pay her salary out of his own pocket he believed in this young women's plight so much. I said that was a non-starter. If he persisted then he could expect to be terminated by KBR, so he should be warned. I said KBR was going to take a dim view of her no matter what the circumstances were. Also, we immediately explained to him that allowing an unscreened/unauthorized person access to a KBR company laptop, flagrant disregard of Security Department orders not to hire anyone without going through IPBD Co. Offices, being in an off-base area which was an immediate firing offense and failing to let the Camp Manager or his supervisors know of this activities were all serious matters. He departed but looking like he had not heard a thing we said.

77. 26 FEBRUARY 2006-CAMP PROSPERITY (E-MAIL)

I get a 'cc' e-mail from Patricia Murphy saying if you need to meet with me, I would appreciate the courtesy of letting me know in advance. No one contacted me about a 16:00 meeting today as was misrepresented to Bobby Burns. (I had no idea what she was talking about.)

78. 26 FEBRUARY 2006-CAMP VICTORY-NORTH (E-MAIL)

Jessie sends me an email off of an e-mail he received from Patricia Murphy about a meeting that R.C. and Tim had in her office with one of the HVAC suspects and she did not know about anything about it (neither did I for that matter). He says to get with me and let me know what is going on. I am getting two different stories on this one and I need it cleared up. Send me something on this by 10:00 tomorrow morning. Thanks.

79. 26 FEBRUARY 2006-CAMP PROSPERITY (E-MAIL)

I tell Jessie that Tim and R.C. will brief you separately on today's incident. I was out of the loop with my own investigations and LN/TCN badging issues at the BCC. But from my end Patricia Murphy continues to hamper my investigation on the HVAC theft and misappropriation of government property with her actions, demeanor, and comments. She is way too personally involved with the major participants from all reports and that close friendship is clouding her professional judgement towards my department and efforts. And I will go on record with that if I need to.

80. 26 FEBRUARY 2006-CAMP VICTORY-NORTH (E-MAIL)

Jessie says to me to let our guys know that they are not required to conduct their interviews with HR present. They can ask employees to write statements but cannot order them or force them to write anything or to answer any questions. You can request individuals to come to the Security Office for interviews or to write statements. Continue looking into your issues and I will handle the complaint side of the house. You guys still have my full support.

Bobby and I spoke earlier tonight, and I also spoke to the HR Manager. Just to make sure R.C. and Tim are careful in their dealings with the employees. The Security Department is always under scrutiny and with what you guys are turning up down there I believe there is a definite possibility that some will try to say things about us. Do not let our guys get into a position that could be used against them.

81. 27 FEBRUARY 2006-CAMP PROSPERITY (E-MAIL)

I tell Jessie I am dragging pretty hard. I am not even banging up KBR for all the hours I am putting in, but my time sheet is still high. All of us are working on not even minimal sleep, we all look like zombies. (At least the Clanton Gang in Dodge City or Tombstone looks MUCH worse, you should see them, they are all very worried. Wonder why?) Glad I am coming up to my R&R roll-out date at the end of my four months stint and not the beginning. I will badly need the break, I cannot wait. Everyone is dragging pretty hard too, but we are solid and hitting the line every time. Tim and R.C. are doing a great job. (Note: another snow job on them to get rid of them) The following topics in no order:

ELECTRICAL THEFT INVESTIGATION: On hold pending other investigations.

PLUMBING THEFT INVESTIGATION: On hold pending other investigations.

POWER GEN THEFT INVESTIGATION: Mr. Lynn Summerville, previous Power Gen Department Head, will be here tomorrow on a site visit (in theory). I will interview him late in the afternoon. "Inshallah!" (Arabic for: "If God Wills It!") Still have to continue our interviews of other former Power Gen LNs. They all want to finish their lengthy statements. In a separate investigation opening the NEW Power Gen Department Manager, Sam Sheppard, is the subject of an inquiry that HE hired a young 'thang' from one of the finest families in the South (of Iraq) so they can 'work very closely together' in his office. He got some local young 'hottie' from some off-limits area and put her at the wheel of one of the KBR laptop computers for a test drive as a typist. He was specifically told 100 times go through IPBD for local staff. He did a spontaneous, voluntary statement and did a massive self-incrimination. Also the IPBD Co. Managers filed a formal complaint against him. We need to type it all up and blow him out of here. Guy is a complete and total dim-wit.

FUEL POINT INVESTIGATION: We finally identified 'Mr. 99' - the owner of the Temporary Fuel Card that was sucked up so much fuel it could have powered the Federation Starship 'Enterprise' on another five year mission to boldly go . . . . . and will interview him shortly. We also found a Mr. Douglas Moore who drove eight kilometers on 1640 liters of fuel in January 2006. Must have either a very bad gas tank leak or probably a bad tune-up from the last Dispatch. He is coming off of R&R shortly and will assist us in our inquiries. Fuel Point scam compiling of data continues, slowly, of vehicles/fuel pumped/kms driven-some interesting numbers.

SST TRUCK INTO CAMP HONOR INVESTIGATION: We got a copy of a letter from the client just now that authorized the same guy who has these SST trucks going into Camp Honor (no U.S. troops there any more) to 'remove' all scrap metal, waste wood, waste copper, spare tubing, etc., from Prosperity - essentially everything junk (or high value/high interest) and truck it off the FOB. Problem is no one (Bobby) authorized it and apparently no one knew about it. (Duh!) Shows where everything is disappearing to now-not off into the "Red/Green Zone" but into the Iraqi Army unit stationed inside Camp Honor. Cute! We continue our interview/statement taking. Looks like there are others involved. Slick scam.

KEN'S ARRIVAL: We all cannot wait. Ken is getting all the meetings, routine reports, administrative whatever. Lucky him!

THE BOTTOM: I have no idea where it is or when we will touch it. Every day brings a new scam; we are in free fall on everything, so do not blow a fuse if some things are running late (just joking). Unbelievable stuff we are uncovering. I mean Wyatt, Vigil and Morgan are faster on the draw than anyone, but you did not tell us the Clanton Gang consisted of 1000+ of them and all working against us (see Patricia in HR).

82. 27 FEBRUARY 2006-CAMP PROSPERITY-MY OFFICE

I was working my next IR (as if I did not have enough IRs to write!). Previous to voluntary statements by Jay Freeman and Michael Peters of the HVAC Department, some 'confidential' sources have now made statements, and further investigations done, that have definitely implicated that Russell Hill and Michael Peters are all heavily involved in the theft and misappropriation of KBR and Coalition Forces GP'ed and non-GPed a/c units, spare parts equipment, Freon gas and other materials from all the camps inside the "Green Zone." Hill was positively identified as the driver of the HVAC Department truck under the 14th of July bridge last January 2006 where he was transferring four non-GP'ed a/c units not Iraqi taxis driven by LNs. USAF SF/IZ Police and KBR USMI Security investigators are looking into the incident. The DCMA, Joe Saladino, already has made a voluntary statement and said he would provide photographic evidence of the transfer and the HVAC vehicle in question.

83. 27 FEBRUARY 2006-CAMP UNION III-KBR SECURITY OFFICE

At about 13:30, R.C., Tim and I were in KBR Camp Prosperity Security Department office when Mr. Simpson entered again. He made another spontaneous, voluntary statement that he had re-hired this young Iraqi woman against what was specifically explained to him at least twice before by both IPBD Co. co-General Managers and myself. He stated again that he was going to again convince IPBD Co. to accept this woman as his employee. He stated again that he had given this woman a typing test on a KBR laptop computer which she admirably passed. Simpson told us that he had met this young woman at an unspecific off-base location and through some personal, but unspecified, contact. He added that she was a young, attractive university professor with good English speaking and typing skills. He again stated that they were going to be working 'closely together.' He again further stated that he liked this young woman a lot. Immediately all of us started to again explain all the company violations that Simpson had committed, to include allowing an unscreened /unauthorized person access to a KBR company laptop, flagrant disregard of Security Department orders not to hire anyone without going through IPBD's offices, being in an off-base area which was an immediate firing offense and failing to let the Camp Manager/his supervisors know of his activities.

My comments finally brought him crashing back to Earth from whatever unreality or stratospheric level he was operating out of. He quickly became defensive, almost paranoid, that the company might actually fire him over this hire. Over the next few days he was seen walking around muttering to himself the company was getting ready to fire him (they were not, we just let it all go with a verbal warning). Within a day or so he quit on the spot convinced his name had already been submitted to the HR Office to have him terminated over his noble, well-meaning humanitarian efforts.

84. 27 FEBRUARY 2006-CAMP PROSPERITY (E-MAIL)

I pass to Jessie that this is a formal Request to Initiate Investigation (RTII) on multiple/interconnected/overlapping investigations we are running, now in conjunction with the USAF SF/IZ Police, AFOSI, the U.S. Army MPs and CID and KBR USMI Security Investigators.

In summary confidential sources, verbal and written statements, unexplained inventory losses, completed and incomplete LDD reports and corroborated and uncorroborated eyewitness accounts have given us strong circumstantial and physical evidence of thefts of a/c units, HVAC spare parts and other related materials from the various camps in the "Green Zone." The investigation centers on two KBR individuals, namely Russell Hill and Michael Peters, Camp Prosperity HVAC Shop Department Head and HVAC Repair Technician, as being the prime persons of interest in this investigation.

There are other U.S. Army and LN personnel involved as main focal points in the continuing investigation.

Request outside assistance in completing this investigation, as the scope has greatly expanded into related and possibly multiple, overlapping, and interconnected investigations into the thefts of U.S. Army and other KBR property, movement of these materials off base for re-sale/trade, production and issuance of ID badges to unauthorized non-U.S. or local personnel and other involvement into insurgent support, illegal activities off-site and criminal gang activities by the persons of interest.

KBR Security will continue to actively investigate these matters until properly relieved by high authority.

85. 27 FEBRUARY 2006-CAMP PROSPERITY-MAIN YARD

Ken Anderson, the new Security Manager, arrived at 17:00. He met with Tim and myself. The first words out of his mouth addressed to me are: "I am taking over all your investigations. Do not do anything more on them." I asked him if he wanted all my notes, witnesses statements and other documentation plus an update or briefing on each of them. "No", he replied. So much for all my hard work and effort on my investigations. Everything was thrown right into the Dempster Dumpster. I immediately suspected he was not smart enough to do that on his own. But he obviously had been told by someone high up in the KBR Security food-chain to kill everything on arrival - fast. This was all a set-up. He was here for only one reason: to shut me down permanently. Except Anderson and the KBR Security High Command HQs did not know me at all. I was not shutting down my investigations. I would just have to tread more carefully from this point forward.

Then he blandly informs all of us that: "Our task is to be 'minions' who 'beat the birds' and 'he shoots them down with a gun.'" Just great, I think, a dangerously incompetent, raging egomaniacal fool - a deadly combination. This was going to end badly for me.

Anderson continued to explain. The first order of business will be the Camp Prosperity DFAC Ballistic Roof Project. Long before I arrived at Camp Prosperity, KBR and the U.S. Army were in a major-league dispute over putting in, or not putting in, a ballistic roof over the DFAC building. Since large groups of soldiers, civilians, TCNs, LNs and other Coalition troops congregate there three times a day for chow; actually there are always people in the DFAC, it was open 24/7, that a well-placed RPG round, mortar barrage or 122mm rocket will kill and wound many of them. A ballistic roof will prevent that by having the explosive detonate as soon as it hit the ballistic roof and thus saving everyone inside. It was a big bone of contention, a real white hot political potato that I was steered immediately away from on the sage advice from Bobby, the Camp Manager, almost from day one at Camp Prosperity. As astute a political operator Bobby was, even he would not go near it. It was pure political drama at its best. I was not sure who was for or against the Project, but I was just as sure I wanted no part of it.

Not Ken.

"I am going to solve the whole problem!" he arrogantly told us with an air of self-confidence and assurance. I explained what Bobby had told me. That the senior KBR management and four-star U.S. Army generals were yapping all about it and had been for a long time. It was a real problem. Even Bobby steered well clear of it and this was his base as the Camp Manager. He just shook his head dismissively and said he would solve the problem. I just shrugged my shoulders and said nothing more.

He then started prattling on about how he was going to be putting in anti-sniper screens on the top all the cinder block walls that surrounded the "Green Zone." These are black mesh plastic screens looking somewhat like cyclone fencing that was held up by metal poles. We has a short stretch of them as a test when I was assigned to Camp Hope. They were expensive, maybe USD$50,000 for 20 meters of them. They came in a few weeks before Camp Hope closed down and turned back to the Iraqi Army. Now Anderson wanted to ring the "Green Zone" with them, the whole place has dozens of kilometers of perimeter walls. It was going to cost a fortune. But he reassured us he was going to make it all happen. I never had heard of any incidents of the "Green Zone" taking any sniper fire. Maybe he had a brother-in-law in the security screening company. Who could say?

The next project was the most important security problem we faced: theft of work tools by LNs. Anderson said that he and Tim would be positioning themselves on the 14th of July Gate to inspect outgoing vehicles for these stolen tools every day. I did not mention that the "Green Zone" has at least half a dozen gates. I did grant him that although all vehicles and persons entering the "Green Zone" were inspected by the U.S. Army gate guards, no one ever checked anyone leaving the base either on foot or in a vehicle. The only problem with this problem is that whole container-loads of everything were flying out all the gates every single day (and night). But obviously Anderson knew what the real problem was here, and he was going to be right on top of it.

Anderson also informed us that he was placing the Camp Prosperity Security personnel back under USMI's 'operational' control. Jessie Rich would remain our Administrative supervisor, but USMI would take control of the Security Department on a day-to-day business. Anderson said he would attend the USMI weekly meetings. We would be reporting to them as it had been done in the past before I ripped us out of their clammy, infuriatingly bureaucratic hands. And I had been telling Jessie in assorted e-mails how much I looked forward to having Anderson show up and help out. That was one of the biggest mistakes I have ever made.

I had to get out of here. Fast.

86. 27 FEBRUARY 2006-CAMP PROSPERITY (E-MAIL)

I tell J.T. I have been specifically instructed to neither confirm nor deny the existence of the KBR Security Department at Camp Prosperity as of 12:00 today by my boss. (Off-the-record, and I will deny I said this: I have to get out of here fast. This is going to be 100 percent looney-tunes.)

87. 27 FEBRUARY 2006-CAMP PROSPERITY (E-MAIL)

Later that evening I told Jessie I had eligibility to transfer. Anderson is on the ground today and is really hard-charging around looking at stuff in his specialty fields. The guy exudes pure energy and enthusiasm in his particular areas of expertise. I am happy for him and he is a super, very well qualified, take-charge kind of guy. He will be a tremendous success here. I can quickly see I have gone about as far as I am going to go here with Anderson on-board. But my work is almost about done. We are quickly stabilizing now, and Anderson's emphasis is well away from all the things I have been tackling. He is focused on certain key areas which I have minimal background, in my opinion. I honestly believe I will not be of much use to his efforts. I feel anyone could come in here now and just take up my new, very simple assigned duties. I am making myself eligible for re-assignment after I come back from R&R on 03 April.

I also had planned to stay until September at the very least when I was eligible for promotion and I had hoped to stay for the required one year especially since Bobby was at the helm. But I know my meagre talents and limited background are not up to what Ken's requirements are. You had offered some remote single G-sites to Tim and R.C. I was wondering you would extend the same offer to me. To be honest I would much prefer to transfer over to my original assignment over to the U.S. Army's SF camp, but I understand that may not be possible. However, I am very happy to go a remote site similar to Camp Hope and remain working with/for you. I will be very glad to remain until you find a suitable replacement sometime in the future. Thanks again for all your support. We could have not come as far as we did in so short a time without your total backing. I sincerely appreciate it and your continued trust. Talk to you in person on about 20 March on my way out on R&R. I will stay for at least one more year as we discussed, with your approval. Thanks again.

(The above e-mail is a desperate scream for a life ring. The last thing I want to do is work for an incompetent, egotistical maniac full of himself. Biting my tongue every second of the day is not how I operate.)

88. 28 FEBRUARY 2006-CAMP PROSPERITY (E-MAIL)

I tell J.T. (off-the-record and I will deny I said this) that all investigations have been transferred to Anderson effectively immediately. Essentially except for LN/TCN badging pure grunt work down at the BCC I am out of a job. Not that grunt work is a bad thing, mind you; at least I am out of the office all day long from 07:00-17:30. I got the very strong impression that these six+ major fraud investigations will all be wrapped up by the time you get here or within the next five minutes (whatever comes first), so we can have idyllic strolls in bliss and idleness. I also have no personal cell phone, but I wish I did. I continue to kowtow the required nine times towards the Emperor in filial obeisance. See you shortly. You will have to exchange verbal communications with my boss on the investigations, as I am now in the Bob Uecker seats waaaaayyyyy back in the stadium. Your most obedient servant.

89. 28 FEBRUARY 2006-CAMP PROSPERITY-MY OFFICE

My took my Field Investigator Notes and wrote them down for review on the LN Plumbers:

1. Raad E. Slawa-LN Lead Foreman Man: Mr. Raad said he was told by Bob (Robert J. Brown) yesterday to junk all the electrical materials found in the conex box. He did that yesterday afternoon. He has no other information concerning these thefts. He stated nothing was ever stolen or taken out of the Plumbing Department. (Note: IPBD stated Mr. Raad is the head of criminal gang doing all the stealing of Plumbing and other materials from Camp Prosperity.)

2. Naoh Thamer Abood-LN Plumber: Mr. Naoh said that Mr. Raad admitted to all the Plumbing Department LNs that he stole everything from the locked conex box the morning of 28 February 2006. He also stated that Bob Villa (former Head of Plumbing Department before Nicholas ('Nick the Plumber') Heckman, Mr.

Villa is now dead) said that one year ago at Camp Graywolf that a U.S. Army conex box filled with plumbing supplies was transferred to Camp Prosperity and all the items were stolen. Mr. Naoh said only Mr. Raad and Heckman had a key to get inside and no one else. He also stated that no one was allowed to touch anything. He stated that the whole conex box was stolen from the U.S. Army by Mr. Raad. He said no one else had any information about this stolen conex box and no one told us anything was stolen. He again stated that Mr. Raad admitted he had stolen all the electrical supplies from the conex box that morning. (Note: IPBD stated Mr. Naoh is working with Mr. Raad on stealing all the Plumbing Department supplies.)

3. Diya Durraid-LN Plumber: Mr. Dhya said he had no information. (Note: IPBD stated Mr. Dhya knows information, but he is afraid and will not speak.)

4. Ghasan Ali Abas-LN Plumber: Mr. Ghasan said that only Heckman (his key was turned over to Bob Villa) and Mr. Raad had the keys to the conex box where the electrical supplies were found in the Plumbing conex box and also in all the Plumbing conex boxes. He said that the plan is Mr. Raad picks up the key during the day from the expats and returns the key when he goes home in the afternoon. He has no other information. (Note: IPBD stated that Mr. Ghasan is Mr. Noah's cousin and is too afraid to speak because Mr. Raad has many relatives, contacts and friends in the "Red Zone" and could kill him.)

5. Mr. Kassem Mohammed Al-Musawy-LN Plumber: Mr. Kassem stated he has no idea what is going on. He said Mr. Raad controlled everything and he heard nothing about any stealing. (Note: IPBD stated Mr. Kassem is honest.)

6. Mr. Emad Kai-LN Plumber: Fired on a week before for going through a trash dumpster. (NOTE: KBR had strict rules that no LN be allowed to go through any dumpster for any reason. He

was caught by the Chief of Services, Robert Uzzle, and terminated on the spot.)

7. Sabe Hazem Daraj-LN Plumber: Mr. Sabe said that he had no information about stealing of electrical supplies from the Plumbing conex box and no information about any stealing. (Note: IBPD stated Mr. Sabe is Mr. Raad's cousin.)

8. Rami Raad-LN Plumber: Mr. Rami was previously fired last week for some offense. (Note: IPBD stated Mr. Rami is Mr. Raad's son.)

9. Aziz Tariq-LN Plumber: Mr. Aziz was absent that day. (Note: IPBD stated Mr. Aziz was Mr. Raad's relative.)

10. Hayder Sabad Abed-LN Plumber: Mr. Hayder stated he had no information about anything. He said he was off for the past three days from work. (Note: IPBD stated Mr. Hayder is clueless about everything.)

90. 28 FEBRUARY 2006-CAMP PROSPERITY (E-MAIL)

I thank Jessie for his support. We know fully well that we can only ask employees to write statements and we all know the employee can decline or refuse to answer any of our questions. There is no question that everyone is watching KBR Security very closely, especially the bad guys, and they would cause us major grief for wrongs or slights real or imagined. But in my dealings with Tim and R.C. they have been totally professional in their demeanor and attitude.

(NOTE: I sent Tim and R.C. a 'cc' of this message. I lied again to throw them totally off. They were doing everything they could to get me fired behind my back.) I have full faith in their abilities to conduct interviews and investigations properly. However, Anderson has command of the organization now and I can quickly see we are headed off into a completely new direction which long needed to be addressed. (NOTE: I also 'cc'ed' Anderson this e-mail to soft-soap him too.) I hope that we can complete five (now six actually) major fraud investigations quickly and can shift our focus to the more important direction Ken is taking us into. Thanks again.

91. 28 FEBRUARY 2006-CAMP PROSPERITY (E-MAIL)

I tell J.T. that Anderson is taking the department in a completely new direction and into an area I am not familiar with, total, radical change of pace. I feel completely inadequate, unworthy to be in the presence of 'The Master,' I shall bow and scrape and back away from his Imperial August Presence, bending low to my simple duties, Sire. (Tugging my forelock all the way.) I 'sleep with the fishes.' I am so outta' here. (That was it. Maybe I can slide over to CVS or something.) Cannot be as bad a place as it will be working for my new boss. Unbelievable. I cannot stay here; it is time to move. Somewhere quiet and remote (like the SF camp). Anyway - see you on 21 March on my way out to R&R. Also the U.S. Army just busted some poor clueless KBR bubba at the APO for trying to mail off a set of desert boots to home he bought at the PX. They told him that NO U.S. Army equipment, uniforms, anything goes out. What do you want me to do with all the gear/medals I got your buddy? I was going to bring it with me on the Rhino when I come to Victory? How do you ship it out? I can dump it back on the U.S. Army. Advise.

"Our task is to be 'minions' who 'beat the birds' and 'he shoots them down with a gun.'" (I am not sure if he meant the game birds or us lowly 'servants.' Maybe he cannot tell the difference between quail and the stable boys/hired hands.) See you in less than three weeks.

92. 28 FEBRUARY 2006-CAMP VICTORY-NORTH (E -MAIL)

J. T. said you may see me before then. Jessie told me to be on stand-by to go to Camp Prosperity and look into whatever it is you guys are doing. We will see! Hey!

93. 28 FEBRUARY 2006-CAMP PROSPERITY (E-MAIL)

J.T. - maybe if we are beating the game birds up for him and he pulls a 'Dick Cheney' on my ass then he will put me out of my misery. When Jessie was down here he offered R.C. and Tim their own G-sites for any little-single man FOB anywhere in D, F, G. I, Q, Z, etc. sites he commands. They have done a great job here. All "Gone with The Wind." See you soon.

Still think all these major, complex, massive investigations will be quickly ended before you arrive. At least one large group of people will be applauding my new boss's arrival - the @#USD$%^&* crooks. Just great-all that effort wasted down the Port-A-Potty. Just great. See you soon.

94. 28 FEBRUARY 2006-CAMP PROPSPERITY-MY ROOM

Something has to give out here soon. Chances are it will be me.

95. 28 FEBRUARY 2006-CAMP-VICTORY-NORTH (E-MAIL)

J.T. tells me I have never worried about terrorists; I know how to deal with them. The powers that be do get upset when I break Security Coordinators, though.

96. 28 FEBRUARY 2006-CAMP PROSPERITY (E-MAIL)

I inform Jessie that based on my new, specialized duties here at Camp Prosperity, and based on Anderson taking the Security Department in a new direction, I believe anyone else who is a hard-charging, motivated, energetic young man who will fit in very well here. We will speak more when I see you. I should be there right on or about 21 March. Thanks again for all your trust and support. You have helped us enormously in setting high standards down here where there were no standards at all. This place was and continues to be the 'Wild, Wild West' although we have made great strides in cleaning up Dodge City in a very short period of time.

97. 28 FEBRUARY 2006-CAMP VICTORY-NORTH (E-MAIL)

Jessie lets me know that he knows Anderson is trying to primarily focus on Force Protection issues, but as I told him there is a lot more to Camp Prosperity than just that. At this time I am not ready to move you to another location. You have been doing a good job down there and I know there are a lot of unresolved issues down there. You are still needed at this site. Force Protection issues and investigations are both part of the security department's responsibilities. We will talk more about this when you come through here for R&R.

98. 28 FEBRUARY 2006-CAMP PROSPERITY (E-MAIL)

I tell Jessie that, yes, I agree with you. There are many issues that still need to be addressed here. And yes, Anderson is primarily focused on Force Protection issues since he arrived yesterday. Yes, I understand that investigations and Force Protection (FP) are important parts of the Security Department. However, based on Ken's specific requirements as what the three of us will be doing down here now, I am totally 'unqualified' for the position. I will talk to you when I come through on R&R. I believe Anderson would be much better served with someone more 'qualified' than me. I understand you cannot move me now. We will talk more.

99. 28 FEBRUARY 2006-CAMP PROSPERITY-IPBD CO. MANAGERS' OFFICE

It was a busy day - and it was going to turn out to be a long, tiring one. At the IPBD's Managers' request they asked me to conduct the interviews of Electrical Department IPBD employees in their office. Mr. Ali, Mr. Khalid, and I planned to interview a number of them of them. No sooner than we finished the first interview when the Electrical Department Foreman, a man named Ronald Battle, entered the interview room unannounced. Battle started loudly complaining to Mr. Ali why did I have to interview these Electrical Department workers. Both Mr. Ali and Mr. Khalid explained calmly that it was part of a sanctioned KBR Security investigation. It had been coordinated in advance with Bobby and IPBD.

Battle turned to Mr. Khalid and started shouting at him: "SHUT YOUR FUCKING MOUTH!" each time Mr. Khalid tried to speak, Battle started screaming again and again: "I AM NOT TALKING TO YOU!" He then left.

I finally intervened and brought Battle and Mr. Ali outside with me, leaving Mr. Khalid inside. I attempted to calm Battle down. I quietly explained to him that Mr. Khalid was a co-General Manager of the IBPD Co., and an equal to Mr. Ali. That Mr. Khalid should have been treated with full respect and complete dignity and allowed to explain his position as a General Manager. I also explained to him that we had the prior approval from KBR and the IPBD Co. Managers for conducting the interviews, the reason for the investigation and the specific procedures about interviewing. I also explained the general circumstances of the thefts. Battle finally regained his composure and walked off without comment.

All the witnesses identified an IPBD employee named Ajo who they tagged as the ringleader of the on-going Plumbing Department thefts. The witnesses stated that Ajo also participated in the theft and misappropriation of items from the HVAC and Power Gen Departments plus the U.S. Army off-load areas. We later heard from an IBPD Plumbing Department employee named Naoh Thamer Abood that only that morning did Ajo inform several Plumping Department Iraqi employees that he stole everything from a locked conex box a year earlier. Abood said a U.S. Army conex box filled with plumbing supplies had been sent from Camp Graywolf to Camp Prosperity. The only people who had keys to the lock were Nick Heckman and Ajo who had given him a key.

We had done a few more interviews when a Black female KBR Electrician named Mattie Van Exel suddenly barged into the room and demanded to sit in on the interviews. Before anyone could reply she started loudly berating me that I had no business interviewing HER Iraqi electricians and no right to fire workers. Van Exel kept up her heated tirade against Mr. Ali, Mr. Khalid and myself beating us for a minute or two before we could slide in a word edgewise. She screamed that she would not tolerate HER workers being questioned and that their rights and her rights were being violated. We all explained that all of her electricians were IPBD employees and they did not 'belong' to her. Van Exel grew more belligerent and shouted at the top of her lungs: "GOD WILL PUNISH YOU ALL!" then stormed out the door.

100. 28 FEBRUARY 2006-CAMP PROSPERITY-MAIN YARD

At approximately 18:00 I asked R.C. by telephone to conduct an investigation and write an IR on a KBR Conduct of Business Code (COBC-Dignity and Respect) Violation by Mr. Ronald Battle, Electrical Foreman and a Ms. Mattie Van Exel, Electrician, that I had personally witnessed concerning Mr. Ali and Mr. Khalid, co-General Managers, IPBD Co., KBR sub-contractor for Labor earlier that day. R.C. agreed to get statements from those personnel involved, conduct an investigation and write an incident report.

101. 28 FEBRUARY 2006-CAMP PROSPERITY (E-MAIL)

I tell J.T. that we will do a sit-down. But all investigations have been ripped out of my hands right now. All the crooks must be laughing their asses off. They are going to get away scot-free. Whatever. I repeated to Jessie that I was totally 'unqualified' for this job based on Ken's exact requirements-let us see how long before Jessie asks me or Ken what they are (hint: minion and game beater). Sorry I do not qualify-move me elsewhere is what I have said twice. Maybe I should go to HR with this one if Jessie balks on moving me which he has said he cannot do it now. He cannot move me yet. I will see what happens when Bobby arrives on the morning helo. He has my back, and we are 'muy simpatico.' When he meets Anderson and his B.S. meter will explode off the scale. Anderson is a pompous, full-of-himself, egotistical maniac. We will see. (Should have held out for the U.S. Army's SF camp).

102. 28 FEBRUARY 2006-CAMP PROSPERITY (E-MAIL)

I tell J.T. a dictionary definition is not KBR Security Department business. Definitions (I knew it anyway) - Minion: a lowly servant or slave, a fawning servile servant to some important personage. Describes me to a T. See you soon sahib.

(Old Sicilian proverb: "The plate of revenge must be eaten cold.")

103. 01 MARCH 2006-CAMP PROSPERITY (E-MAIL)

I am not turning down . . . . . oops! Excuse me! ('The Sun King' reigns down here at Camp Prosperity now! It is his domain, and not mine anymore.) I would not have turned down any offer of help and have gladly welcomed you to the 'Wild, Wild West.' The deeper we dig the more we find out-there is no bottom to this quagmire, we are overwhelmed with now six major investigations. The crud levels go totally down to the center of the earth. Anyway, us simple menials are not intelligent enough to deal with such lofty ministrations of the Royal Personage. I just recommended to Jessie by e-mail a few minutes ago that a much more experienced individual like Josh or Matt be transferred here. All the job requirements from 'The Sun King' are now are to be 1) a 'minion' and 2) a 'game beater.' I thought Josh and Matt (NOTE: two very young KBR Security Technicians at CVN) would be PERFECTLY well suited for that role. I am simply not qualified. I shall gracefully resign myself to a job more suited for my humble talents somewhere else. See you soon.

Ciao, a lowly slave toiling in the fields of the Lord of the Manor.

(Have to practice now: "Yes, Bwana, no bwana. Yes, sahib, no sahib." I think I got it.) Stay safe. It is not just the Islamic Jihad terrorists we have to worry about.

104. 01 MARCH 2006-CAMP PROSPERITY-MAIN YARD

Anderson approaches me in the Main Yard and then buttonholes me. He tells me in no uncertain terms that I am not to discuss anything about TCN or LN CAC cards or ID badges that were retrieved by the IBPD Managers from all the fired workers in each department. He is emphatic that I completely shut my mouth about the subject and if anyone asks tell them: "I have no information." He repeats what he just said to me to make absolutely sure I have heard exactly what he said, and what he wants me to say. Then he stalks off.

I have absolutely no idea what he is talking about. Of course, the IPBD Managers will pull all the ID badges or CAC cards from the fired workers. That is a routine procedure. I am unsure how the ID badges or CAC cards are to be disposed of having never had to deal with the problem before. I guessed they would all be turned into whatever badge-issuing authority that handed them out for destruction. They would naturally keep a record of all the badges issued and turned in for shredding. None of this made any sense to me.

Shortly thereafter, the two IPBD Managers buttonholed me in the Main Yard. They explained that short while ago R.C. strode into their office, under the direct orders of Anderson, and demanded that all the fired workers ID badges or CAC cards be handed over to him immediately. He gave them no reason why he wanted them but made veiled threats against the two Managers of the consequences if they did not fork them over on the spot. So they handed them all over. Again none of this made any sense to me. I had to tell them I had no information on the matter which was actually true. They said they were going to bring the matter to Bobby's attention to get the matter resolved. I said that was an excellent idea.

105. 01 MARCH 2006-CAMP UNION III-FUEL POINT

At 13:30, I went to the Fuel Point but did not see any supervisors there. I inquired with the workers about the supervisor and was informed that: "Mr. Burgess had walked off without telling anyone where he was going." They had no idea when he would be back.

106. 01 MARCH 2006-CAMP PROSPERITY (E-MAIL)

I tell Jessie that based on Anderson's 'new requirements' for these security positions that I cannot possibly meet perhaps I should run this through HR. Since I understand there is a new HR person coming in here to deal with HR and security exclusively (Patricia is being delegated to non-security HR issues from what I was informally told) maybe I need to dump this in their lane for resolution. Of course, I would like to handle this in-house, but I feel now I am not getting much attention. These new 'requirements' are what we call in the U.S. Army as 'Mission Failure' and it is causing me a lot of problems in even trying to think about meeting them. I cannot even begin to measure up to them. This has put me in an impossible situation. I have every confidence that you will resolve the dilemma quickly and efficiently.

107. 01 MARCH 2006-CAMP VICTORY-NORTH (E-MAIL)

Jessie says he has no idea what I am talking about. Please expound on this.

108. 01 MARCH 2006-CAMP PROSPERITY (E-MAIL)

I tell Jessie - simple. Anderson briefed Tim and me outside of the Operations Office in the parking lot at approximately 17:00 the day he arrived. (Not sure when he briefed R.C.) He said the requirements he needed from us is that we are going to be his 'minions.' He said that we are going to be his 'game beaters,' and make the game birds fly and he was going to shoot them down with his 'gun.' A definition of a 'minion' (from what I remember) is a 'slave' or 'lowly servant.' It also means a 'fawning sycophant' and/or a 'game beater.' I am totally unqualified to remain in my security position. So as not to cause additional friction or problems for you and Bobby, my request to be transferred to another assignment after my R&R is completed will be submitted. Right now my personal feelings are I would rather work for Russell Hill (HVAC Department Head under investigation for running a massive theft ring) than Anderson. At least Hill has three things going for him: 1) he treats me with respect, maybe he says bad things about me behind my back, but to my face he is respectful, treats me as an equal or as a professional and is never condescending; 2) he listens to me very, very carefully and I listen to him very, very carefully; I can probably remember everything he has said to me so far and I am sure he can do the same thing over the past four weeks and 3) at least Patricia Murphy likes Russell Hill-that says something.

I have had people down here scream in my face in the past four weeks, tell me every nasty name in the book, back-stab me left and right (up through HR) and it does not bother me in the slightest. Because I know three things: 1) I am doing my job to make this place better and doing it right; 2) Bobby has my back and 3) you have my back. But to have your new boss show up and call you, in effect, his/a 'slave' is too much. I have some pride in what I do, but I also have a 'hot button' and he hit it with a sledgehammer. I have every confidence you will straighten this organization/problem out quickly as you always have. See you in 20 days.

109. 02 MARCH 2006-CAMP PROSPERITY-MY OFFICE

"It's not our problem." No matter how many times I went in to see U.S. Army MP units or the U.S. Army CID offices everyone said the same thing: "It's not our problem." I went into as many units as I could. It made no difference. Actually, everyone in the KBR Security was on very specific orders from the KBR Security Supreme High Command HQs NOT to go to see any U.S. Army MP or CID units for any matter. I ignored those orders. I went to each U.S. MP unit and CID HQs in the "Green Zone" and Camp

Prosperity when I could only in an effort to see if I could find someone in the U.S. Army to care. It was no use. No one cared.

110. 02 MARCH 2006-CAMP PROSPERITY-MAIN YARD

J.T. arrived to "See what you guys are doing" on the orders of Jessie. Anderson, Tim and R.C. wisely made themselves invisible for the whole time J.T. was on the ground. If Anderson had taken over all my investigations then he never showed up to insist only he speak to J.T. He was no doubt scared of what tongue-lashing he would endure from J.T. about anything moronic he would definitely say about anything. J.T. had a fierce reputation and did not tolerate any ignorant, stupid, or bombastic statements from anyone. Everyone steered well clear of him while he was on the ground. We sat down each day and went over all the IRs, witness statements, photographs, whatever else I had uncovered.

We hit all the bases in the "Green Zone" for the Grand Guided Tour, spoke to Joe Harris at the AFOSI, talked to the commander of the USAF SF/IZ Police and hit the Fuel Point over at Camp Union III. I gave him a tour of the lay-down yard crime scene where all the generator sets, light-alls and other Power Gen equipment had been methodically dismantled and spirited away outside into the "Red Zone." I explained the inter-locking thievery as coordinated by the IPBD LNs and who were the lead criminals who had organized the other Iraqi thieves. A fair amount of time was spent with the IPBD Managers in their offices. We also paid a courtesy visits to the Camp Manager, Bobby Burns, and Art Shook over at USMI Security.

The plan was to have Jessie submit an RTII right after J.T. had returned to CVN. Then, if all went well, outside 'corporate' investigators would swoop in from Dubai and look at everything we had uncovered, then the start dismantling the place piece-by-piece.

However, J.T. was not optimistic that event would be done properly or professionally. He explained that in the living memory of KBR Security in Iraq there was only one time that an outside 'corporate' investigator had come in here off of an RTII. He said that one investigator came in on one important incident of some massive thievery, had spent all his time shopping in the PX or screwing off having fun for a few days, then finally had shown up in the CVN Security Office, copied the Security investigator's IR word-for-word, then departed only to file that as his 'report.' He never talked to anyone, never investigated anything, and did not lift a finger but to plagiarize the IR. Not a good sign. But I knew by the time J.T. had departed he would have a full picture of what I was doing and there was to be absolutely no questions in his mind I had uncovered some major criminal activity here. But in the whole of Iraq, the exact same thing was happening. J.T. knew that before he had come down.

111. 03 MARCH 2006-CAMP PROSPERITY (E-MAIL)

I tell Jessie that, with your permission, based on initial multiple and now a combined, greatly expanding, investigation, Joseph Saladino, DCMA, Quality Assurance Representative (QAR) has authorized the following personnel to be issued a U.S. Embassy-Baghdad Yellow-stripe with Escort Privileges ID Badge effective immediately:

RICH, JESSIE: D, F, G & I-SITES AREA SECURITY MANAGER
BURNS, BOBBY: D-2 CAMP MANAGER
SEMMES, J.T.: D, F, G & I-SITES AREA SENIOR INVESTIGATOR
LE BLANC, LEONARD: SENIOR SECURITY TECHNICIAN

Mr. Saladino advised that if anyone at USMI-Baghdad/Task Order 100 Security Department had any questions or concerns about this authorization he would be very happy to speak to them personally about the importance of issuing these US Embassy-Iraq badges.

112. 03 MARCH 2006-CAMP PROSPERITY-IPBD MANAGERS' OFFICE

The IPBD Managers asked me to come to their office. They quickly unraveled the mystery of why Anderson and R.C. wanted to keep the fired IPBD LN workers CAC cards and ID badges. They explained that the USAF SF/IZ Police and the AFOSI had just told them they wanted to interview all the fired workers about all the thievery, especially in the Power Gen and HVAC shops and get their statements. But without having a CAC card and ID badge none of the workers could re-enter the "Green Zone" to be interviewed. So that action of pulling and keeping everything completely blocked any more evidence to be gathered from the fired worker's witness statements.

There was more. They also said one of their spies inside the "Hausassem" or Army of Thieves attended a meeting the night before. R.C. had attended the meeting and explained when all the workers who had been fired and would be fired from IPBD would be getting their CAC cards and ID badges BACK for use. That none of the CAC cards and ID badges were going to be turned back into the U.S. Army for destruction. Then, the fired workers could freely enter all the camps and bases inside the "Green Zone" and continue their stealing and looting on a free-lance basis. Slick. All I could do is wait for Bobby to send up a slap-flare or emergency signal rocket to alert Jessie and get his attention and get the whole mess turned around. So much for everyone else's honesty in the Camp Prosperity Security Department.

113. 03 MARCH 2006-CAMP UNION III-FUEL POINT

Starting on 26 February and continuing up to today, I visited the KBR Fuel Point office whenever I had some spare time to gather information about daily vehicle fuel issuance records for January and February 2006 and all fuel card issuance records for a preliminary incident report on theft of fuel from the Fuel Point and very poor records keeping of those fuel cards. I frequently interacted with Lee Evans, the new Fuel Point Manager, who has given me his full cooperation and been very helpful in his support of my efforts.

Often Lee Evans is busy on some business inside the Fuel Point office, so I normally wait outside at the Fuel Point where I have frequently observed Lamel Burgess, Fuels Specialist. I have immediately noticed that he was completely inattentive in his management of the Fuel Point. For example, Burgess spends almost all or all of his time either reading a newspaper, talking on his cell phone, listening to his music on a personal CD player with headphones while sitting in an easy chair and then as often as not sitting down reading a newspaper and listening to music with the headphones on without once looking up at the Fuel Point operations.

At 17:00 I stopped off at the Fuel Point to ask Burgess about a statement I had requested from him on Fuel Point operations prior to Lee Evans arriving to assume responsibility several days prior. I again saw Burgess sitting in a collapsible easy chair, listening to his CD player with his headphones on and reading a newspaper. I stood there for several minutes watching and then asked him to include additional information about the previous year's Fuel Point operation in his statement. Burgess nodded and then right back to what he was doing before which was reading and listening to music. At no time did I see him look at seeing what vehicles were being fueled or what problems were occurring.

One other specific example happened back on 28 February 2006. I had to obtain a new fuel card for my Chevy Tahoe, which had been apparently lost/stolen while the vehicle was being routinely serviced at the Operations Department Dispatch Office. I was attended by one of the Fuel Point personnel who asked me to please wait while they took measurements of the fuel tanks and they would print me a copy of my new fuel card when finished. While I was waiting outside I observed Burgess on his cell telephone for 25 minutes talking without his once looking at what was going on at the Fuel Point. The Fuel Point workers continued to dispensing fuel without any KBR supervision. Burgess was always looking away from the Fuel Point.

114. 03 MARCH 2006-U.S. EMBASSY MAIN BUILDING, DCMA'S OFFICE

J.T. and I went into the heavily defended U.S. Embassy complex not far from USMI. We were on a mission. The DCO, Joe Saladino, wanted to report a 'drug deal' that went down under the 14th of July bridge he had witnessed several months in January. When seated, J.T. did all the talking. After exchanging the usual greetings, they quickly established that they had a number of mutual friends in the Broward County, Florida Sheriff's Department where John has worked for several years and also on the Florida Highway Patrol where he had been a sworn officer for a stretch. They immediately established an easy rapport. Joe Saladino also explained he was a retired New York City patrolman who moved down to Fort Lauderdale in Broward County, Florida before he signed on as a DCO.

Mr. Saladino started in by loudly complaining about the 'drug deal' he had witnessed and the dozens of other incidents of thefts, stealing, rip-offs and misappropriation of U.S. government property since he landed the previous summer. He said he could not get a single person interested in the U.S. Embassy or in any outside organization or agency including law enforcement. Everyone poo-poo'ed the idea of the stealing, just casually dismissing everything he saw out-of-hand. They said it was not enough to be bothered about. All these blasé attitudes infuriated him. He exclaimed that J.T. and I were the first people to show any interest in his observations and he welcomed our visit.

Then he immediately broke into a highly detailed, very animated description of what he saw had happened. He said as soon as he noticed what was occurring he knew there was something illegal going down. He had seen these 'drug deals' go down all during his career on the streets as a beat cop. He was in a vehicle passing by under the turn-around loop under the bridge and instantly told his driver to slow to a crawl so he could catch as many details as possible. He described a man who matched the exact description of Russell Hill, right down to the blue denim bib overalls, scruffy white beard, black-rimmed glasses, and long-sleeve red checked shirt he always wore. He was carrying a package a/c unit from his maintenance truck KBR over to an Iraq's pick-up and slid it into the truck's rear bed. The Iraqis had several look-outs standing around.

Mr. Saladino had previously given a positive identification of the KBR vehicle that was involved. I had already determined that two individuals, Russell Hill, and Clinton Towery, possessed keys to the truck. J.T. had six photographs. Included were these two individuals along with four other similar photographs, a standard six photo line-up. These were presented to Mr. Saladino. He immediately and unerringly identified Russell Hill as the driver of the truck which carried the a/c units and went on to describe Hill's actions in parking, exiting the vehicle, helping to unload the truck, and exiting the scene. Mr. Saladino indicated the photograph he had selected by initialing the photo.

Joe Saladino also said he had previously identified Russell Hill as the driver of the truck to the AFOSI investigators. He was told that the investigators had obtained several SORs for the a/c units about the time of the incident. The investigators also told him that they had identified the drivers of the two taxis as KBR Iraqi HVAC employees: Mr. al-Atar and Mr. Rasheed Achmend. Both men were interviewed and admitted to the investigators that they drove the two taxis in question that contained the stolen a/c units. Both taxi drivers admitted they believed the a/c units to be stolen.

Our next stop was the AFOSI office. There was an agreement between the two major U.S. military forces in the "Green Zone" for territorial jurisdiction. Common-garden varieties of crime (assault, minor theft, vehicle accidents, etc.) were handled by the U.S. Army's MPs. But for crimes against government property (fraud, misappropriation, waste, etc.), we had to see the AFOSI detachment. We spoke with a Special Agent Garfield 'Joe' Harris. From his age, demeanor, and vocabulary I guessed he was a MSGT. I already know from my time as a USAF Security Police (SP) officer back in the mid-1970s that AFOSI Special Agents never used their ranks. We briefed him on what we had found. Joe Harris listened attentively but took no notes. He was professional, polite but non-committal.

J.T. and I went back to Camp Prosperity. On the ride back we discussed what we had found and what to do next. I know that my part of the investigation would lead right back to the HVAC Shop. As has been said many times before, an investigator follows a lead no matter where it goes. I spoke with Russell Hill. He denied he was the person who was seen by Joe Saladino under the 14th of July Bridge since he stated he was on leave that during time period. That was a very easy claim to check with Operations who kept who was on leave at any one time and when. He also insisted he had given the keys to his truck to Clinton Towery. I checked with Towery, but he flatly denied ever having the keys. He said Russell Hill was the only person allowed to drive his truck as he did not trust anyone else to operate it. I went back to Russell Hill to discuss the discrepancy with him. Then Hill stated he had given the keys to Jack Callison and he had operated the truck. I interviewed Callison. He was very adamant in his denial of ever having operated Hill's truck. He confirmed what Clinton Towery had said-no one was allowed to operate his vehicle under any circumstances. But there was also one small problem. Callison also said he had not been hired on by KBR at the time in question. I checked. He was right. That left Russell Hill as the only culprit in the theft.

I told J.T. the whole camp was like a huge sieve. Storage containers holding hundreds, or thousands, of valuable spare parts, supplies, equipment, materials, and other gear were always left unlocked day and night. Equipment, materials, and supplies were haphazardly scattered around the camp everywhere. Vehicles were always left unlocked, almost all of them carrying valuable testing instrumentation, supplies, spare parts, and special tools. Baghdad was at the end of a very long supply line. But everyone's attitude was one of 'could not-care-less'. In the evening I started 'stealing' everything of value in every unlocked vehicle I found, including keys, vehicle registrations and valuables. I turned my 'loot' over to Bobby in his office the next morning. The offending or negligent driver had to come to retrieve their goods and vehicle registration then receive a royal ass-chewing as punishment. I was far from the most popular person on the camp site. But my job was not trying to win any popularity contests here. My job was to make the camp as safe and secure as possible. But I could not do that alone. I needed everyone's cooperation. I was not getting it. So it was obviously I would have to force the issue by being strict. I had no choice.

115. 03 MARCH 2006-CAMP PROSPERITY (E-MAIL)

J.T. sent Jessie and me an e-mail which is a supplemental report to his IR. He said at 08:00 this date a meeting was held with Joseph Saladino,

DCMA QAR, regarding the incident that occurred beneath the 14th of July Bridge and the photographs he had taken of the incident. Saladino had previously given a positive identification of the KBR vehicle involved in the incident. It was determined that two individuals, Hill, and Clinton Towery, possessed the keys to the truck. Photographs of these two individuals along with four other similar photographs, a standard six photo lineup, were presented to Saladino. Saladino immediately and unerringly, identified Russell Hill as the driver of the truck who carried the air conditioning units and went on to describe Hill's actions in parking, exiting the vehicle, helping to unload the truck, and exiting the scene. Saladino indicated the photograph he had selected by initially the photo.

116. 03 MARCH 2006-CAMP PROSPERITY-MAIN YARD

I received a telephone call from Mr. Ali informing me that R.C. has been in their office and he asked Mr. Khalid and Mr. Ali to write statements about the COBC Violation and they agreed to do so. However, he immediately informed me that R.C. then asked them to have a Mr. Haji Naji, Power Generation Administrative Assistant, to write a statement about the Theft and Misappropriation of U.S. government property in the KBR Power Generation Shop. R.C. began questioning Mr. Ali and Mr. Khalid about specific details concerning the investigation that I was actively conducting by specifically asking who had written what statements concerning the Department, what those statements contained, all details of my current investigation, copies of all statements written in English and/or Arabic, what the statement writers knew about a Lynn Summerville, former Power Generation Department Head, now Central Iraq Area Power Generation Manager, who was a prime suspect of my investigation into these thefts and misappropriations, and any other information they knew about of my investigation.

Mr. Ali became quite alarmed as he knew I was conducting this investigation, knew from personal experience that R.C. and Summerville had been and were still close personal friends from Summerville's tenure here and knew that Mr. Haji Naji had been cleared of any suspicion of involvement plus he specifically been asked not to write a statement due to his complete non-involvement after my initial investigation. That is why he called me.

I called R.C. and simply said in a friendly tone of voice: "Hi, R.C., what's going on?" He immediately became very defensive. He quickly denied that he was in or had ever been in Mr. Ali's Office, stated he knew nothing about the Power Gen theft and misappropriation of U.S. property investigation and stated he was declining to investigate the COBC Violation without an explanation and hung up. I never asked R.C. anything about him being in Mr. Ali's Office or either the Power Generation or COBC investigation.

117. 04 MARCH 2006-CAMP VICTORY-NORTH (E-MAIL)

Jessie asks were statements taken from Mr. Ali and Mr. Khalid reference the possible COBC dignity and respect issue that occurred yesterday? If so, I would like those sent to me. If they have not been taken yet then I would like for you or Tim to go and request a written statement from each of them on the issue. Thanks.

118. 04 MARCH 2006-CAMP PROSPERITY (E-MAIL)

I pass to Jessie that actually Mr. Ali's statement was just finished a few minutes ago and Mr. Khalid's statement is still being written. It is my investigation. They have been busy with a few dozen statements in general about assorted subjects as you know. But I will get them scanned up to you hopefully by tomorrow. We are all working as a team, although I only see everyone else at noon at our daily meeting. And perhaps in passing at best. I see no problems on this end with us working together overall.

119. 04 MARCH 2006-CAMP PROSPERITY (E-MAIL)

I tell J.T. sorry, I fell half-asleep and sent an incomplete e-mail by accident. I need to call it a night. I will finish now:

JESSIE: Sending Jessie e-mails and including comments on how we are a real 'team' down here.

ANDERSON: Although R.C. is extremely strained, extraordinarily taut, and keenly wary, Anderson is also in a panic, but clueless. He is not getting much sleep either. The edge is really off his arrogance and condescending attitude now. He is not sure of himself and he does not know why, something he cannot figure out. Like the solid ground is slowly starting to move between his feet, imperceptibly twisting and turning, sliding, and bending, and he cannot comprehend what is taking place to react to it since the ground was always solid before. None of us are getting much sleep from the extreme stress to be honest. Anderson (and Tim) has no idea the raging firestorm about to break loose.

HVAC EXPATS: Now Michael Peters is talking real trash to everyone (well, not me anyway, I am just a 'minion') on the camp about how he is waiting for a 'public apology' (in front of everyone) from the Security Department over our 'harassment' of the HVAC Department for no reason. Apparently the storm passed overhead without a drop and the foul balls have dropped back into complete complacency. Hmmmmmmmmmmmm. OK, I will get back to you on that one Peters. "The plate of rev. . . . ."

IPBD LNs: Tomorrow they will see all the scumbags get canned and their badges pulled and destroyed by me-personally. Stand by.

ZZZZZZZZZZZZZZZZZZZZZZZZZZZZZ! (I am dead.) Until tomorrow, same Bat-time, same Bat-channel. . . .

120. 04 MARCH 2006-CAMP PROSPERITY (E-MAIL)

I pass to J.T. the following commentary:

EXHAUSTION: I am there, I rarely get to sleep before midnight and keep waking up at 05.15 for some strange reason. Now I have the endless task of writing everything I have uncovered and back it up. Happy to go out on R&R in about two more weeks. I think I will sleep for the whole two weeks I will be gone. We are getting closer every day now.

RESPECT: Before you arrived I was being shouted at in my face, cursed, defiled, belittled, run-down, etc. Since you departed it is rare to see anyone not tug their forelock (male) or curtsey (female) to me at all hours. Even people I have never even seen before say hello to me or use my name in the greetings. Even people who would not have even looked in my direction before are at least nodding and acknowledging my presence, always with a genuine smile. You have made me into a true 'Man of Respect'. A real 'pezzonovante,' a .90 caliber. (Grazi.)

TEAM PLAYER: Rah, rah, sis boom bah! Go Team! Yaaaahhhhhhh! (I love acting, I am such a ham.) I smile a lot to Anderson, R.C. and Tim, bow and scrape, agree with everything they say, extravagantly praise Tim and R.C. constantly and tell Anderson it was his great ideas (even when they were mine). And just keep my mouth shut around them. I tell Anderson what a genius he is and try not to blast him too many times for his endless moronic ideas (like guide him away from the helm of the Titanic.) They have a false sense of security now, all except for . . . . .

R.C.: He is very much worried, has a very concerned, strained look on his face. Tim and Anderson are totally clueless. But R.C. is extraordinarily wary now, right on the knife edge. He knows something is going on behind the scenes, but not what-sort of like a semi-transparent/opaque screen. He also knows something is terribly wrong, but he cannot put his finger on it. He is like a rat in the night. He knows the cat is out there waiting for him somewhere with better vision, he senses it with very nerve wracking ending, but he cannot see it. It is just too dark. He seeks an edge (he is constantly asking people (and me) for info on what is going on, but not too overtly). Mr. Ali and Mr. Khalid have brave Iraqis coming forth now and they are watching for his daily arrival over at 215 Apartments (he has a little sweetie on the side there). He is talking to all the bad guys now: Summerville, Mr. Raad (Plumbing LN Chief Thief), etc., all the scumballs out there. Now I am waiting for the 'call' to take him down. We shall see. Should not be long now.

MR. KHALID AND MR. ALI: They are furiously writing their statements on everything. I just make minor, slight corrections to spelling and grammar to make it half-way readable, but not too much mind you. It is brilliant stuff if I may say so myself! Let us just say I make sure their 'core' information matches my 'core' information in general. The little petty details may be omitted or skewed slightly, but the overall fundamentals are intact and readily apparent.

121. 05 MARCH 2006-CAMP VICTORY-NORTH (E-MAIL)

Jessie tells me that he is still waiting for the military's report on Michael Peters, and the statements from Mr. Ali, et. al., as well as some more LN statements on HVAC and Power Gen Departments in particular.

122. 05 MARCH 2006-CAMP PROSPERITY (E-MAIL)

I tell Jessie that I am finally getting a few stray minutes to wrap up other badly back-logged statements as I start to dig out from under a mountain of everything. These statements (on Nicholas Heckman, Sarah Smith, Patricia Murphy, Samuel Simpson and R.C.'s statement on Nicholas Heckman that were attached to the e-mail) do not rate an IR in my book unless they tie-in to other investigations (Samuel Simpson will rate an IR as soon as I finish the investigation on him). I believe the rest will fall under 'HR/Management /Supervision' issues that touch on us in some way. Let me know if you want me to initiate an IR on each one. Some go into people's personnel files and the rest are handled at the supervisor level for further action (counseling, disciplinary action, transfers, remedial training, termination, etc.). I do not know what is in someone's personnel file, of course, maybe the file is jammed with problems. But at least there is a record. Thanks for your support and backing through this very trying and difficult time.

123. 05 MARCH 2006-CAMP PROSPERITY (E-MAIL)

I pass to Jessie that my take on this one (the interruptions of the Electrical Department interviews in the IPBD Managers' office by the KBR Electrical workers Van Exel and Battles) was it was more an 'HR/Camp Management' problem than a 'Security' problem per say. I was a 'witness' to the event, but I would not have said they were 'impeding' or 'hampering' my investigation into everything that is going on as they want 'clean' employees just as much as we do. It is your call, of course. I will do as you advise. I did not do an IR on it or tie it into the big one. The IPBD Managers are sending their statements directly to Bobby as this is a matter between KBR employees and IPBD Management. We were/I was just a spectator(s). (And like I needed to write another IR!) Let me know. But I will 'cc' you with Mr. Ali and Mr. Khalid's statements today on the incident.

124. 05 MARCH 2006-CAMP VICTORY-NORTH (E-MAIL)

J.T. tells me that Jessie will look into the badge issue, but he agrees that it is a Site Manager problem and could be corrected with a phone call. He also pointed out that you work for him, not me, and he would appreciate more direct communications from you that he can address these problems in a more expeditious manner. I think he may also get his feelings hurt when he hears second hand information (I know it pisses him off). So remember, Jessie gets a copy of everything and all reports filed within 12 hours, complete or not. You can ask Bobby . . . nothing is more aggravating than being in charge and not knowing about some particular incident when asked by a higher up. Please get me what you can on Peters. Thanks.

125. 05 MARCH 2006-CAMP VICTORY-NORTH (E-MAIL)

Jessie says that all the badges that are still in the possession of the Security Department will be returned to the IPBD Manager by tomorrow. Confirm for me when they are returned. I have been told that the IPBD Manager did not want them back and that is why they were distributed back to the Department supervisors. Please confirm or deny this for me from the IPBD Manager. Thanks.

126. 05 MARCH 2006-CAMP PROSPERITY (E-MAIL)

I tell Jessie you were told 100 percent wrong. Mr. Ali and Mr. Khalid have been complaining about these badges ever since R.C. was told by Anderson to remove them from the IPBD offices. The loss of badge control meant the bad guys took over again and were giving the badges back to their little buddies, so they both knew R.C. and Anderson were tied directly into them 100 percent at their direction. I was ordered to stay completely away from this problem, and I did. I can have Mr. Ali and Mr. Khalid confirm the above to you tomorrow directly by e-mail. What you are being told by either Anderson or R.C. is pure fantasy. I will confirm tomorrow what was returned, but who knows what badges have been actually returned into the field and what badges were not. It will take a while to head-count and sort out the mess. R.C. just went in there and snatched them all right off the desk according to Mr. Ali and Khalid. It may take a while to re-confirm what badges R.C. and Anderson distributed to the workers. I repeatedly told Anderson and R.C. this IPBD badge issue was going to get people into trouble (like a good 'Team Player'), but they blew me off totally.

127. 05 MARCH 2006-CAMP PROSPERITY (E-MAIL)

I tell J.T. I am in 'gridlock' - to wit:

USAF FP/IZ POLICE: They aren't moving to do anything because they do not have Mr. Safaa to interview (he doesn't answer his phone now) and any of the rest of the HVAC guys to interview like they wanted, and they do not have the photos of the HVAC/Power Gen Iraqis to show to the Iraqi taxi drivers for them to finger (They only know the faces very well. And maybe one named Bashaam) who helped KBR Security are from last year and not all the Iraqis now are working (like our two suspects) were photographed.

And none of the HVAC/Power Gen/other Iraqis is in the door anyway to be finally photographed by me/us/IPBD because of . . . .

ALL BADGES: R.C. and Anderson are sitting on all the Iraqi badges that are sitting on R.C.'s desk and not giving them back at all and everyone is screaming for them to be given back. I was told to give them all to IPBD (which I did) and I was told to back away from the disaster and shut my mouth (which I did) and I said like: "I have no information" to anyone who asks (which I did) when the Trades Department Heads come to me shouting where are our badges and I say: "I have no information." So they run off to IPBD and IPBD tells them to see R.C. and Anderson and they are extremely 'scarce.' So IPBD thinks or has been told that Anderson and R.C. are doing some sort of a 'drug deal' on the side of some sorts with these badges now (rumors are flying everywhere). So when I saw (Don't you love this? I do.) Anderson today at breakfast I started yanking on his chain very hard a few thousand times (just like I did yesterday) about all of the above and said (I am TRYING to be a 'team player' here which is what Jessie wants now) I really DID NOT APPRECIATE WHOMEVER HAS THE BADGES AND I AM NOT SAYING WHO SINCE I DO NOT KNOW as they are causing me a lot of problems and headaches with, say, everyone on the FOB. So the HVAC/Power Gen people cannot be photographed or interviewed because they cannot get on the FOB because (MR.'TEAM PLAYER OF THE YEAR' (I love this)) Anderson and R.C. are having me in total gridlock.

STATEMENTS FROM MR. ALI AND MR. KHALID: Mr. Khalid's relative died, and he is at a funeral all day today and Mr. Ali is doing payday today. We are scheduled for a 15:00 appointment.

LYNN SUMMERVILLE: JUST walked into Mr. Ali's office and I have to run.

TEAM PLAY: Well, Jessie sent Anderson down here and now Jessie wants all these investigations done el mucho pronto and I would suggest Jessie have his wayward step-son Anderson start doing his job-whatever that is-and perhaps give everyone their badges back. Just a suggestion. Film at 11. ("The plate of rev . . ." even for Jessie. He sent this Frankenstein monster down here to the FOB, let him gather up the simple villagers and try to catch the monster. The buzzards are coming home to roost.)

128. 05 MARCH 2006-CAMP PROSPERITY (E-MAIL)

I pass to Jessie the latest on updates:

USAF IZ/SF POLICE: I will get them/try to get them what they want ASAP. To take down the KBR three HVAC shop expats they need: 1) a statement from Mr. Safaa implicating them in the theft ring and 2) photos of the HVAC LNs who took the a/c units off of the back of the KBR truck under the 14th of July Bridge with Russell Hill so they can show them in a Photo ID line-up to the Iraqi drivers to finger. This is enough to bust them out. I will ask Joe Harris for a short statement on R.C. and what he asked them about my investigation and also get Mike Peter's statement from them from his six-hour marathon data dump/gut-spill IF it is ready for pick-up. It was not the last time I checked.

STATEMENTS FROM MR. ALI AND MR. KHALID ON R.C.: Tomorrow I will have them consolidate a huge statement on R.C. and ship it to you. Will have them write it in Arabic and you can have someone translate it. Much faster.

PHOTOS OF THE HVAC LNs FROM THE CAMP PROSPERITY MAYOR'S CELL ID BADGE FILE: I will get the names of the HVAC LNs, download the pictures from the Camp Mayor's cell ID Badge file, print them, get them to the USAF IZ/SF Police investigators and have the taxi drivers finger them from a photo ID line-up.

OTHER IRAQI LN STATEMENTS ON THE THEFTS/WHATEVER: I will send them untranslated/in Arabic to you directly.

129. 06 MARCH 2006-CAMP PROSPERITY (E-MAIL)

I pass to Jessie the following topics in no order:

MR. ALI'S STATEMENT ON R.C.: Mr. Ali just walked out of here with a copy of his signed statement going to Jessie via Bobby and a courier hand deliver on the Rhino tonight direct. Standing-by to stand-by. All statements we could get or have gotten (unless one of the fired workers shows up to drop the dome on someone) are now done and shipped. I am done.

O/T: According to Anderson at our Daily Meeting the PM is going to a) cut my head off for all my O/T I was authorized to have and put on my timesheet, b) fire me and c) get me into hot water. Not sure in what order these events will happen. I see-bust my ass 18-19 hours/day for a whole month, only charge KBR for 15 hours for two weeks of O/T, get yelled at for breaking six major investigations and then get threatened or fired for my miserable efforts. What is wrong with this picture? Hey! Maybe I can become a scumball, spend all my time STEALING everything, make millions on the side and NOT get fired for my efforts! Hey! Sounds like a plan! In fact, Lynn Summerville got PROMOTED to Area Manager and he is even a bigger thief than Russell Hill. I have been doing it all wrong all these years-I should have been a lying, stealing, backstabbing slimeball crook instead of an honest, upright, hardworking, clean citizen! Silly me.

MY IMMEDIATE BOSS: Can his ego get any bigger? Unbelievable.

About it for now, see you when I see you-like tomorrow or no later than 21 March.

130. 06 MARCH 2006-CAMP VICTORY-NORTH (E-MAIL)

J.T. forwards me the one-page, simple request for the RTII. It would be routed up through the KBR Security chain-of-command for approval and then be sent to the outside 'corporate' investigators in Dubai for action. The RTII simply understated the allegation that LN SCWs, KBR HVAC, and KBR Power Gen personnel possibly involved in the unauthorized/movement/selling of government/KBR property off camp. The synopsis of the allegation read: There are numerous allegations and reports of property being transported off site by the Local National sub-contract workers with the assistance of personnel within the KBR HVAC Department and the Power Gen Department at Camp Prosperity. There are various investigations currently being conducted on numerous client Departments to include USAF SF/IZ Police investigators, AFOSI, DCMA and U.S. Army CID. Attached are incident reports and written statements as supporting documentation of these actions.

Now all we could do is wait and see what happened next. It was out of our hands.

131. 06 MARCH 2006-CAMP PROSPERITY (E-MAIL)

I tell J.T. I guess I am getting what-worn out-from everything. I am trying to follow Jessie's specific orders - be a 'Team Player,' follow the chain of command, do this, and do that. And then when I do those things I get beaten up for doing them. Example, follow the chain of command, I work for Anderson, but then Jessie tells me the Site Manager can have Anderson return the badges. Anderson does not work for the Site Manager; he works for Jessie. Can I go to the Site Manager about the badges? No, I am given specific orders to steer all Security Department business away from Bobby and keep it in-house. And these badges are not even my concern as I was told specifically to keep my nose out of it, because normally IPBD can go to the Site Manager, but they know Anderson is in control of everything through R.C. and they know Anderson works for Jessie and not Bobby plus they are very afraid since R.C. is in bed with the criminals. And then I am supposed to go through the chain of command and be a 'Team Player.' Do I tell Anderson to return the badges? No - I am not Anderson's boss. I politely advise Anderson that the badges are a surface-of-the-sun hot issue and to keep away from it, as a 'Team Player' should do. Does he listen? No, I get the hard blow-off every time. Jessie tells me to be a 'Team Player' but being a 'Team Player' is not ratting out your scumball buddies, so I do not rat them out to Jessie, but then Jessie wants to know exactly what is going on. So when I do not tell him everything about my scumball co-workers then I get it in the shorts for not telling him and

I hurt Jessie's feelings. I had this investigation ready to break open in less than 24 hours when someone (no names mentioned) sent Anderson down here. And things have been horribly screwed up ever since. And I have been fighting to get it back to where it was before he arrived.

There are two military management styles I have been under. One is Command by Control-you do exactly what you ae told and nothing else. USAF and probably the USMC, except they do not have checklists-unknown about the U.S. Army). Everything is written down and everything has a checklist. Deviate from the checklist and you get your head handed to you. The other is Command by Negation (USN). The USN tells the ship's Captain to go from, say, San Diego to Yokosuka, Japan. The big Admiral does not tell the Captain what his specific route is, but to leave on this date and be there on that date. The USN figures the Captain is smart enough to work his way around or avoid islands, typhoons, other ships, rocks, shoals, bad weather, waterspouts, Islamic Jihad terrorists in dinghies, whatever and arrive safely. If they see the Captain is headed in the wrong direction (like he is going through the Panama Canal and across the Indian Ocean to Japan), then they 'negate' his course and route him around through the Pacific. Jessie wants to micromanage running my ship from CVN and it is not happening. He is giving me constant conflicting orders and then he is not happy because I cannot do 50 things at the same time exactly the way he wants. Jessie is a great guy; he is a great boss. But he either decides Command by Control is going to work (it is not going to; I can tell you right now) or Command by Negation is going to work (it will). Either Jessie trusts me to work all this out in some way (avoid the rocks and shoals) or he can tell me what to do each time step-by-step (USAF style) and I will sit and wait for orders. And I am sorry Jessie has his feelings hurt, but if it will make him feel any better he can come down here and have some of these very nice people scream in his face for a change for doing his job. See you in two weeks. "The plate of re . . . . . the wheels of justice . . . ." (Sorry for venting, I have no one else to vent to except Bobby and he has far more problems than me. I will get you what you want ASAP.

132. 06 MARCH 2006-CAMP PROSPERITY-IBPD CO. MANAGERS' OFFICE

Mr. Khalid made the following written statement:

"Before five or six days ago Mr. Le Blanc gave me the ID badges for the people who were terminated from the IBPD Co. Mr. Le Blanc told me to keep these badges with me. The same day after I found out that R.C. and Anderson came in the office and they took away from me all the badges from all these guys. And I told them that Mr. Le Blanc told me to keep these badges with me and they ordered me to give them the badges and they told me: "They will take the badges." And I gave them the badges and said: "However it doesn't make a difference to me." Now today they returned back the badges before a couple of days ago and I refused to take the badges from them, and this does not make sense. I wonder why they took it from me first and now they returned it today. And why they say to Mr. Jessie that they gave the badges back and they did not."

133. 06 MARCH 2006-CAMP PROSPERITY (E-MAIL)

I tell J.T. the following topics in no order:

SOMEONE PUT THE HEAD OF A CAMEL UNDER KEN'S BEDCOVERS: According to 'informed and highly reliable sources' someone put the head of a camel underneath Anderson's bedcovers. Reportedly Anderson just had all of his appendages chopped off (including his tiny weenie) and then had what was left of him pounded severely and mercilessly by a large sledgehammer by someone in the higher chain of command for several hours. He got blasted badly (I assume by Sandy Darden, who took over as Area KBR Security Manager when Frank Russell de-mobed). That might be the reason he has looked a bit in 100 percent complete shell-shock these days. Hhhmmmmmm! The young lad (Anderson) is totally catatonic. Anyway - it was apparently explained to him that if ONE of these ladies went out and sued KBR about these allegations on R.C. using the threat of 'investigation'/pressure against these ladies for some totally illegal on-the-side 'nookie' the lawsuit(s) that would result would be massive and national headlines would occur. But the BAD thing was how our lad Anderson handled all of it-did he go right to Sandy Darden as soon as he heard all the allegations from Dan Stack on R.C.? Are bears Catholic? NO, he does what he always does-he went right to R.C. with it to cover it all up! HELLO! DUH! EARTH-TO-MARS!?!?! And then all of these other allegations came pouring forth against him, R.C., etc., on how things were NOT getting handled AT ALL when all these problems surfaced-all of them got buried. Anyway-everyone who came to me was told go DIRECT to Dan McGuire with a 'c.c.' to Sandy Darden (just like you said). All the people here who came to me with complaints KNEW I had been: 1) ordered off the case; 2) placed on thin ice over everything that has happened by R.C., Tim, Anderson, etc.; 3) at least I was trying to help them out and 4) gave them some hope, however slight. And ditto on the U.S. Army; apparently their formal complaint(s) is/are on the way and . . . . .

TOMORROW IS ONLY A DAY AWAY: The formal, written statements by these several/many ladies on the allegations against R.C. are being transmitted tomorrow to the High Supreme Command HQs. THAT is what everyone is waiting for, then appropriate action should commence from there. THAT is what all of the people here were waiting for-written statements. We shall see. I trust there will be a formal HR Investigation (and not Security) and results to follow soon enough. Interesting.

OUR LAD (KEN ANDERSON): He actually spoke to me today! I was in shock-true stuff! Really. He seemed very confused and very dazed, but the words coming out of his mouth made sense. He asked me for some help finding a vehicle we both know is still at Camp Victory being 'repaired.' Maybe it was an excuse to speak to me. I said I would 'make some inquiries' for him. He was very subdued, mild, no ego, nothing but . . . . . what? Well, nothing.

AN OFFER HE CAN'T REFUSE: From all reports Anderson is spending massive amounts of time on the phone and doing e-mails: constantly/night-and-day. I do not think he is playing computer games or talking to his bookie or stockbroker these days. The word from the herd is he is frantically looking for another job - FAST. Even he knows the wet cement overshoes he is now wearing (while sitting dockside) is about dry now. The scoop from group is it will be any day now for his fate. I believe it was recommended from someone/people here that his move from Camp Rustimayah to Camp Prosperity was a terrible, terrible mistake and he has 'lost the confidence' of the high command in his further tenure as the local 'El Supremo.' It appears he is 'lacking' in many areas. Hmmmmmmmm! What a surprise!!!! All I can say is: "Could not have happened to a nicer guy!" So we shall see.

About it here - I am still playing 'The Three Monkeys' gag. I am actually enjoying not having any of the security guys speak to me. I am sort of my own mini-security department of sorts, just on nights. So far, so good. I do miss the 'making inquiries' hot action, but I am now mellow and serene. Just being patient. See you when I see you. I signed the e-mail off as Chief Inspector Dreyfus.

134. 07 MARCH 2006-CAMP PROSPERITY (E-MAIL)

J.T. forwarded me a copy of an IR submitted today to Jessie. No doubt Jessie sent it to J.T. for commentary or to check out my take on it since my name is included in it. It is all about how Anderson and I went together to all the investigative entities in the "Green Zone" to check up on their involvement into all the investigations we are currently conducting. That included meeting with Rob Akers over at USMI, AFOSI Special Agent 'Joe' Garfield over at the USAF SF/IZ Police, people at the U.S. Army CID office, that we met with SFC UFN Cardone at the U.S. Army MP shop and with the AFOSI. Everyone denied knowing anything about any on-going investigations from our end in the "Green Zone" or anywhere else.

The only problem is I never went anywhere at any time with Anderson. The whole IR was all pure fabrication, a lie, made-up B.S. Since Anderson hit the ground seven days ago and called us all 'minions,' we rarely met and spoke less. He, Tim and R.C. scattered to the four winds and did nothing all day. It was rare now when I saw them too. Anderson never visited anyone. If he had he would have known that Joe Garfield was assigned as an AFOSI Special Agent, not as a USAF SF/IZ Policeman. Yes, I suspected 'Joe'

Garfield was a MSGT, but the AFOSI never used their ranks or grades. All of these entities knew all about our investigations since I had periodically told them about it in person.

I had no idea what Anderson is doing. Maybe he was trying to prove to Jessie he was 'Actively on the job here, earning his high salary!' But I knew one thing - he has no idea what he was doing either. He was criminally incompetent. I just let it go. Contacting Jessie to contradict Anderson and his idiotic bogus IR would do nothing for me or my cause.

135. 07 MARCH 2006-CAMP PROSPERITY-IPBD CO. MANAGERS' OFFICE

Mr. Khalid contacted me. He wanted to hand me a written, signed statement on that wonderful piece of humanity R.C. and what he had just done. Mr. Khalid wrote:

"We were going to terminate laborers from our company of course after they had done something against the rules of our company or KBR Company, R.C. always came to us (Mr. Khalid and Mr. Ali) and explained to us if we fired this person from his job and of course you live in the "Red Zone" and he too (the fired worker) lives in the "Red Zone" then people will watch you and maybe you will be killed by their hands because they know you fired them. This is like threatening us. So it means do not make us fire someone and it makes us shut our mouths for every single bad thing they make it. Especially what was going on before in the Camp Honor FOB with the HVAC Group when we found some guys who were guilty when we discovered something was missing from the HVAC Shop. And he told us no one can fire anyone; we are the ones who decide who gets fired and who does not. Also from my information I know he has a relationship with a girl. Her name is Hamsa. She works like an interpreter and he got her cell phone number and he calls her. And he talks bad words to her, and I got a witnesses to that. When he rides with us in his vehicle, Mr. Ali, and myself, especially Mr. Ali recognized her as she worked for him before like an interpreter position in one of the Main gates in the "Green Zone"."

136. 07 MARCH 2006-CAMP PROSPERITY-CAMP MAYOR'S CELL

I was in the Camp Prosperity Mayor's Cell office turning in eight Camp Prosperity 'Green' ID Badges for destruction obtained from recently terminated KBR IPBD Company sub-contractor Iraqi LN workers. A SSGT UFN Jordan, U.S. Army, Assistant Camp Mayor, was looking at the badges one-by-one and commented "D." I said: "D?" He said two of these recently terminated Iraqi LN workers had been authorized by someone, most probably their supervisors, entry into the DFAC, the 'D' meaning unescorted entry into the Camp Prosperity DFAC and showed me both badges. I said that was impossible. I said there were dozens of messages, orders, directives, statues, memos, letters and other official U.S. Army and KBR missives categorically stating that no LN workers are allowed in the DFAC unless they are interpreters and then escorted by an expat. This was all based on the incident of an Iraqi suicide bomber penetrated security in the Mosul DFAC and detonated his explosive-laden vest, killing hundreds of innocent personnel.

I knew there were thousands of Iraqis that entered the "Green Zone" daily. There were political figures, U.S. government officials and employees, civilian service workers of all nationalities, delivery workers and residents. Everyone had to carry some sort of identification or ID card that granted some access privileges, but some carried ID cards that allowed their holders to enter and exit the "Green Zone" without being searched. For security reasons, U.S. official policy required meticulous background checks before any ID card was issued to them. The problem was some KBR employees corrupted the procedure for obtaining ID cards in ways that enabled fraud, theft, and misappropriation.

I was hardly surprised that some KBR workers improperly obtained and distributed ID badges to their Iraqi workers without having conducted the standard vetting or background checks on them. So these badges allowed them to access areas they would not have been ordinarily allowed to enter or escort non-badge holders they would not have ordinarily been not been allowed into these camp areas. This both endangered lives and facilitated thievery.

I asked SSGT Jordan to allow me to examine the ID badge issuance records to spot when these badges were illegally issued. We both checked and found the eight badges of the recently terminated IPBD employees were issued on 15 January 2006 by Michael Peters and Richard Kolivoski, both in the HVAC Department; Noe Morin, Electrical Department, Michael Jackson, Labor Department; a former KBR Power Gen Department employee named Fergus Johnson. All of them falsified ID badge applications to allow two IPBD workers access to the Camp Prosperity DFAC.

I then remembered that Michael Peters made a spontaneous and voluntary statement in the KBR Security Office back in mid-February about how he illegally obtained a Yellow-stripe CAC card for Mr. Safaa in exchange for three tanks of helium to fill the intelligence and observation balloons suspended over Baghdad. I spoke with SSGT Jordan further. He explained that KBR employees had requested all documents reflecting the loss of Security ID cards or badges be shredded to keep LOGCAP III contracting officers in the dark from learning about these losses. From everything I had seen so far that sounded accurate. He added that the U.S. Army did not care, they were not beholden to LOGCAP III civilians or KBR.

I brought all this to the attention of Anderson. I said a serous security breach happened in issuing these badges. He emphatically told me to "shred all the documents." I reminded him what had happened at the Mosul DFAC suicide bomber attack. Anderson told me again to either "toss out" or "trash" the documents. As he walked away he waved his hand in the air and said: "Get rid of the documents and we'll not discuss the matter again." I took everything to my room, typed up an IR and sent it with all the attached evidence to Jessie.

137. 07 MARCH 2006-CAMP PROSPERITY-ELECTRICAL DEPARTMENT OFFICE

Another IR: At about 07:15 I found the same situation as before with the Electrical Department door being wide open again with the same set of keys on the same center desk. I waited five minutes inside, but no one came. I closed, but did not secure, the door. At 07:45 I saw Donald Walker outside the Electrical Department office. I approached and told him about the same, unresolved situation as of almost one month ago. I asked him did he get the extra sets of keys made for his Department personnel to secure his office door. He stated he had not. I asked him why not and he said the 'key maker' for Camp Prosperity was the Billeting Department and their rules limited two keys to be made for every door and one of those keys must be retained by the Billeting Department. I stated that only applied to rooms/LSAs controlled by the Billeting Department and not to other office spaces. I asked him if he had spoken to the Camp Manager about his security/key problem. He stated he had not. I asked him why. He did not give me an answer but stared at me. I strongly directed him to immediately see the Camp Manager and finally resolve this pressing security issue. He gave me no indication he would resolve this issue.

In my opinion, due to Walker's lackadaisical, totally uninterested, attitude towards security in his department, I recommend some remedial action be taken to resolve the matter quickly and finally. Walker has shown by his actions he is indifferent towards security. I believe his whole department may share his poor attitude.

138. 10 MARCH 2006-CAMP PROSPERITY-MY OFFICE

The RTII was supposed to have been sent off to the outside 'corporate' investigators today. Back to waiting for something positive to happen - for a change. But I was not going to hold my breath on anything.

139. 11 MARCH 2006-CAMP PROSPERITY-NIGHT PATROL

Since I had already set-up the LN/TCN Badging Program in automatic. Everyone was doing everything they needed to do and make appointments. Right after Ken's arrival last month, R.C. decided to jump right in and hi-jack everything to replace me of the responsibilities. It was an extremely smart thing for R.C. to do. This did two things: 1) Ken would never check on R.C's activities as long as no one complained about the Badging Process. He could sleep all day, party hearty all night out in the "Green Zone" and then just before he went to bed he could check up on the daily busloads of LNs and TCNs going down to the BCC every morning at 08:00 and then pick-up the future appointments at the BCC before going back to sleep again.

Since I had no desire to see anyone in the Security Department I volunteered for 'Night Patrol Duty.' I would do walking tours of the whole camp starting at 18:00, then hit the sheets at 06:00. I would be up by the daily 14:30 Security Department meeting of everyone. It was a total waste of my time - all the investigations had been shut down hard and everything written was promptly trashed or ignored by Anderson, so there was little to talk about except Anderson and Tim 'inspecting' out-going vehicles of LNs for 'stolen' hand tools at closing time. That was all they did for the day to earn their pay except do nothing. Even though I had been specifically 'ordered off' from doing any more investigations, I ignored those idiotic orders. I kept on doing whatever investigations I could between the time of our daily Security Department meeting after I got up and when I reported for 'Night Duty' a few hours later.

I would keep a low profile and keep working 'Night Patrol' until I left on R&R in about 10 more days. The plan worked. No one bothered me at all.

140. 11 MARCH 2006-CAMP PROSPERITY-IPBD CO. MANAGERS' OFFICE

I passed the following statement from Mr. Ali and Mr. Khalid:

"I have been told by many of my IPBD Company workers that R.C. has been seen in 215 Apartments, even at night. And he has been seen in his shady truck (with black or tinted windows) with one LN female hugging and kissing outside of the 215 Apartments. And I have been told by many of my workers who live in the 215 Apartments that R.C. has gone to Mr. Raad (Plumbing Department Lead LN, now fired) having a party there, drinking liquor and having fun. And the people there have said they have seen him with female interpreters having fun, especially one who has a shaky reputation. One guy has always been fighting in the Laundry dept., named of Mr. Allaa, with the other workers. He was told to stop it by the other workers he said all he had to do is go and see R.C. to clear his name. One worker who was hit by this Mr. Allaa and Mr. Allaa made his mouth bleed and eyebrow bleed and he said that he would make the man he beat up to get fired because of the power of R.C. Mr. Allaa said hush your mouth or I will get Mr. R.C. and get you fired. Mr. Allaa is the cousin of Mr. Raad who also had R.C. in his apartment at 215 Apartments because they live close together, so if R.C. is not at a party with Mr. Radd and is at a party with Mr. Allaa. There have been numerous stories about Mr. R.C. have illegal sex with female LN interpreters some of it is unusual.

Six months ago there was an incident between R.C. and Mr. Robert Uzzle, Camp Prosperity's Chief of Services. The allegation was Mr. Uzzle touched or put his hand or hands on Mr. R.C., but Mr. Khalid was the witness and stated that Mr. Uzzle was not even close to R.C. during this incident and never touched him. However R.C. came to Mr. Khalid and put his arm around his shoulders and said to him in a low voice: "Why do you want to be a witness against me? I was touched by Mr. Uzzle and you saw that did not you?" And Mr. Khalid told R.C. that he did not see anything. Mr. R.C. became upset and since that day has always been hostile towards us for all matters.

According to my information R.C. came to KBR as a General Labor Forman and he was pushed here almost one year ago. After a while he became a security person. For a while he was the only security person here at Prosperity. We understand from a worker who has left that he found a female soldier and took her to his hooch. He heard this story many times from the workers. One of the workers told us he was hugging and kissing a white female soldier. He took her to his hooch and stayed there for almost two hours. And one day they found he took he took a Black female soldier until one day by we heard that R.C. had been punished and they brought him to Robert Uzzle's office as he was the Labor Brokers office and R.C. was sent back to Labor Foreman. And everyone refused to talk as it was Top Secret and the stayed as a General Labor Foreman. Then Roger, the Security Manager, was out of it, but he quit and went back to America, then someone new was hired and transferred R.C. back into Security. When R.C. came back and then everybody was talking about R.C. about his doing stuff and the LN female interpreters who working in Prosperity they caught him in his hooch with bad sex magazines and a female with him she was a soldier. This is all what I hear from my workers. And when the story of Troy (Williams) happened the workers said that R.C. cannot find Troy not because he is tracing him, because he has the same stuff in another apartment, because he had to capture Troy because Troy is doing the same stuff in the 215 Apartments as R.C. is doing."

141. 11 MARCH 2006-CAMP PROSPERITY (E-MAIL)

I tell J.T. the following topics in no order:

THE INVISIBLE MAN: I remain 'The Invisible Man.' Anderson just walked in here (the Little Internet/Phone Room) where I was checking my e-mails and did not say a word. He sat right next to me too. Was in here about 10 minutes and walked out without a peep. I did not make eye-contact as I was deep into my own stuff, but I knew it was him. Anyway-same-same, none of the Security people even acknowledge my existence. I am no longer a 'threat' to them, I do not exist. Whatever.

YOUR GOODIES: If I CAN ever get someone to give me a ride (I have had several 'appointments' set up with R.C. to take me over to the APO-all blown-off of course, what a surprise!) I will mail you your last 'war souvenirs.' If not then I will have to bring them with me when I move within (I assume) the next 24-48 hours or whenever. STILL want to stay down here (until September), just have Sandy Darden send me two more new Security Technicians and we can run it with the five of us. Figure the two new guys here now are salvageable, once the 'truth' gets explained to them and they get 'de-programmed' from their complete 'brain-washing' done by Anderson, R.C. and Tim about me/the real situation here. Just a suggestion. You said Jessie offered me any job within the D, E, F, G, H, I, etc. sites. I asked for the SF Camp and CVS: closed/no jobs. OK, no problem-then next option is 'stay here.' I did not do anything wrong, just clean out the Security scumballs which is what is needed anyway. Can do easy, no sweat, GI.

THE THREE BRASS MONKEYS: Still playing 'The Three Brass Monkeys' to the hilt ("Hear no evil see no evil, speak no evil"). Out of character for me, of course. But maybe it is my greatest role! DO NOTHING FOR A CHANGE! And I am doing absolutely completely nothing. Still on nights, do not say anything to anyone, do not see anything, do not hear anything.

OK-stay safe, keep me posted on events. Good luck and see you when I see you. Ciao, Chief Inspector Dreyfus.

Is Inspector CLOUSEAU coming down here from Dubai so I can confess that I was impersonating an 'Inspector' as opposed to an 'Investigator' and that I DID steal the 'Pink Panther' diamond? Just curious.

142. 11 MARCH 2006-CAMP PROSPERITY (E-MAIL)

I pass to J.T. the following topics in no order:

FRUSTRATION LEVELS: True, extremely high (however much less now that I have spoken to you a while ago). I was worried that the Supreme High Security Command HQs types were all 900-lb. gorillas. Not that they did anything they wanted, but that they slept all day, woke up for a few hours, yelled and screamed Tarzan-like sounds while running-around the jungle, pounding their chests with their fists, and then went right back to bed. End results: Nothing accomplished. However . . . . .

DEER-CAUGHT-IN-THE-HEADLIGHTS-LOOK HAS CHANGED: .... 30 seconds after I got off the phone with you I walked into the Ops Office to drop off a few extra things I had. Anderson was sitting in there slumped down. He has had this 'deer-caught-in-the-headlights' look. Today's look was classic. He looked totally stunned. I mean in real shock. Almost physical ill, like someone whacked him across the back of the head with a 2x4 (hard). So maybe it has 'started' - that is what Dan Stack has intimated. He said he got the call first thing this morning and it is 'rolling.' Saw Bobby when I came out of Ops. He looked 'happy.' And as for me? My name is . . . . .

MY NAME IS NOBODY: I am on nights, rarely (if ever) see anyone from Security and if I do they never speak to me anyway, get no reports from them, only report to Anderson what vehicles are left unopened and then locked when I do occasionally see him, just do my job, and make no other moves. I am just sitting on the bench and watching the game progress. However, just remember what it says on this movie tombstone: "Nobody was faster!" I continue to physically and verbally 'pack-out' to move elsewhere (this is for everyone's notice, especially Security's). Just to throw smoke clouds out in large amounts. Three Brass Monkeys.

Not much more-stay in touch. Stay safe (Genius at work up there!). Something tells me I will see you shortly.

143. 11 MARCH 2006-CAMP PROSPERITY-NIGHT PATROL

I am really at the end of my rope. But working the 'Night Shift' has helped to take a lot of the pressure off of me, allowed me to stretch my legs for 12 hours and given me time to think about everything. But I know this situation cannot go on forever.

144. 19 MARCH 2006-CAMP PROSPERITY-IPBD CO. MANAGERS' OFFICE

Haji Naji had previously written out a statement on all the stealing that had been going on in the Power Gen Department which the IPBD Managers had translated and transcribed. They handed the written statement to me today.

"We had generators here that belonged to KBR. We were told the story about those generators is that they were not important and replacement parts were too expensive, so they were taken outside of the "Green Zone" with items to be fixed, or so it appeared at the time. I remember asking Leith and Lynn about this several times and was told this is none of your business. Do not interfere with my business is what Lynn told me. I remember one time I told him that the part he needed was outside (in the Iraq market). He advised me to compromise my remembrance.

Summerville also tried to cause conflict between me and my co-workers. He defended their position and threatened of my removal from camp. He talks to me with lack of dignity and I try to avoid him. He treats me like I do not see what he sees and do not hear what he says and acts accordingly.

Once Summerville talked to me in an aggressive manner about distributing my work to the rest of the crew, how the work should be done, the sequence in which it should be done. Leith did whatever he said. Lynn would show preference to Leith, Riyadh, Tony, and he preferred them because they were involved in the theft. The rest of the workers are only there to work and be in the background.

I felt compelled to try and resolve that issue and tried to bring it up to Mr. Russ, Patrick, and Conrad. Nobody did anything and I think they were afraid of him. Some of them said they did not want to get involved because he is close friends with R.C.

In regard to military generators, we had only one here. Now there are two additional smaller units. A new 'chassis' (or engine) and electrical setup were deliberately sabotaged and transferred to KBR generators. Those parts as well as other part including gas (switches or pumps) are brought to the yard after having been pulled out of military generators. They then stay in the KBR work area for some time until they are forgotten. Then Lynn gets with someone with a DOD badge then gets with Leith, Riyadh, or Tony then they are escorted out of the gate where they take the parts and sell them individually or in bulk in the Iraq market, depending on the demand. They take things from generators, electrical, plumbers and the military. New and used cables are taken to the electric shop and cut down in size using the yellow table saw and carried out in vehicles by Leith or Troy (KBR).

Before Summerville handed the operation over to 'Red' Johnson he wanted to get rid of the whole crew. Leith spoke on behalf of Feras and Ghasan to keep them on site. There was an argument between me and Lynn before he flew out about an increase in my pay. Lynn told me right there that he could not give me a raise because KBR did not have the funds. I told him thank you and KBR.

One month after the hand-off to 'Red,' there was a theft of parts (Sylvan Dynamos) and other parts and equipment belonging to KBR that are used for work. Red did not do anything without consulting Summerville and Leith helped in this regard.

I then tried to talk to 'Red' about the military generators taken out of the work area. I tried to get him to include me, but 'Red' said the same thing Leith said which was no matter what I did there is no way I could take Leith's place even though I do speak better English. Summerville heard about my conversation from Leith and there after Riyadh, Tony, Ghasan and Feras bullied and talked bad to the rest of the crew.

Summerville treated the guys that helped him better. This even applied to the food he brought. He brought them more and better food and asked them to choose what they wanted. He would allow Leith to come in early so he could leave early and tend to their business. If there was a get together for lunch he would only invite the guys in their loop, invite them to good helpings, and they would eat together. You can ask Patrick, Conrad, and Mr. Russ about that.

After 'Red' and Sam Simpson came, Leith and Summerville tried to convince Simpson of letting them bring three generators until they can move them out. He could not sway Sam, so their business was at a stand-still. They wanted to hide them there until they could sneak them out and sell them in the market.

Summerville tried to get rid of Simpson by causing him problems after that. He did this by damaging one part in the generator at Tower Three and the seals inside another generator at the Investigation Headquarters.

When Lynn made it back from the airport he set up a meeting with me and Manuel and talked in an aggressive manner with us. I tried to explain some of the problems I was running in to and he would not listen and told me to take a vacation without pay. I asked, "What am I going to do with time off?" He told me to do whatever I want to with it. I replied, "I will take the days off, but I will address another problem with you when I come back until it is resolved."

I saw some empty oil barrels with Leith, and he started asking me about the number of barrels needed to supply a generator for a given time. I told him I did not know what the amounts are. I do not know what amount was taken.

On Thursday 21 February 2006 Mr. Khalid came and took Leith with him. When we saw that we assumed termination of our contracts was in the works. When Leith came back with Riyadh behind him he told the rest of us to go to the security office and that they only want to know about the Sylvan-Dynamo. When they took our badges, Leith, Riyadh, and Ghasan were scared that they may have been caught.

Riyadh said I need someone to "raise my leg" (implying he needed help). Leith was red and his expression gave him away. They were both waiting to be escorted out to the gate.

The next day, the calls began, and Riyadh and I talked on the phone (around that time Tony left work around Noon). Riyadh said he would not be returning to work and said: "Ahmad quit the job and do not come back. If you come back they will lock you up." I told him: "You know I did nothing wrong". He said it does not matter and that Lynn called Leith and told him the same thing. Lynn told him not to worry and that in a week he would bring us back and do not worry about what was said or the security guy."

145. 20 MARCH 2006-CAMP PROSPERITY (E-MAIL)

I say to J.T. thanks for the encouraging news. Joe at DCMA? Why didn't I think of that! (Know why? Because I am a 'TEAM PLAYER!' Ha, ha!) Guess where my first stop will be after schmoozing with Bobby to re-establish our 'muy sympatico-ness'? Straight down to Joe's office for a little 'consultation'/'advice' with our 'Padrone.' See what happens. It is my pleasure as the Iraqis say. I can also go to the 'client' and schmooze as well (not sure who to go to yet with the Army-someone with 'gravitas'), ditto to the USAF SF/IZ Police, if needed. Whatever it takes. I had put 12 bad guys on the radar scope for 'shoot-down-in-flames' and seven more bad guys for 'force-downs' (shoot up their engines/wings, make them crash, etc.), not thieves per say, but guys like Ron Battle who got a terminal case of diarrhea-of-the-mouth to Mr. Khalid or Nick the Plumber who said: "Let the Iraqis steal @#USD$%^&*! everything, I don't care." Some hard HR slap-downs/write-ups/eventual resignations. We will see. I had four of the 19 gone on my scorecard (including Lynn Summerville if he jumped and maybe not R.C., I assume he did not move yet either-then three out of 19). OK - you may see me earlier then 04 April, maybe time to head back to Dodge City for the titanic struggle. Not desire, but cash flow - plus if I am out on LWOP somewhere, then I am 'losing' money, not making it. My batteries are about to charged up once I am in Thailand. My strategy will not change on my return, head right back to Mids. See what happens. Thanks again. See you when I see you. Stay in the bunker.

146. 20 MARCH 2006-CAMP PROSPERITY (E-MAIL)

I respond to J.T. by saying what a surprise! Tim and Anderson back-stabbed Jessie on the transfers? Anderson finally has an area big enough that almost holds his ego: The "Green Zone." And he has a sycophant to constant feed his massive ego - Tim. For them to lose all that easily is not going to happen without their furiously struggling to fight tooth and nail to prevent that. Tim loses his 'Sugar Daddy' and Anderson's ego is hard stuffed back into the little confines of a much smaller place. That is going to hurt them on both counts. What gets me here is Jessie obviously thought all the little participants of this chessboard game were going to meekly just allow him to be moved around as 'pawns.' No way, Jose. At least I have pure motives here in trying to make the organization better. If I thought for one minute by going over to CVS would help make things better in the organization, sure - why not? I have pride in what I do, and I am actually a 'Team Player' in spite of some reports. But Jessie must think I am totally brain-damaged that I was buying into all of this on being moved to CVS. The best thing I can do for the organization is to get back to Camp Prosperity and sweep the rest of the scum off the streets THEN move to CVS/wherever. Cannot do that on vacation buried in a useless back-water job on nights at CVS. And - anyway - I was having so much fun at Camp Prosperity. I still do not appreciate how it was done or the now many lies that went along with it. Not done professionally. Good intention overall, bad execution.

OK-enough of this goofiness. Thanks again for the update and I would mucho appreciate any new posts as they come up. I am sure you cannot even keep up with the changes now as the 'death struggle' for control of Security continues unabated. I actually just hope Jessie finally wins.

See you when I see you. Stay in the bunker. Good move (and smart too) on keeping a low profile.

147. 20 MARCH 2006-CAMP PROSPERITY (E-MAIL)

I tell J. T. I am on it. Joe is still very 'hot' about this a/c investigation and where it has been (not far apparently except what we have done) and where it is going (only where we push it). You and I both know he wants SOMEONE to do SOMETHING about the mess and no one (outside of you and me) has expressed the slightest interest in lifting a finger, maybe the USAF SF/IZ Police. So we have a strong ally in Joe. Not a problemo, I will pass him (and Bobby) the report and ask him for his assistance to put this back to Jene Harper with a recommendation. Didn't Jessie put in the formal request with the USAF Analysis and Information Section to get a copy of the final USAF Report on the results of Russell Hill off-loaded the a/c units into the taxi? I already know the answer anyway - all requests have been quashed. Jessie did not have the time or was told not to (or more probably even if he did have time it will take only one-two years for them to crank out a scrubbed unclassified copy of the damn thing). Typical USAF. OK-next week I am on it. One small advantage of being back at Camp Prosperity is that people do not want to touch badging (they consider it as hot as nuclear waste), then they will leave me along as long as I stay off the radar scope. So I can get into the U.S. Embassy for 'consultations' as needed. This could work to our advantage.

I think Abraham Lincoln once said that all the evil people in the world need to get away with bad stuff is for the good people to remain silent. Nnnnaaaaaaaaaaaa! But I will put a sock on it for the greater, long-term need. I have to keep a low-profile now, not that I minded keeping a high-profile against the local bad guys, but it is really bad when you have to keep a low-profile from getting shit-canned from your evil 'superiors' for doing your job. Whatever. See you when I see you. Stay in the bunker, we will have to ride it out.

148. 20 MARCH 2006-CAMP PROSPERITY-MY OFFICE

Before I was dropped off at the Rhino pick-up point for my well-deserved R&R I took one more look again at everything I had accumulated as far as the investigations were concerned. Then something odd caught my eye. I doubled checked all the statements again R.C. has used a completely different six-digit KBR employee number on every statement he ever made on the IRs. Not one of them was a duplicate. R.C. - that slimy, corrupt bastard. I wondered if he was even officially a KBR employee at all, or he was just snuck into Iraq by his 'Godfather' or 'Sugar Daddy,' Remo Butler. Maybe R.C. was wanted back in the U.S. by the police or authorities for who knows what? What better place to hide out on the lam than in the Big War Zone? Especially when the person who wielded the real power in Iraq and Kuwait fended off every effort to get R.C. fired. I knew he had been closely protected from talking to the IPBD Managers and R.C.'s conversation with Remo Butler about "taking care of me" last month after I had interviewed another of Butler's favorite little 'pets,' Lynn Summerville, another serial criminal on the loose inside of Iraq.

In one meeting I had in Bobby's office earlier in the month. He told me that R.C. had worked for him at another base somewhere in Iraq some time ago. Bobby said he had plenty of evidence to fire him on the spot for countless illegal activities, but Remo Butler had swooped in, got that action squashed then had him transferred to another base out of harm's way. The impression I got from Bobby that R.C. was another serial criminal. Bobby was very frustrated to be thwarted this way. That R.C. had caused nothing but serious trouble for Bobby and was a low-life to boot. Bobby also said he was not happy that R.C. was already here at Camp Prosperity when he was transferred in last year. But with Butler's backing, R.C. was completely invulnerable. I just shook my head in disgust and commiserated with Bobby on the R.C. problem. The best I had hoped for was to have him transferred elsewhere and out of my hair along with Tim. They both had jumped right into bed with Anderson and gave him their full support. It was a mutually incestuous relationship among the three of them.

149. 21 MARCH 2006-CAMP VICTORY-NORTH-KBR SECURITY OFFICE

I sat with J.T. in the Security Office before I had to go to BTC, catch the bus to go to BIAP for my flight to Dubai and then Bangkok on R&R. As always, virtually everyone else in Security was out running around with their hair on fire doing nothing to earn their high salaries. So I knew we would remain undisturbed. We spoke of the past and the future. Every time we got together we talked about the book I would write. He would help me out by saving all the e-mails, investigator reports, photographs, witness statements and whatever else we could. No time line was set to do the book. I said I had vague notions about suing KBR for massive high crimes and misdemeanors or allowing them to happen. But I added finding a law firm meant I needed deep pockets to pay for their services and with no guarantee I would win. No law firm was going to do 'pro bono' work on this lawsuit. I was sure KBR had massed legions (or whole armies) of lawyers to fight off every legal attack and lawsuit. They had much more firepower than I could ever hope to muster. I was not sure what I was going to do about KBR, but all I had was a book on this sordid saga. J.T. said he would look forward to reading what I was going to write as he liked my unique 'style' of writing with lots of colorful phrases and insightful similes. I thanked him.

J.T. confirmed everything I had found out: there was massive stealing going on all throughout the "Green Zone" and all over Iraq at every single base. And nothing was being done about it. Not only in virtually every department at Camp Prosperity, but throughout the whole country. I had asked Jessie Rich what our next move was. He said he would submit another RTII. This was a form that went from KBR Security to the outside contracted professional 'corporate' investigators sitting in some Dubai fancy, plushy upholstered high rise office building, all sitting fat, dumb and happy. The plan was for them to come in and take over everything from us since we were not 'qualified' to handle such weighty matters such as massive stealing and other major crimes like rape, armed robbery, major drug or alcohol distribution and the like. Jessie informed us he would submit the RTII to the High Supreme Security Command HQs the next day. He said the orders would be to stand down, do nothing, stop all our investigations, and wait for the 'corporate' investigators to arrive. We were finally done. But I could not relax.

I finally asked J.T., in some exasperation: "Who-in-the-hell hired all these incompetent security people?" J.T. had called some of them, more than a few times, "street thugs." He explained that Remo Butler, who is Black, had hired some of his 'Bro's' - R.C., 'Tony' Bryant and his son, plus Summerville to specifically name four of them that we knew about. All of them were turning out to be criminal predators, street hustlers, small-time losers, and petty hard-core thieves with no doubt long rap sheets from what I had seen so far of them. A classroom of kindergarteners would have been more effective as security troops than the motley crew we had with rare exceptions.

Then it suddenly all clicked together. The one-sided conversation with Frank Russell I had had the previous year, when he verbally scaled me to death over asking a simple question about my old work buddy's resume for Security, made perfect sense now. Someone very high up was ONLY hand-picking almost overwhelmingly, completely incompetent Security people way outside of KBR HR's control to work in Iraq. It was all deliberately done. In fact, there were obviously more than a number of pure predatory criminals on the payroll, Summerville, R.C., and doubtless more than a few others, that Remo Butler was protecting.

"Remo Butler," he replied.

Remo Butler. DPM for Iraq and PM for Kuwait. Butler held all the real power for all practical purposes in both countries. He was virtually autonomous. J.T. explained he was a retired U.S. Army SF Brigadier General (BGEN) and a reputedly widely-known, even notorious, self-promoter. I did not doubt that statement for a second. I thought then why would Remo Butler hire almost totally moronic, completely incompetent idiots, and predatory criminals to be in KBR Security? Brain-damaged, drunken circus clowns were more competent than almost all the people we had in Security. That absolutely made no sense. So finally I asked:

"Then who-in-the-hell hired Remo Butler?" I asked.

"Donald Rumsfeld."

Donald Rumsfeld, the Secretary of Defense. This was not looking good-at all.

"Then who-in-the-hell hired Donald Rumsfeld?"

"Dick Cheney."

Dick Cheney. Vice-President of the United States and hand-picked running mate of President George W. Bush. He set off all the events into motion in Iraq. Cheney was also the former President of Halliburton, corporate parent of KBR. He was widely known to have millions of shares of KBR or Halliburton stock. Undoubtedly Rumsfeld has the same stake too. But neither of them ever had to do a financial disclosure for U.S. government service. Every other elected official has to do so; they were strangely exempt from the requirement. You could not slide the sharpest, hardest, thinnest razor blade between Cheney and Rumsfeld. They were the closest, absolutely tightest of friends, virtually Siamese twins. Cheney was constantly hard-wired into

Halliburton and thus all activities of KBR and especially in Iraq. He knew exactly what was going on here in Iraq as did Rumsfeld-then this whole scenario was all obviously rigged by them from the get-go. The whole thing was a set-up, a monstrous scam to steal hundreds of billions of dollars while KBR Security either looked the other way, or helped the thieves load their trucks with loot and waved them bye-bye out the main gate. That meant I was literally a dead man if they set up this whole massive, unbelievable scam.

Then we only had one chance and one chance only. A miracle. That the outside professional 'corporate' investigators, sitting fat, dumb and happy down in Dubai, would come in here and totally rip the whole place apart. The odds were impossibly long on us succeeding. All we could do now is wait. And I was going out on a very badly needed, very well-deserved R&R to Thailand today.

Author's Biography

Leonard Henry Le Blanc III is the Dean and Vice-President of Institutional Advancement for the American University Sovereign Nations (AUSN), a new, on-line, de-colonized institution of higher education with an international campus. He is also the General Manager of SEATE Services, Prop., a firm that provides Arabic-English translation services, sells new and used books and sells and distributes the IRAQ COMMITMENT MEDAL and official award certificates from the Iraqi Government for all military members and civilian workers who were in Iraq during Gulf War II.

He has earned a B.S., Geography, Kansas State University (1973); M.A., Management. Webster University (1989); B.A., History, The University of the State of New York (1991); B.S., Individualized Studies, Charter Oak State College (2003); M.A., International Relations, Webster University (2012); M.S., Bioethics & Global Public Health, The American University of Sovereign Nations (AUSN) (2016); Ph.D., Bioethics & Global Public Health, The American University of Sovereign Nations (AUSN) (2017); M.S., Technology and Sustainability, The American University of Sovereign Nations (AUSN) (2019); and M.S., Public Health, The American University of Sovereign Nations (AUSN) (2020).

He has written four books about deep U.S. government corruption and massive thievery along with several U.S. defense contractor also involved in collusion or participation together; has lived and worked in Japan, Thailand, Iraq, Nigeria, Bosnia, Kuwait and Afghanistan for over 25 years total. He has also written academic and historical articles for various publications and journals; has been a writer and story contributor for TIME Magazine; has been a freelance reporter for THE BANGKOK POST, and an English Language Consultant to THE NATION MEDIA GROUP (Thailand); he was also the Literary Editor of the PATTAYA TRADER MAGAZINE (Thailand) and has been a Contributing Editor of EXPAT LIFE IN THAILAND Magazine.

He retired from the U.S. Naval Reserves in 2000 after more than 26 years of combined active and reserve service. He has visited or lived in 72 countries. He and his wife Lena and two children, Leonard IV and Lujane Jasmin currently live in Bangkok, Thailand.

Leonard H. Le Blanc III
JUSMAGTHAI
P. O. Box R3521
APO AP 96546-5000
12 April 2015

The Hon. Eric H. Holder, Jr.
The Attorney General
Department of Justice
950 Pennsylvania Ave., NW
Washington, DC 20530-0001

Dear Secretary Holder-

This letter will serve as a formal request for an investigation into the lack of action by the Department of Justice (DOJ) on the handling (or mishandling) of my federal whistle-blower (FWB) lawsuits against two notorious US defense contractors, namely Kellogg, Brown & Root Services, Inc. (KBR) and Combat Support Associates, Ltd. (CSA). These firms were deliberately responsible for massive stealing, fraud, misappropriation, destruction of records, double, triple and even quadruple billing plus numerous other high crimes and misdemeanors against the US government before and during Gulf War II (GWII).

In summary, I filed a FWB lawsuit against CSA (Atch. 1) on 12 December 2006. After numerous prods and various legal actions by my law firm, Grayson & Kubli, DOJ eventually authorized an investigation which commenced on or about January 2009. The Lead Investigator, Mr. Art Coulter, was assigned to the case. Mr. Coulter passed occasional status reports along to my lawyer, Mr. Cliff Holmes, Esq., confirming what I had stated in my FWB lawsuit; i.e., that CSA was deeply involved in massive fraud, chicanery and thievery. In fact, the DOJ investigators reported they found overwhelming evidence, including interviewing two ladies who worked for CSA, Ltd., in a secret, locked room at Camp Doha, Kuwait hand-writing bogus time sheets for "ghost" CSA employees so CSA could collect on their "salaries". Eventually the case was partially unsealed for CSA's commentary. However, Mr. Coulter continually declined every offer from Mr. Holmes to personally interview me which I thought was very strange.

Sometime around June 2010 Mr. Holmes met with Mr. Coulter at his office with the other DOJ investigators. According to Mr. Holmes, Mr. Coulter repudiated every single piece of evidence his team had uncovered. Mr. Holmes was incredulous. He asked Mr. Coulter what happened and why. Mr. Coulter stated that "Department of Defense (DOD) officials requested DOJ drop its investigation into CSA's activities as they might need to use CSA's services again in the future." Mr. Coulter stated DOJ would decline to intervene in the matter.

Not only is this totally preposterous and unprofessional it is also completely negligent and most definitely a criminal collusion on the part of Mr. Coulter and some other slimy confederates at DOD. The FWB lawsuit then foundered and was dismissed without prejudice by the federal district court as no other law firm would case without DOJ's intervention.

Immediately after the CSA lawsuit was dismissed I filed a formal request for an investigation with DODIG into CSA's criminal activities. Nothing has been done to date. No one contacted me for an interview, nor has DODIG lifted a single finger to investigate. Obviously the same people at DODIG are still blocking any investigation into CSA.

My FWB lawsuit against KBR was filed on 17 June 2009. (Atch. 2). From periodic reports DOJ investigators said they also found massive fraud and thievery by KBR in Iraq. Eventually the case was partially and then fully unsealed by the court for KBR's comment. Over the years several Lead Investigators pled for more time to investigate until the federal court grew exasperated by the repeated requests for extension and the case was ultimately dismissed without prejudice. DOJ neither confirmed nor denied they were intervening, but my lawyer was informed by DOJ they would file an administrative action in federal district court to demand KBR release records proving the massive fraud. Supposedly, unconfirmed reports stated DOJ discussed a settlement. That was back in November 2013. Nothing has happened since that date. The lawsuit remains stalled.

Normally a letter such as this would immediately go into the proverbial 'rotating file' or be 'lost' behind the radiator. However, there is one small problem here. Back in August 2013 an Investigative Reporter, a Mr. Billy Kenber, on assignment to the WASHINGTON POST (WP) newspaper (he sat next to Bob Woodward in the newsroom; was on a one-year Fellowship from the TIMES OF LONDON), requested we do a telephonic interview about a certain company, namely CSA, and my inert FWB lawsuit. I am not sure who or what led him to the topic, but our interview was long and intensive including details of the criminal actions of Mr. Coulter and the unsavory characters over at DOD. He also interviewed other former CSA employees from what I heard through back-channels. We did not discuss the KBR case as it remained under confidentiality at the time.

When the CSA story finally hits the front page at the WP one of these fine days (after they receive all the multiple FOIA requests) I am positive the White House will have someone important standing at the brace in front of the President Obama's desk and being asked two important questions: "What did DOJ know? And "When did DOJ know it?" This letter concisely answers both questions.

I am sure there will be Pulitzer Prizes again for whatever investigative reporter that fields these FWB lawsuits as they will be explosive, headline-banner exposés (who already have at least one of them): Seymour Hersh (NY TIMES), Mark Thompson (TIME Magazine), Bob Woodward (WP), etc.

Like Yogi Berra is always fond of saying: "It's Abu Ghraib/My Lai/Bernie Madoff déjà vu all over again." The US government has long known about all these notorious atrocities from other stalwart whistleblowers but had chosen to ignore them until they actually got into the news. The CSA and KBR cases are the exact same scenario.

This matter can go only one of two ways. First - DOJ will re-activate both lawsuits by declaring they will intervene in the lawsuits so justice can finally be done. Or second - the matter will remain permanently buried behind the radiator courtesy of Mr. Coulter and the coterie of other low-ranking perps inside DOJ and the cabal of high-ranking perps over at DOD. Then the "Department of Justice" will become an oxymoron with no "justice" being served in either case.

I feel it is as unconscionable as it is inconceivable that DOJ will allow such massive stealing of the government's money on such a titanic scale to go unpunished or even unchallenged unless there is collusion or incompetence. I trust neither is true. Unless DOJ has the same feelings that one law firm out in San Francisco expressed to me when they were exploring taking over the case from the first law firm I employed. They ultimately declined because they simply said they were "very afraid" of KBR and its fanatic, rabid, pit-bull defensive tactics against all forms of litigation.

I also trust it is not a lack of intestinal fortitude on the part of DOJ for its inexplicable inaction to expeditiously move forward on these cases.

However, I am also mystified with other similar, but lesser cases that have gotten great international attention. GEN Petraeus sends his "girlfriend" some cute "love e-mails" and hordes of DODIG investigators come out of the woodwork to investigate these little "mash notes" with the attending titanic 24/7 news coverage. Conversely Hillary Clinton sends her husband Bill invitations for lunch using her private e-mails from her DOS office and masses of DOS investigators plow through them looking for clues on the Benghazi fiasco with press reporters swarming all over the front page story.

So it is most curious CSA and KBR brazenly steals multi-billions of dollars from the US government and neither DOJ nor the national press makes a single mention of this fact. The national press's reasons I can understand. They are chasing the hottest story of the moment – what Kim Kardashian's little sister's maid's best friend's dog had for breakfast this morning – highly important news. Yet KBR's and CSA's galactic-sized thievery goes unmentioned and unpunished. This is unfathomable. If DOJ can form a joint government task force to combat trade in world-wide illegal animal parts (USD$20 billion/year) then they can chase KBR and CSA (roughly the same amount was stolen by them).

Like Sherlock Holmes and THE HOUND OF THE BASKERVILLES, the monstrous dog that did not bark at midnight when someone was murdered inside the home he was guarding, there is a mystery here. Both KBR and CSA remain unpunished in spite of the overwhelming evidence of guilt. The only conclusion can be – Elementary, my dear Watson – collusion between nefarious, odious DOD and DOJ officials to prevent justice from finally being served.

This is the epitome of irony. Where does someone go to get real justice when some sleazy people in the DOJ (and DOD) are part of the effort to block that justice? It is not that CSA and KBR remain uninvestigated. In fact both firms have been repeatedly investigated for over a decade – the FBI, US Army Contracts Command, DODIG, US Army Criminal Investigation Division, etc. Nothing has happened to either firm for well over a decade. What is the real mystery answer here? Someone, or some people, high up in the US government are blocking all these investigations.

      I can only hope that I will one day see both FWB lawsuits re-activated and the wheels of jurisprudence to grind fine and on now quickly to an ultimate successful conclusion of justice finally being done and all the criminals punished.

Best regards,

LEONARD H. LE BLANC III

CC: Victor Kubli, Esq., P.C., SECDEF, Robin C. Ashton
       File.

U. S. Department of Justice

Civil Division

Office of the Assistant Attorney General   Washington, D.C. 20530

FEB - 5 2018

Mr. Leonard H. Le Blanc III
1401 College Avenue
Apt. C107
Manhattan, KS 66502

Dear Mr. Le Blanc:

This is in response to your March 1, 2017 request to Senator Jerry Moran for assistance arranging a meeting with Attorney General Sessions concerning two qui tam actions you filed under the False Claims Act (FCA). Your inquiry was forwarded to my office for a response. In your request to Senator Moran, you state that your lawsuits are "stalled" because all federal whistleblower lawsuits have been "shut down by DOJ." This understanding is incorrect. As discussed below, although the government declined to intervene in your actions, you had the opportunity to pursue them yourself, but elected not to do so.

The FCA authorizes a private person, commonly referred to as "relator," to file a suit on behalf of the United States alleging fraud or false claims against those who have wrongly claimed money or property from the U.S. Government. The FCA allows the United States to investigate the allegations, and to make a decision whether it will intervene and take over the litigation. If the United States decides not to intervene, the FCA allows the relator to litigate the case on his own. 31 U.S.C. § 3730(c)(3) ("If the Government elects not to proceed with the action, the person who initiated the action shall have the right to conduct the action.").

Here, after conducting an investigation, the United States exercised its discretion not to intervene in your lawsuits. *See U.S. ex rel. LeBlanc v. Combat Support Associates Joint Venture ("CSA") et al.*, No. CV06-7862 JSL (JWJx) (C.D.Cal.) and *U.S. ex rel. LeBlanc v. Halliburton, Co.*, No. 1:09-cv-01113 (D.D.C.). As noted, you then had the opportunity to pursue the cases on your own. Indeed, the courts in both cases issued orders notifying you, through your attorneys, of your option to proceed with the litigation by serving the complaints on the defendants. In neither case, however, did your attorneys serve the complaints. In July 2011, the court in the *CSA* action directed that by November 1, 2011, you either serve the complaint or otherwise explain in writing why the case should remain open. On November 7, 2011, after you did not respond to the court's order, the court dismissed the case. In your case against Halliburton, your lawyer, on your behalf, voluntarily dismissed the case on July 15, 2014. I have attached the pertinent orders and notices in each case.

Mr. Leonard H. Le Blanc III
Page 2

As your cases were dismissed long ago either voluntarily or as a result of inaction on your part, you no longer have any FCA cases pending in any federal court. For these reasons, we do not believe a meeting with the Attorney General about these cases would be fruitful at this point. We hope this response was helpful.

                          Regards,

                          Chad A. Readler
                          Acting Assistant Attorney General

Enclosures

JS - 6

UNITED STATES DISTRICT COURT

CENTRAL DISTRICT OF CALIFORNIA

UNITED STATES OF AMERICA ex rel. LEONARD H. LE BLANC III., Plaintiffs, v. COMBAT SUPPORT ASSOCIATES JOINT VENTURE; et al., Defendants.	Case No. CV 06-07862 DDP (JWJx) **ORDER OF DISMISSAL**

THE COURT having ordered the Plaintiff to show cause in writing, not later than November 1, 2011, why this action should not be dismissed for lack of prosecution and Plaintiff having failed to respond,

THE COURT ORDERS that this action be, and hereby is, dismissed without prejudice for lack of prosecution and for failure to comply with the orders of the Court, pursuant to Federal Rule of Civil Procedure 41(b).

The Clerk shall mail, FAX or E:mail a copy of this Order to all counsel.

Dated: November 7, 2011

DEAN D. PREGERSON
United States District Judge

cc: Generic Civil AUSA

UNITED STATES DISTRICT COURT
CENTRAL DISTRICT OF CALIFORNIA
CIVIL MINUTES -- GENERAL

Case No.   CV 06-07862 DDP (JWJx)   Date   July 1, 2011

Title   UNITED STATES OF AMERICA ex rel. LEONARD H. LE BLANC III. -V- COMBAT SUPPORT ASSOCIATES JOINT VENTURE; COMBAT SUPPORT ASSOCIATES, LIMITED; AECOM GOVERNMENT SERVICES, INC.; RESEARCH AND ANALYSIS MAINTENANCE, INC.; AND SMI INTERNATIONAL CORP.

Present: The Honorable   DEAN D. PREGERSON, U.S. DISTRICT JUDGE

John A. Chambers	None Present	N/A
Deputy Clerk	Court Reporter / Recorder	Tape No.

Attorneys Present for Plaintiffs: Attorneys Present for Defendants:

NO APPEARANCE   NO APPEARANCE

Proceedings:

MINUTE ORDER (IN CHAMBERS)
ORDER TO SHOW CAUSE RE DISMISSAL FOR LACK OF PROSECUTION

Plaintiff(s) is ordered to show cause in writing no later than November 1, 2011 why this action should not be dismissed for lack of prosecution.

The Court will consider the filing of the following, as an appropriate response to this OSC, on or before the above date:

- Proof of service of summons and complaint.

In accordance with Rule 78 of the Federal Rules of Civil Procedure and Local Rule 7-15, no oral argument on this Order to Show Cause will be heard unless ordered by the Court. The Order will stand submitted upon the filing of the response to the Order to Show Cause. Failure to respond to the Court's Order may result in the dismissal of the action.

:   N/A

Initials of Preparer   JAC

Leonard H. Le Blanc III
2165 Prairie Glen Place
Manhattan, KS 66502-4779 USA
15 February 2018

Mr. Chad A. Readler
Acting Assistant Attorney General, Department of Justice, OAAG,
Civil Division, Room 3141, 950 Pennsylvania Ave., NW
Washington, DC 20530-0001

Dear Mr. Readler -

This is in response to your welcome letter dated 05 February 2018. Please note my new address as your letter went to my previous residence. It would take a very long book to respond to the many points you raised in your letter about my now dismissed federal whistleblower lawsuit against KBR. Fortunately, I AM writing a book about it - two books in fact. I have two publishers lined-up willing to print the books and 3 printers if I wanted to self-publish the works.

I wanted to share a brief scene, a vignette, in the book (as Tom Wolfe always like to in his books) to illuminate the whole matter in contrast. My lawyer, Mr. Victor Kubli, arranged a meeting with your attorneys, specifically Beverly Russell and several others since he knew I was returning to the U.S. on one of my rare appearances here. We met in their office in about April/May 2010 prior to my departure for training as a US Army GS-13 civilian and later deployment to Afghanistan. I had just flown in from Thailand where I have lived.

At the meeting was Ms. Russell and several other DOJ attorneys. They introduced us to two young "investigators" working on my KBR lawsuit. I started right in on my narrative: how there was a titanic theft ring run by a certain BGEN Remo Butler, USA, who was KBR's Deputy Country Manager for all Iraq bases. He, in turn, was directly hired by a certain nasty piece-of-work named Donald Rumsfeld. Who was Donald Rumsfeld's closest, bestest, tightest friend in the whole universe? A former President of Halliburton, the

KBR parent, name of Dick Cheney. I also detailed how many KBR personnel and their legions of Iraqi minions (or workers) were selling the goods outside the bases to a 100,000-man national "Theft Ring" controlled by an Iraqi mater criminal called "The Hausaman." This massive thievery was going on ALL military/KBR bases inside of Iraq. He, in turn, gave some of the proceeds to the insurgents to fund their operations, buy weapons, recruit other insurgents, etc. Additionally, KBR and Iraqis were scouring any scrap of aluminum they could find to send to the Iranian Revolutionary Guards to make EFPs - Explosive Formed Projectiles - that could blast through any armor the U.S. had.

I also detailed how KBR Security personnel were all hand-picked by Butler to be hired. This was all done outside of normal KBR HR procedures. (Still not sure why I got hired on.) But the key thing here was there were not enough of them. Many small bases in Iraq had NO security personnel, and even the major bases had a few. In the Green Zone there were two (2) people when I arrived in February 2006. But the few KBR security people in Iraq were either grossly incompetent, had no security experience at all or, as we later were to find out, had criminal records. But the higher up you went in KBR Security you went the stupider people became.

I then detailed how the people in KBR Security, including all my close co-workers (except for two men) plus many other non-KBR security personnel blocked, interfered with, hindered or hampered my investigations. I explained how whole container-loads of goods were flying out the gate around the clock - everything was disappearing - and had been from all reports from the start of GWII. No investigations were done except in a cursory manner. But I had accumulated photos, investigation reports, witness statements, e-mails, documentary evidence, etc. detailing everything. A formal written request was sent by my boss to outside KBR-contracted "Corporate Investigators" sitting in the UAE to come and investigate the matter. No one ever came' no one ever would. All investigations remained shut down long after I had departed Iraq.

I detailed how once I connected all these dots together in late March 2006 tying Butler-Cheney-Rumsfeld- "The Hausman"-the insurgents-KBR thieves, etc., three things happened in quick succession: 1) Remo Butler SHUT DOWN ALL INVESTIGATIONS IN IRAQ EFFECTIVE IMMEDIATELY. Not even a lost ID badge/CAC card could be investigated. KBR Security was totally emasculated; 2) I was quickly booted out of KBR Security (no reason tendered) and 3) Remo Butler abruptly quit. (What is wrong with this picture?)

I talked for perhaps five (5) hours. No questions. We had blown past lunch. No one spoke a word. In fact, everyone looked as if they were bored to tears (excuse me, to death). Finally, one of the investigators (he looked like he was about 18-years-old) asked me a question: "Do you know what happened to the Phi-Jamma-Slamma-Frizzle-Frazzle-Left-Right-Wing-Nut-Agitator that was at Camp Swampy, Anbar Province, Iraq at 3:00AM on the morning of Friday, July 10, 2005 in the F-100 locked storeroom on the upper shelf, left-hand side with dust on it?"

"Hello!" I replied. "I was in KBR Security, not Supply. How in the hell am I supposed to have that information? It's impossible!" Two more similar questions followed. I repeated what I had said. We broke from the meeting. Finally, on the way out, Beverly Russell said the investigators were having a very hard time finding internal e-mails of people who worked for KBR. I said that is like saying Saudi Arabia has no sand. KBR was extremely fanatic about keeping e-mails. I said I will pull off e-mail addresses from a weekly general safety newsletter e-mail that went out to like 150 people in the Green Zone in Baghdad and send it to you. I did. Then after several more years the lawsuit was dismissed for LACK OF PROSECUTION in the part of DOJ after the court grew completely exasperated with the endless delays by DOJ that they couldn't find enough evidence to go forward. (What's wrong with this picture?)

Flash forward to late last year. I requested a FOIA from DCIS to see if anything was done on my lawsuit investigations through DCIS. One redacted investigator report came in with the batch. The "investigators at the 2010 KBR meeting at DOJ were not from DOJ but DCIS. They basically stated: "Yah, we met with this Le Blanc guy for a few minutes. He denied everything, denied he had any evidence, denied knowing any facts, denied he knew what was stolen or when or couldn't even answer a single one of our questions, he knew nothing. We talked to a few other people around here and there and everyone denied that anything could have been stolen in Iraq. They all said that government procurement or contracts management people had the tightest lid on everything there. They said that it was totally impossible to have had anything stolen anything in Iraq at any time. We are recommending you close the case. Le Blanc also said he didn't even know why he filed the federal whistleblower lawsuit in the first place"

I also did a FOIA to DOJ on my federal whistleblower lawsuit also last year. Guess what came in? ONLY the 220 pages I sent, or my lawyer sent to DOJ, plus the lawsuit and some court records. There wasn't a scrap of evidence that DOJ EVER DID ANY INVESTIGATION TO START WITH FROM DAY ONE ON MY KBR LAWSUIT. (What's wrong with this picture?)

I will make sure you receive a very prominent mention in my book (I know the author very well). I have many dozens of examples similar to the one above. I am sure it will make fascinating reading for all.

Regards,

LEONARD H. LE BLANC III
LCDR   USNR (Ret.)

Leonard H. Le Blanc III
2165 Prairie Glen Place
Manhattan, KS 66502-4779 USA
16 February 2018

Mr. Chad A. Readler
Acting Assistant Attorney General, Department of Justice, OAAG
Civil Division, Room 3141, 950 Pennsylvania Ave., NW
Washington, DC 20530-0001

Dear Mr. Readler -

I am compelled to do a follow-up answer to your most welcome letter of 05 February 2017. Before I commence, I must state several disclaimers. First, I started doing investigations into large theft rings back at U-Tapao Air Base in Thailand at the end of the Vietnam War in 1975. I was a young, shave-tail, whippersnapper U.S. Air Force Security Police officer 1st LT at the time. Since then I have conducted seven (7) major investigations into large public and private theft rings. In fact, I have written four (4) books (all for sale on www.Amazon.com) about those investigations. Additionally, I have already successfully defended my Ph.D. dissertation proposal in Management a number of years ago at an international university in Thailand on how to detect U.S. government/public and private theft rings since they are all operated exactly the same way. I plan to go back and complete my Ph.D. in 2019. So, I can state with confidence that I have had some experience in investigating large theft rings, especially U.S. government-operated and U.S. defense contracted-operated rings, especially in a war zone, unlike the Department of Justice (DOJ) who has NEVER investigated a single large U.S. contractor-operated theft ring or supported a single federal whistleblower lawsuit in federal court (to date).

Second, I freely admit I was wrong when I told Sen. Jerry Moran (KS-R) that DOJ "shut down the investigation" into KBR in Iraq during GWII. That is incorrect. DOJ never shut down the investigation into KBR because DOJ NEVER STARTED ANY INVESTIGATION! I have not been able to find a single scrap of evidence to show DOJ even broke the cellophane on a new box of paperclips on an investigation into KBR at all. I shall inform Sen. Moran of my error.

To return to your letter, I can confidently state that your missive will be held up one day in some major university American Literature class as a classic example of a Kafkaesque-like, bureaucratic-type non-response of obfuscation and blame-shifting. That KBR went out and stole hundreds of billions of dollars in Iraq at the behest of high-ranking Bush Administration officials (namely Donald Rumsfeld, Dick Cheney, et al.); then they were aided and abetted by a cover-up orchestrated by DOJ and the Department of Defense (DOD) and other U..S. government entities, but IT IS ALL MY FAULT BECAUSE I DIDN'T HAVE THE MILLIONS OF DOLLARS NEEDED TO SUE KBR IN FEDERAL DISTRICT COURT NOR DID MY LAWYERS!

Even the newest law school graduate (as the class anchorperson) already knows that: 1) Without a DOJ intervention in any federal whistleblower lawsuit that lawsuit will be fatally weakened in court; i.e., "Why didn't DOJ investigate this matter and intervene if it is true?"; 2) "What law firm in the known galaxy will risk millions of dollars in investigation and court costs to support a lawsuit DOJ did not intervene in with the chance they might lose?" (A: No one.)

But, again, according to your letter, the blame rests solely with me for not acting. You have stated that DOJ is totally blameless in the matter and it is closed. Perhaps your letter will also be used in Literature class as a perfect example of extreme absurdity, incredulity or ridiculousness. I hope you don't think I am even going to take your statement at face value. Perhaps you think I am extremely stupid.

In any event, DOJ has left too many 'smoking guns' lying about. One perfect example was Mr. Art Coulter, DOJ Supervising Investigation

Attorney, who told my lawyer at the time (2011) in a meeting inside DOJ that DOJ was instructed by DOD to shut down my federal whistleblower lawsuit that I had filed against a fly-by-night, notoriously corrupt U.S. defense contractor in Kuwait called Combat Support Associates (CSA), Ltd. This was because, as Mr. Colter explained, "DOD MIGHT USE CSA AGAIN IN THE FUTURE!" That is like putting all the foxes back into the chicken coop to guard it. I estimated CSA only stole USD$1.0 billion over eleven (11) years of their contract. At least from all reports DOJ DID do at least a cursory investigation into CSA's thievery and confirmed they found reams of damming evidence before permanently ending their investigation. The owners of CSA? All high-ranking U.S. Army generals.

I close my letter by repeating the quote that I used in my first book "AIRBASE": "Quis custodient ipsos custodies?" (Juvenal (d. 127 A.D.), Satire 6.346-8, late 1st century/early 2md century A.D.) "Who watches the watchers?" Where does an honest person go for justice when DOJ is just as totally corrupt and notoriously evil as the U.S. defense contractors they are supposed to be investigating to protect the public treasury? I have no answer. But I am working on one, hence my forthcoming books.

I will do my best to portray all the perpetrators inside DOJ as accurately as I can. I do not anticipate a rebuttal book by anyone from DOJ to proclaim their virgin-like innocence or pure-as-snow chastity. Thank you for adding a valuable contribution to American Literature and Crime. I am confident that the Attorney General and you will get at least some decent billing in my effort as will many others. This should be a real page turner about everyone who sold their country out for. . . .what? Money, yes - in the case of KBR. Otherwise, like DOJ? I do not know. Perhaps you can tell me the reason why in another letter that is more informative than this last one.

Regards,

LEONARD H. LE BLANC III
LCDR   USNR (Ret.)

Cooper & Kirk

Lawyers
A Professional Limited Liability Company
1523 New Hampshire Avenue, N.W.
Washington, D.C. 20036

Charles J. Cooper
(202) 220-9660
ccooper@cooperkirk.com

(202) 220-9600
Fax (202) 220-9601

March 6, 2019

Leonard H. LeBlanc III
2165 Prairie Glen Pl.
Manhattan, KS 66502-4779

Dear Mr. LeBlanc,

    I represent former Attorney General Jeff Sessions, and I am writing to you at his request. I understand that you have sent him an excerpt from what appears to be a book entitled "War Whores!" [Copy attached.] You have included on that excerpt what appears to be a quote, or "blurb," that you attribute to General Sessions and that references certain "whistleblowers lawsuits." Please be advised that you are not authorized to attribute this quote, or any other quote, to General Sessions in connection with this book or any other publication. To the contrary you are instructed not to attribute any quote or blurb to General Sessions in any way. Please be further advised that if you fail to abide by this instruction, General Sessions will pursue any and all available avenues of relief.

    Sincerely,

    Charles J. Cooper

    Charles J. Cooper

Leonard H. Le Blanc III
2165 Prairie Glen Place
Manhattan, KS 66502-4779 USA
08 March 2019

Mr. Charles J. Cooper, Esq.
c/o Cooper & Kirk, L.L.C.
1523 New Hampshire Ave., N.W.
Washington, DC 20036-1203

Dear Mr. Cooper-

This is in response to your most welcome threatening letter of 06 March 2019. Your attention is directed to Attachments # 1, 2 and 3. These will detail my final attempt to contact Mr. Sessions while he was Attorney General (AG) and speak to him about my three (3) inactive federal whistle-blower lawsuits. Mr. Sessions directed his Assistant Attorney General-Civil Division to respond to my request through my senator, SEN. Jerry Moran (R-KS), back in 2017. As you will read HE BLAMES ME FOR EVERYTHING! That I could not find a deep-pocketed law firm to represent me in my lawsuits totally absolved the Department of Justice (DOJ) from intervening or supporting my lawsuits is ALL MY FAULT. This is totally absurd.

    I sent Mr. Sessions, while AG (and others inside DOJ), several letters detailing the corruption inside DOJ such as DOJ investigators lying about the investigation and admitting to my lawyer at a DOJ meeting they were going to cover-up and stop the investigation on one federal whistle-blower lawsuit at the request of the Department of Defense (DOD) even though they found and admitted they found massive piles of evidence of fraud and over-billing, the collusion between DOJ and other U.S. government entities, namely DOD, the DOD Criminal Investigation Command, the U.S. Army Criminal Investigation Division (CID) and other government organizations, all in an effort to block, impede or stop any investigation into U.S. defense contractor thievery in Iraq during Gulf War II (GWII). Mr. Sessions never responded. However, NO FEDERAL WHISTLE-BLOWER LAWSUIT HAS EVER BEEN SUPPORTED BY DOJ starting with the Bush Administration in 2000 and continued through the Obama to the Trump Administrations. None. In spite of overwhelming evidence of U.S. defense contractor over-billing, fraud, stealing and other high crimes and misdemeanors, Mr. Sessions did nothing.

Now your threatening letter has arrived. You are stating Mr. Sessions is in the injured party here. I sent him a draft summary of my forthcoming book for commentary, correction, change or detection of error. Perhaps you missed (or slept through) the class called "Absence of Malice." I have given Mr. Sessions the opportunity to correct anything wrong or add his own commentary to the book's narrative. All I received was your threatening letter. This shows to me what I have written is accurate.

Perhaps you missed (or cut) another class called "Libel/Slander/Defamation of Character." Mr. Sessions is a "public figure". I am not slandering him, libeling him or defaming his personage in the book's summary. I am quoting him. I am writing in my book what I believe to be factual and correct. I offered Mr. sessions the chance to respond. He has refused.

However, I wish to be fair here. I wish Mr. Sessions no personal ill will. I do demand and expect justice. I have never gotten any. My book is historical, a recitation of the facts. However, I propose a compromise solution which will be very easy for Mr. Sessions to implement. Mr. Sessions simply has to call the new AG, Mr. William Barr. He can explain DOJ's almost two-decades long failure to support any federal whistle-blower lawsuit. He can explain about all the corruption, collusion and the conspiracy inside DOJ to deny justice to federal whistle-blowers like me. I will assume Mr. Barr is an honest person (as I assumed Mr. Sessions was). He can conduct an internal investigation of DOJ and my federal whistle-blower lawsuits. He will find everything I have said is accurate. Mr. Barr will declare that DOJ was in grave error in not supporting my federal whistle-blower lawsuit in federal district court and DOJ has decided to finally intervene in each one.

Since Mr. Sessions was a highly-respected, long-serving Senator, he can simply call all his former Senatorial colleagues and request legislation be passed or the current laws amended, or an extraordinary exception be made on the time limits in reactivating these federal whistle-blower lawsuits. It is also a widely known fact in legal circles that DOJ crafted internal DOJ procedures to also block or greatly impeded any federal whistle-blower lawsuits. These DOJ regulations must be scrapped or at least re-written to help federal whistle-blowers. The federal whistle-blower lawsuits will then proceed to federal district court (again) this time supported by DOJ. Since the evidence is overwhelming the verdicts in each case will be a slam-dunk. Then the poor U.S. taxpayers will get back hundreds of billions of U.S. dollars that were stolen by these notoriously corrupt U.S. defense contractors. Then I am sure Mr. Sessions' name will disappear from my book and enjoy an anonymous retired life. I cannot be fairer to him.

If not, then I will see you and him at trial. He will have to testify WHY he continued the DOJ policy of deliberately not intervening in any federal whistle-blower lawsuit, testify to why he deliberately ignored my letters detailing corruption inside DOJ and collusion with DOD, et al., testify to why he should not be held accountable when he was in charge of DOJ as AG in light of all the facts. Or as we call the DOJ "The Department of Injustice." The trial will be a sensation - another Scopes Monkey Trial. It will enter into American history.

Thank you - you have given me exactly what I have been waiting for 12 years - finally - my day in court. I look forward to that day in either scenario. I fervently hope it will be at several federal whistle-blower lawsuit trials. However, right now Mr. Sessions is slated to be a central (and historical) figure in my three books about the whole sordid matter for doing nothing and ignoring the mess which he knew about, unless I receive some justice in this matter.

Best regards,

Leonard H. Le Blanc III
LCDR, USNR   (RET.)